Leading Your Healthcare Organization to Excellence

A Guide to Using the Baldrige Criteria

Leading Your Healthcare Organization to Excellence

A Guide to Using the Baldrige Criteria

Patrice L. Spath

Health Administration Press
Chicago, Illinois

Your board, staff, or clients may also benefit from this book's insight. For more information on quantity discounts, contact the Health Administration Press Marketing Manager at (312) 424–9470.

09   08   07   06   05   5   4   3   2

Library of Congress Cataloging-in-Publication Data
Spath, Patrice
   Leading your healthcare organization to excellence : a guide to using the Baldrige criteria
  /Patrice L. Spath.
    p. cm.
  Includes bibliographical references and index.
  ISBN 1-56793-233-9
   1. Medical care--United States--Quality control. 2. Total quality
management--Awards--United States. 3. Malcolm Baldrige National Quality Award. 4.
Organizational change--United States--Management. 5. Health services
administration--United States. 6. Health facilities--United States--Administration. I. Title.

RA399.A3S62 2004
362.1'068–dc22

                           2004042385

The paper used in this publication meets the minimum requirements of American National Standard for Information Sciences—Permanence of Paper for Printed Library Materials, ANSI Z39.48–1984. ⊗™

Acquisitions manager: Audrey Kaufman; Project manager: Joyce Sherman; Cover designer: Betsy Pérez

Health Administration Press
A division of the Foundation of the
   American College of Healthcare Executives
1 North Franklin Street, Suite 1700
Chicago, IL 60606–4425
(312) 424–2800

This book is dedicated to the Excellence in my life, my four grandsons: Gary and Jacob Young and Nathan and Edward Fine.

Contents

Foreword

Ian Morrison, a recognized futurist with a special interest in healthcare, published a book entitled *The Second Curve* in 1996. His fundamental concept was not original. The idea of "first curve, second curve" dates at least to Thomas Kuhn's work on the concept of paradigm, or, more specifically, paradigm shift. Morrison specifically addresses healthcare in his book, suggesting that several years ago healthcare was in the infancy of its transition from a first-curve to a second-curve paradigm. It is my observation after three decades in the professional practice of (a) caring for patients and (b) healthcare quality consultation and learning facilitation that very few people within the health caregiver community have understood that healthcare has been struggling for more than 20 years now to escape its first-curve paradigm, even as it struggles inevitably toward its second.

Patrice Spath is one of those rare people who understands and communicates this genuine paradigm shift. *Paradigm* is defined simply as a model or pattern. The model or pattern of healthcare quality thinking prior to 1979 was based primarily on what I call the *craft model* (Merry 2003). This model is based on a concept that dates to medieval days. A craftsperson was one who spent years learning a skill, such as medicine or clock making, and who, on completion of this rigorous training, was honored by being granted extraordinary autonomy and respect as he (typically) plied this skill.

In 1979, the Joint Commission on Accreditation of Hospitals (now the Joint Commission on Accreditation of Healthcare Organizations) announced its Quality Assurance Standard for hospitals. Though it certainly was not the Joint Commission's intent, this event was what I consider to be the end of first-curve healthcare's total focus on the craft of medicine as defining healthcare quality. I now perceive the Joint Commission's move as a landmark intuitive recognition that the quality of patient care was no longer totally locked into the craft concept related to the skills of individual craftspersons (physicians, nurses, and other caregivers). Quality in 1979 and forever after would relate intimately to management competencies within caregiver workplaces, such as hospitals. Though most of us in healthcare did not fully realize this at the time, this shift signified that healthcare was moving from a model or pattern (paradigm) that defined quality in terms of the skills of individual craftspersons to one that integrated broader notions of how institutions such as hospitals, via their management systems, influenced these craftspersons in their daily work, and thus influenced quality as experienced by individual patients.

Extensive research in healthcare quality over the past 20 years has validated Morrison's prediction that this first-curve to second-curve paradigm shift is well underway. It is now accepted that the quality patients receive is related not just to the skills of individual caregivers but also inextricably to the ability of healthcare facilities to provide a complex array of quality-enhancing structures and processes that support those individual caregivers. Patrice has been a creative force in this first-curve to second-curve transition, indeed from its inception in the early 1980s. For more years than we both might wish to admit, she and I from our respective West and East Coast locations have been pursuing parallel careers trying to envision and facilitate healthcare's transition from its first-curve ability to miraculously cure but also to harm, to its second-curve ability to cure without harm. Finally, we both envision a healthcare world in which caregivers might experience purely the satisfaction that their calling both to cure and to care without harming implies.

In addition to her excellent consulting skills—this book is replete with case examples of her successful client work over the past 20 years—Patrice has been a prolific contributor to the literature of healthcare quality. She has consistently been on the leading edge of introducing essential quality concepts to her clients and to all of us seeking to facilitate a transformed healthcare system. In her prior works, she has documented both the progressive theoretical frameworks of quality and the impact of these concepts in actual client settings. Her recent book on patient-centered care is in the distinct tradition of first-curve to second-curve healthcare (Spath 2004). This latest work carries that tradition into the future.

There is no shortage of articles and books these days directing readers from healthcare's first curve to its second curve. So what is unique about Patrice's latest contribution? In my opinion, the answer to this question boils down to the following points:

1. Patrice has wisely focused on the criteria of the Baldrige National Quality Award as the fundamental framework for the executive who wishes to transition his or her organization from healthcare's first curve to its second curve. This is especially important now that healthcare boasts three institutions (the first of which was chief executive officer Sister Mary Jean Ryan's SSM Health Care in 2002) that have achieved this highest U.S. recognition of system quality.
2. This book offers explicit and precise guidance on how to follow this nationally recognized model for leaders who seek to transform their organizations from a first-curve to a second-curve paradigm.
3. Patrice offers helpful instruments derived from her extensive consultation and learning-facilitation experience. These tools, which are labeled as Key Points, Self-Assessments, and Reflections, are placed throughout the book and make this work an invaluable aid. They constitute a "speed read" option for busy executives who may wish to scan this work prior to reading it for a more in-depth analysis. My hunch is that those executives who adopt this speed-read approach—be they chief executive officers or chief medical officers—subsequently will slow down to read more thoroughly what Patrice offers in this book. Further, my guess is that, even after a speed read, these executives will distribute copies of this book to everyone in their organization: senior managers, middle managers, frontline supervisors, direct caregivers, and, yes, even physicians.

I am honored that Patrice has asked me to contribute to this book, her most recent and excellent work. I endorse it wholeheartedly. It is truly a blueprint for senior executives who seek to lead a genuine first-curve to second-curve healthcare journey.

Martin D. Merry, M.D.
Senior Advisor for Medical Affairs
New Hampshire Hospital Association and Foundation
for Health Communities
Adjunct Associate Clinical Professor of Health Management and Policy
University of New Hampshire
Durham, New Hampshire

REFERENCES

Merry, M. D. 2003. "Healthcare's Need for Revolutionary Change." *Quality Progress* 36 (9): 31–35.

Morrison, I. 1996. *The Second Curve*. New York: Ballantine Books.

Spath, P. L. 2004. *Partnering with Patients to Reduce Medical Errors*. Chicago: American Hospital Association.

Preface

How can you tell if your healthcare organization's performance is less than optimal? It's easy: just think about where the chief executive officer (CEO) spends the majority of his or her time in any given workday. What percentage of time is spent in the following activities?

1. Discussions/meetings responding to customer problems (e.g., dissatisfaction with services provided, delays in health services delivery) or work process problems (e.g., interdepartmental squabbles, resource allocation, poorly designed tasks)
2. Discussions/meetings responding to problems resulting from miscommunications, low employee morale, lack of training, deferred preventive maintenance, missing or misapplied policies or procedures, and so forth
3. Visiting patients and other customers, employees, and work units; congratulating people; celebrating success; exchanging information with people; and reinforcing the organization's mission, vision, values, and initiatives like quality and patient safety improvement
4. Diagnosing the changes in the healthcare industry, reassessing the truths and assumptions regarding your organization, building a flexible and learning organization, and reinventing the organization's present and future

If the CEO and other senior leaders are spending the majority of their time in the first two areas—solving work process or management issues—organizational performance is less than optimal. Acknowledging the need to change the system is the first step in moving from mediocrity to excellence. Practically speaking, such acknowledgment means that senior leaders allocate some portion of time to something that will take time and effort. This may be hard to do. But the degree to which the need for change is acknowledged indicates how likely the organization is to explore alternatives for effectively addressing the complex healthcare environment.

This book is about options—what leaders can do to advance performance excellence within the context of the organization's mission, vision, values, and available resources. The first step toward exploring those options is recognizing the role of leadership in advancing excellence. "Solving the problems begins with owning the problems," says Roger Pearson, CHE, CEO of Ellsworth County (Kansas) Medical Center. Pearson's realization of personal accountability marked the start of an effort to improve performance at his hospital. "Because I am responsible for the design and support of the systems currently in place, I am part of the problem," says Pearson. "To begin improvements, I must ask, 'Why have I allowed this system to be the way it is?'"

In his book *Good to Great*, Collins (2001) describes several factors that are exhibited in high-performing companies. Surprisingly, good-to-great companies eschew flashy management strategies in favor of a consistent, day-by-day commitment to do the right things. By exercising tenacity and faithfully staying the course, these companies are able to outperform competitors. How do they do it? Leaders do not lurch from strategy to strategy searching for a magic pill in reaction to each new failed improvement initiative. Instead, the momentum along the excellence journey builds gradually, with evolution giving away to revolution only after long, patient years of preparation. The good-to-great principles, as well as the principles of many successful management strategies, are evident in the criteria of the National Baldrige Quality Award. The Baldrige Criteria are used in this book as an analytical framework or diagnostic system for understanding the enablers that drive healthcare organizations to their highest levels of sustainable achievement. The criteria are now widely accepted as the de facto standard for performance excellence.

Healthcare organizations can use the Baldrige Criteria to identify organizational strengths and key areas for improvement. Though the criteria are connected to a National Quality Award process, organizations do not have to apply for the award to benefit from the criteria. The criteria stimulate organizational excellence without being prescriptive; the choices of actions necessary for advancing performance are left to the judgment of senior leaders. The criteria do, however, guide those choices in some important ways. The Leadership category focuses on the actions of senior leaders to create and sustain a high-performance organization. In the Strategic Planning category, the Baldrige Criteria emphasize the importance of well-thought-out actions based on a solid understanding of patients, other customers, and the market. An explicit focus is placed on organizational alignment, staff motivation, and systematic process management. The Measurement category makes clear the need to act on the basis of understanding rather than assumptions. In all of these ways, the Baldrige Criteria very much echo the ideas articulated in Collins's *Good to Great*.

The Baldrige Criteria are effective for advancing performance excellence in healthcare organizations for several reasons.

- Baldrige provides a proven quality system. The Baldrige Criteria were designed by leading U.S. quality and management experts representing a wide variety of industries, companies, and backgrounds. A systematic process is used to conduct an annual review of the criteria to continually refine and update the program.
- Baldrige Criteria are applicable to all stages of excellence. Healthcare organizations just embarking on the performance excellence journey can use the criteria to broaden their understanding of their management systems and prioritize improvement activities. Organizations further along on the journey can use the criteria to pinpoint trouble spots and instill a process of continuous improvement. The potential for positive, long-term improvement is unlimited. Positive changes in the organization and its attitudes, services, processes, measurement, planning, leadership, and patient satisfaction can all be inspired by the Baldrige Criteria.
- Baldrige Criteria are a valuable self-assessment tool. When people work in a healthcare organization for any length of time, they are prone to develop blind spots more easily. "Business as usual" prohibits the kind of ongoing and fresh analysis needed for

continuous improvement. Using the Baldrige Criteria as a self-assessment tool forces the organization to study its entire management system and the assumptions used to judge performance.

Rather than an ill-defined management fad whose use-by date has expired, the Baldrige Criteria represent an interrelated collection of time-tested principles, procedures, and techniques that turn performance excellence from an abstract (and empty) notion into an operationally useful management model.

Are all of the Baldrige Criteria covered in detail in this book? Most likely not. The criteria represent an overarching management philosophy that, when thoroughly studied and articulated, would fill several volumes. Describing how each of the Baldrige Criteria can be applied to performance excellence initiatives in healthcare organizations would be like answering the question, How big is the universe? One way to get people to appreciate the size of the universe is to have them hop on stepping-stones to bigger and bigger places, starting with the earth and then to the moon, the solar system, nearby stars, the Milky Way galaxy, clusters of galaxies, and, finally (in the words of Buzz Lightyear from the film *Toy Story*), to infinity and beyond! Most of the stepping-stones of an organization's performance excellence journey are found in this book; however, readers are encouraged to refer to the current edition of the Baldrige Criteria for more details. By using the criteria as a self-assessment tool, senior leaders can further explore all of the ways in which the organization can rethink and redesign certain practices, strategies, and structures.

In balancing the need for specific details and the desire to be succinct, some of the subjects are purposely only briefly covered. After all, entire books are devoted to topics such as Six Sigma and strategic planning, and it would be foolhardy to attempt to adequately address these subjects in just one book. Throughout this book readers will find suggested additional resources to supplement the learning experience. What is most important to understand is how the grab bag of various performance tools and strategies fits into the bigger picture of organizational excellence. Once that is well understood, senior leaders can adapt the tools and strategies to the behavior and management needs of the organization. The Baldrige Criteria can serve as a detailed, informative tool for creating lasting organizational change, or they can become just one more doomed quality initiative. The character and choices of the leaders involved will be the deciding factor.

Patrice L. Spath
Brown-Spath & Associates
Forest Grove, Oregon

REFERENCE

Collins, J. 2001. *Good to Great: Why Some Companies Make the Leap . . . and Others Don't.* New York: Harper Business.

Acknowledgments

Countless friends and colleagues assisted me in the preparation of this book, and I am sincerely grateful to everyone for their support and words of wisdom. Several people deserve special mention and my heartfelt thanks.

To Roger Pearson, CHE, CEO, and all of the managers and staff members at Ellsworth County Medical Center, Ellsworth, Kansas, for their exceptional commitment to performance excellence and willingness to share their successes as well as missteps along the excellence journey.

To Kate Garber, assistant vice president at Blake Medical Center in Bradenton, Florida, for her devotion to organizational learning and willingness to go the extra mile to ensure that other facilities might learn from Blake's experiences.

To Dennis Hamilton, CHE, president and CEO of FHN, a health network in Freeport, Illinois, for advancing everyone's understanding of performance excellence principles by freely sharing the FHN performance measures and targets.

To Jack May, president and CEO of Sebasticook Valley Hospital in Pittsfield, Maine, for his enthusiasm and dedication to helping make Sebasticook the best small hospital in Maine and for his spirit of teamwork in contributing to this book.

To Virginia Bynum, Ph.D., CHE, vice president at Sioux Valley Hospitals and Health System, based in Sioux Falls, South Dakota, for willingly volunteering information about what her organization is doing to advance performance excellence.

To Don Sibery, FACHE, former CEO of Central DuPage Health in Winfield, Illinois, for his candid and sincere assertions about what leaders can and should be doing to create learning organizations.

And most of all to Audrey Kaufman, acquisitions editor at Health Administration Press, whose idea this book was in the first place and whose patience and unending encouragement helped bring it to closure.

CHAPTER ONE

Advancing Healthcare Excellence

I N 1971, GEORGE C. SCOTT won an Oscar for his starring role in the black comedy *The Hospital.* At one point in the movie, the hospital chief executive officer (CEO), played by Scott, yells to a group of community protesters something like, "You want to run this hospital? Fine. It's yours." He then storms out the door. Practically speaking, being a senior leader in a healthcare organization usually ensures one thing: No matter what choices you make, a sizable group under you will be disappointed by your decision. That cannot be avoided. What can be avoided is less-than-optimal organizational performance.

Achieving organizational excellence is not about passing surveys, saving money, or effectively marketing your services, though all of these are necessary activities. It is about taking a hard look at the organization as a system and understanding the implications of that view for what it means to performance. An organization is made up of parts. Each part affects the ways other parts work, and the way all parts work together determines how well the system works. Managing a healthcare organization by managing its separate parts causes suboptimal performance; the parts often achieve their goals at the expense of the whole.

Organizational excellence is not about doing things right. It is about doing the right things to promote operational effectiveness and efficiency. Inadequate systems often impose conditions that limit, constrain, or in other ways control people's behavior in ways that produce mediocrity. A systems view of the organization shows the fallacy of categorizing performance problems as people problems ("If only they would just do it."). Failures in cooperation, poor morale, and conflicts among departments are symptoms, and their causes lie in the system. For example, training staff members to provide better customer service assumes that if people do "as they should" with patients and their families, satisfaction levels will improve. In practice, staff member behavior is governed by the system in which they work. Many improvement initiatives fall far short of success because they do not change the system.

Organizational excellence is not about achieving world-class quality. It is about focusing everyone's energy on what matters most to the organization: the mission, vision, and strategic goals. All healthcare organizations are made up of people who have a wealth of knowledge and desire. Senior leaders must channel this energy toward achieving optimal performance. Whatever point you aim for on the good–better–best continuum, it is imperative that organizational energy be focused on priorities. To do otherwise means that your organization will always be stuck in a reactive mode. Excellence has less to do with how much an organization has than with how much it can do with whatever it has to ensure high performance in the context of goals, objectives, and strategies.

Finally, organizational excellence is not about people working harder. The workweek does not need to bleed from 40 hours to 55 to 60 . . . or more. Excellence is about making knowledge-based decisions that are critical to the organization's success with appropriate urgency. Planned management replaces stress-inducing crisis management. It is incumbent on senior leaders to be sure that everyone knows the difference between what is critical and what is marginal so that limited personal and organizational resources are used in a priority-anchored manner.

In today's organizational milieu of cultural diversity, open systems, flattened hierarchies, decision-making transparencies, and customer demands for better access to and better service from all healthcare providers, senior leaders must optimize organizational performance. Is your organization in need of change to achieve the best possible performance? How many of the disabling symptoms listed in Figure 1.1 do you recognize in your organization?

Change for improved performance means changing the system, and this requires a long-term commitment. The good news is that the journey does not have to be too complicated or all that difficult; it just has to be active.

Figure 1.1 Symptoms of a Problematic Organization

Leadership Issues

- Senior management's directives disappear into a black hole.
- Too many management levels exist between senior leaders and staff members.
- There is no organizational vision.
- Strategic plans have little impact on day-to-day activities.
- Operational decisions are made at too high a level in the organization.
- There is no visible leadership.
- The focus is on doing things right rather than doing the right thing.
- There is a reluctance to innovate (e.g., "We don't do it that way here.").
- Leadership is stuck in the status quo (e.g. "We've never done it that way here before.").
- The focus is all on financial success.
- The organization is too bureaucratic.
- Staff members will not deliver bad news.
- Information flows down the organization, but not up.
- Personal and departmental conflicts are rarely acknowledged or dealt with.

Performance Issues

- There is a high rate of waste or non-value-added activities.
- The amount of time between problem identification and resolution is excessive.
- Lots of activity takes place without corresponding performance gains.
- There is a lack of ownership for quality and patient safety.
- Many complaints are heard from customers (e.g., patients, families, physicians).
- There is excessive paperwork.
- While lots of data are available, little worthwhile information is provided.
- Individual performance problems are not confronted or honestly communicated.
- New procedures fail more often than not.
- Staff turnover is high.
- Staff morale is low.
- Overhead costs are high.
- The market share is static or declining.
- Patient retention is low.

HOW TO USE THIS BOOK

This is a self-help book for healthcare organizations wanting to achieve higher levels of performance. You will discover the critical enablers of performance excellence and learn how you can incorporate these enablers into your organization's daily practices. Enablers are mechanisms, attributes, or characteristics that, if present, make an organization more likely to achieve high performance. There is nothing magical about the excellence enablers. In fact, some are fairly basic concepts that most people learned in undergraduate-level management classes. However, all too often organizational improvement initiatives are begun without a clear understanding of the totality of the commitment needed for the endeavor. Well-intentioned efforts to advance healthcare excellence are frequently stymied by impediments that leaders just do not see coming. By being aware of the enablers of success, leaders can anticipate and properly prepare before starting down the road to major organizational improvements.

What you will not find in the book is the one "right" way of advancing excellence. Through the use of case studies and examples, you will learn how other healthcare organizations have incorporated the excellence enablers into their business practices. In some instances, what other organizations have done may be the best thing for you to do also. However, each example must be considered within the context of your organization: your culture, customers, available resources and technologies, competitive strategies, and so forth. As the poet Antonio Machado (1978) writes, "*Caminante, no hay camino. Se hace camino al andar,*" or, "Searcher, there is no road, the road is made by walking."

An important element of any self-help book is the opportunity for personal contemplation. Therefore, scattered throughout the chapters in this book are contemplation places labeled as "Key Point," "Reflection," and "Self-Assessment." The key points are issues that significantly affect an organization's ability to achieve a high level of performance. The reflections are intended to be thought-provoking introspections about how excellence can be advanced in your organization. The self-assessments are exactly what the title implies—opportunities to evaluate yourself or your organization. Often the mind-set of organization leaders is "Just do it! Fix performance improvement." Unfortunately, that bias toward just fixing it typically guarantees less-than-optimal organizational performance down the road. The contemplation places in this book are intended to help change that bias, especially if the subjects are honestly and thoughtfully considered.

Advancing excellence requires an understanding of the complex factors that affect performance—leadership, strategic planning, human resources, process management, information and knowledge management, and customer expectations. Performance excellence is not a quick-fix strategy. According to Lulla (2002),

> One Japanese expert on [organizational quality] likens the need for patience and discipline to that of the bamboo farmer. Once the bamboo seed is planted, the farmer must water it every day for four years before the tree breaks ground. But when it finally does, it grows 60 feet in 90 days.

ADVANCING EXCELLENCE

In the second half of the last century, the pace of new business performance improvement techniques quickened considerably. We have seen the following theories and methods (not in chronological order and not a complete list):

- Management by objectives
- Theory X and theory Y
- Theory of constraints
- The matrix organization
- Organization development
- Total quality management
- Downsizing
- Organizational learning
- Systems thinking
- Team building
- Cultural change
- Benchmarking
- Core competencies
- Business process reengineering
- Lean thinking
- International Standards Organization certification
- Customer relationship management
- Knowledge management
- Chaos theory
- Six Sigma
- Breakthrough improvement
- Small- and large-system change
- Rapid cycle improvement
- Balanced scorecards

These quality techniques have sometimes been considered management fads—innovative concepts or techniques that are promoted as the forefront of management progress and that diffuse very rapidly among early adopters eager to gain a competitive advantage. When organizational leaders suspect such a concept is falling short of its expected benefits, the technique is quickly discontinued or drops back to very modest usage. Some techniques fail—or are at least dropped from the repertoire—because they are too costly. This was the case with business process reengineering (BPR). Many companies, including healthcare organizations, quickly realized that the costs of carrying out BPR throughout the organization would be crippling (Hall, Rosenthal, and Wade 1994). The costs involved in implementing Six Sigma also appear to be a barrier to adoption, especially for small companies with less than 500 employees or receipts of less than $50 million (Dusharme 2003).

Many concepts, such as total quality management (TQM), need visible leadership commitment and support for the full benefits to be achieved. Regrettably, when implementing TQM, some healthcare leaders adopted a "throw it against the wall and see if it sticks" attitude. Skeptical about the benefits of the concept and yet required by accreditation standards to use some of the techniques, management took a long, hard look and decided, "We really don't want to spend much time or money trying this out." The bulk of TQM implementation was delegated to middle managers and the quality director, with little or no senior leader involvement.

Healthcare organizations that dismiss quality concepts as "not working" often fail to get to the essential ideas. Implementation of improvement strategies is more than the random application of a combination of management tools or techniques. There is often confusion surrounding the relationship of the work environment and the tools, such as problem-solving tools, statistical process control, process mapping, and the like. The tools do not by themselves allow the organization to achieve excellence. The conceptual issues such as leadership, training, and empowerment must also be addressed.

 KEY POINT

People like General Electric's former CEO Jack Welch and SSM Health Care's CEO Sr. Mary Jean Ryan had a single goal in mind: to make their businesses as successful as possible. They knew it would take more than the tools of the quality profession to achieve this goal; they also had to create a vision and a framework for excellence to support the tools.

It would be wrong to presume that all of the innovative quality concepts or techniques lacked effectiveness when applied in healthcare organizations. For instance, the methods of TQM are very much alive, although the vocabulary may have changed. Some TQM methods (e.g., process improvement techniques, customer focus, employee involvement) are ingrained in the environment of many healthcare organizations. Over the course of the various starts and stops of improvement strategies, healthcare workers have begun to develop new values and belief systems. The new values include empowerment (make the right decision for the patient and other customers), accountability (take ownership for your work), and continuous improvement (look for ways to improve everything you do, every day). Significant positive results are being achieved in those healthcare organizations that have effectively harnessed the talents of all who are connected to the organization. Some healthcare organizations involved in Six Sigma projects are reporting noteworthy success in reducing undesirable variation in key processes (Barry, Murcko, and Brubaker 2002; Gaucher and Linton 2002).

Healthcare organizations have not needlessly suffered through decades of constantly changing performance improvement strategies. Numerous benefits have been derived along the way. It is entirely natural that new business improvement ideas get put forward. All fields of human endeavor typically depend on newer methods building on or being added to the best parts of older methods. It is counterproductive to see new methods as being in conflict with each other or replacing an older method. Once one reconciles the vocabulary differences, one usually finds considerable overlap among the supposedly new methods.

All of the models for business excellence have a similar structure. The prime focus is on leadership, continuous improvement of key performance measures, customer satisfaction, effective use of information, good people management, and quality processes. The message of business excellence has not changed much over the years. And yet the real world of many businesses, including healthcare organizations, continues to struggle with implementing this message.

Starting the Journey

As does any journey, the journey to performance excellence requires a starting point. Where does your organization need to start? The starting point depends on the maturity of your quality efforts. One way to characterize this is to describe the quality values that drive the organization. These values change as the organization advances along the performance excellence journey.

- Stage one: Performance is based solely on rules and regulations.
- Stage two: Good performance is an organizational goal.
- Stage three: Performance can always be improved.

At stage one, senior leaders and managers view performance improvement as an external requirement and not a dynamic that will help the organization to succeed. There is little awareness of behavioral and attitudinal aspects of performance excellence and no willingness to consider such issues. Performance is seen very much as a technical issue; mere compliance with rules and regulations is considered adequate.

At stage two, leaders and managers perceive good performance as being important even in the absence of external pressures. Although awareness of behavioral issues is growing, this aspect is largely missing from improvement actions. Technical and procedural solutions are proposed when problems arise. Performance is defined in terms of targets or goals. The organization has begun to look at the reasons why performance sometimes reaches a plateau and is willing to seek solutions from other organizations.

A healthcare organization at stage three has adopted the ideal of performance excellence. It places a strong emphasis on communication, training, management style, and improving efficiency and effectiveness. Everyone in the organization can contribute. People are aware that some behaviors enable improvements to take place and, on the other hand, some behaviors act as barriers to further improvement. Consequently, people understand the impact of behavioral issues on performance improvement. The level of awareness of behavioral and attitudinal issues is high, and measures are being taken to improve the work climate. Progress is made one step at a time and never stops. The organization reaches out to other organizations and asks how it might help them improve their performance.

Healthcare organizations are at various stages in the excellence journey. Some have already begun the journey and are far along in the never-ending challenge of performance excellence. Other organizations have institutionalized a quality culture and are now working to put the right systems in place to support this culture. Some remain satisfied with just meeting externally defined regulations with little focus on overall

systems improvement. Most organizations find that they exhibit characteristics found in every stage of the performance excellence journey.

Begin by determining where your organization is now along the
journey to excellence. The following self-assessment provides you with a
better understanding of your organization's strengths and weaknesses.
In addition, you will learn more about the characteristics found in stage
three organizations—those that have embraced performance excellence
as an ideal.

✓ SELF-ASSESSMENT

How many of these characteristics can be observed in your organization? In each
stage, check all that apply.

Stage One: Performance is based solely on rules and regulations.
- ❑ Problems are not anticipated; the organization reacts to them as they occur.
- ❑ Communication between departments and functions is poor.
- ❑ Departments and functions behave as semi-autonomous units, and there is little collaboration and shared decision making among them.
- ❑ The decisions taken by departments and functions concentrate on little more than the need to comply with rules.
- ❑ People who make mistakes are simply blamed for their failure to comply with the rules.
- ❑ Conflicts are not resolved; departments and functions compete with one another.
- ❑ The role of management is seen as endorsing the rules, pushing employees, and expecting results.
- ❑ There is not much listening or learning inside or outside of the organization, which adopts a defensive posture when criticized.
- ❑ Performance improvement is viewed as a required nuisance.
- ❑ People are viewed as "system components"; they are defined and valued solely in terms of what they do and what they contribute to the bottom line.
- ❑ An adversarial relationship exists between management and employees.
- ❑ There is little or no awareness of the work processes.
- ❑ People are rewarded for obedience to rules and results, regardless of long-term consequences.

Stage Two: Good performance is an organizational goal.
- ❑ The organization concentrates primarily on day-to-day matters; there is little in the way of strategy.
- ❑ Management encourages cross-departmental and cross-functional teams and communication.

- Senior managers function as a team and have begun to coordinate departmental and functional decisions.
- Decisions are often centered around cost and function.
- Management's response to mistakes is to put more controls, via procedures and retraining, in place. A little less blaming takes place.
- Conflict is discouraged in the name of teamwork.
- The role of management is seen as applying management techniques, such as management by objectives.
- The organization is somewhat open about learning from other organizations, especially new techniques and best practices.
- People think that *best practices* means higher costs and reduced productivity.
- The relationship between employees and management is adversarial, with little trust or respect demonstrated.
- Awareness is growing of the impact of cultural issues in the workplace; however, people still do not understand why added controls do not yield the expected performance improvement results.

Stage Three: Performance can always be improved.
- The organization acts strategically with a focus on the longer term as well as an awareness of the present. It anticipates problems and deals with their causes before they happen.
- People recognize and state the need for collaboration among departments and functions. They receive management support, recognition, and the resources they need for collaborative work.
- People are aware of work processes and help managers to manage them.
- Decisions are made with full knowledge of their impact on performance as well as on departments and functions.
- There is no goal conflict between performance improvement and productivity, so performance is not jeopardized in the pursuit of efficiency targets.
- Almost all mistakes are viewed in terms of the work process or systems involved. The important thing is to understand what has happened rather than find someone to blame. This understanding is used to modify the way work is done.
- The existence of conflict is recognized and dealt with by trying to find mutually beneficial solutions.
- Management's role is seen as coaching people to improve performance.
- Learning from others both inside and outside of the organization is valued. Time is made available and devoted to adapting such knowledge to improve performance.
- Quality and productivity are seen as interdependent.
- Short-term performance is measured and analyzed so that changes can be made to improve long-term performance.

- People are respected and valued for their contributions.
- The relationship between management and employees is respectful and supportive.
- There is awareness of the impact of cultural issues, and these factors are considered in key decisions.
- The organization rewards not just those who produce but also those who support the work of others. In addition, people are rewarded for improving processes as well as results.

Advancing performance excellence in a healthcare organization requires systems thinking. But what does that mean exactly? The short answer is that senior leaders need to understand the following:

- How the organization performs as a web of interrelated, interdependent processes and functions
- What underlying performance factors are common to all organizations and how these factors affect the organization's ability to improve performance

In the next chapter, the reader is introduced to a time-tested model of organizational excellence that incorporates systems thinking.

REFERENCES

Barry, R., A. C. Murcko, and C. E. Brubaker. 2002. *The Six Sigma Book for Healthcare: Improving Outcomes by Reducing Errors.* Chicago: Health Administration Press.

Dusharme, D. 2003. "Six Sigma: Big Success . . . But What About the Other 98 Percent?" *Quality Digest* 23 (2): 24–32.

Gaucher, E., and R. Linton. 2002. "A Tale of Two Six Sigma Implementations." Presentation to the National Forum on Quality Improvement in Health Care, Orlando, FL, December.

Hall, E. A., J. Rosenthal, and J. Wade. 1994. "How to Make Reengineering Really Work." *McKinsey Quarterly* 2: 107–28.

Lulla, S. 2002. "Quality Leadership—Role Model for Recovery." [Online article; retrieved 2/04.] www.indiainfoline.com/nevi/qule/qu01.html.

Machado, A. 1978. *We Make the Road by Walking: Selected Poems of Antonio Machado.* Translated by Betty Jean Craige. Baton Rouge, LA: Louisiana State University Press.

CHAPTER TWO

Blueprint for Excellence

ORTUNATELY, HEALTHCARE organizations have at their disposal a proven blueprint for performance excellence—the criteria of the Malcolm Baldrige Quality Award. The U.S. Congress established the award in 1987 to recognize organizations for their achievements in quality and business performance and to raise awareness about the importance of quality and performance excellence for achieving a competitive edge. The U.S. Commerce Department's National Institute of Standards and Technology (NIST) manages the Baldrige National Quality Program in close cooperation with the private sector. The American Society for Quality (ASQ) assists NIST with the application review process, preparation of award documents, publicity, and information transfer. ASQ is a professional, not-for-profit association serving more than 80,000 individual and 700 corporate members in the United States and 62 other nations.

For the first ten years, the annual awards were limited to three eligibility categories: manufacturing, service, and small business. In 1998, two additional eligibility categories—education and healthcare—were added. In 2002, SSM Health Care, based in St. Louis, Missouri, became the first winner of the Baldrige Award in the healthcare category.

The Baldrige model is a systems perspective of the organization as a whole. According to Kofman and Senge (1995), "fragmentation is the cornerstone of what it means to be a professional, so much so that we call ourselves 'specialists.' Accountants worry about the books . . . nobody worries about the business as a whole." The importance of a systems perspective for advancing performance excellence was not readily apparent to Roger Pearson, CHE, CEO of Ellsworth County (Kansas) Medical Center (ECMC), when he embarked on a project to fix the quality improvement program at this 20-bed rural hospital. His introduction to the Baldrige Criteria and the realizations that came with this introduction are detailed in the case study below, as related by Pearson.

ECMC CASE STUDY

The first hospital in Ellsworth County, Kansas, was established in 1900 and has gone through many changes in its 100-plus-year history. The original 18-bed building was replaced in 1921 with a 40-bed, 4-story brick building. During the next 70 years, four major renovations were completed, which raised the licensed bed count to 72. The utilization and financial fortunes of the hospital improved dramatically with the start of Medicare in the mid-1960s.

However, 20 years later the hospital found itself unable to remain financially stable. This resulted from changes in the federal reimbursement methodology and reductions in traditionally high hospital utilization practices. By 1992, the hospital had shrunk to 44 licensed beds and had gone into bankruptcy. To ensure that health services would still be available locally, the citizens of Ellsworth County approved a tax referendum that included purchasing the assets of the hospital and converting it into a county hospital. On August 1, 1993, the newly reorganized, publicly owned hospital began operation. This coincided with the start of my tenure as CEO.

At that time, ECMC was debt free and had 15.4 days of cash in the bank. The long-range plan was to make it to the end of the week with enough money to make payroll. The immediate concern in 1993 was to stabilize the hospital's financial position. Once that occurred, the need for a new facility became apparent. The hospital built in 1921 was replaced in 1999 with a new facility at a different location within the city limits of Ellsworth. Along with the new building came upgraded diagnostic and rehabilitation capabilities as well as improvements in direct patient care services.

In 1998, five years after emerging from bankruptcy, ECMC was surviving. The old facility had been replaced with a new building, utilization of services was on the rise, and the organization had a stable base of staff members and medical providers. And yet, only an external transformation had occurred. The question that still needed to be answered was, "How do we improve to ensure our long-term survival?" Together with the director of systems improvement, I reviewed the effectiveness of our long-established quality improvement (QI) program. What we found was a system in need of repair. Departmental improvement projects were diffuse, without a customer focus, and in some cases just did not seem to be on topics of great importance. Some departments consistently reported performance measurement results, while others were "just too busy" to get their reports done on a timely basis. It was evident that our QI activities needed an injection of new energy and direction if our efforts were to ever answer the "So what?" question: "Now that we've done what we've done, have we done any good?" Realizing that the effectiveness of our current improvement efforts was related to our own past decisions, external assistance was sought to revitalize our efforts. My initial reaction was to "fix" QI. Once that was done it seemed that our internal transformation would be complete. Little did I realize how wrong I was.

Financial constraints kept ECMC from engaging someone from a large national consulting firm. A QI consultant I had met through some prior networking activities in Kansas was contacted. Because he was local I felt that he would best understand the rural Kansas culture and also be conservative in his fees. In 1999, the consultant met with the systems improvement director and me to develop a strategy for what needed to be done. I wanted him to provide me with recommendations of how the QI program could be modified to propel ECMC to the next level. In other words, I asked him what we needed to do to fix our program. In early 2000, the consultant toured the ECMC facility, reviewed written documentation, and interviewed all 12 of our managers. As the discussions progressed I began to wonder if the consultant really understood what I wanted. His questions and comments did not seem to focus on identifying which QI processes, statistical analyses, or measurement methodology needed fixing. He asked questions such as the following:

- How do senior leaders communicate and evaluate organizational performance expectations?
- What is your strategic planning process, and how is the strategic plan communicated to the entire hospital staff?

- What is your process for identifying patient expectations and requirements?
- How do you gather and analyze data to support strategic decisions?
- How is your education and training system tied to your strategic plan?
- How does your organization manage key processes to support daily operations?
- What are your key patient-related service results?

The report we got back from the consultant identified our strengths and opportunities for improvements in seven specific categories: leadership, strategic planning, patient/customer/market focus, information and analysis, staff focus, process management, and organizational results. The feedback report read in part as follows:

> Based on the written documentation and the interviews conducted at the hospital, we believe that Ellsworth County Medical Center would score in the 150 to 200 range on the Baldrige 1,000-point scale. While the scores for most categories fall into the 20 percent to 30 percent range (200 to 300 out of 1,000), the lack of measurable results prevents the total score from reaching that level. We think that Ellsworth County Medical Center has significant opportunities for improvement given the assets currently available to the hospital. These include a dedicated and cohesive management team, a new facility, and a competent staff who truly care about the hospital.

You have to realize that people at ECMC were actually feeling pretty good about our accomplishments over the prior five years. We were surviving financially, we had a new building, we had an improved image in the community, and we were experiencing an improving culture that recognized some value in teamwork and cooperation. The consultant's report was somewhat disheartening. Not only did I not learn how to fix QI but ECMC also scored a miserable 20 percent on this thing called a Baldrige 1,000-point scale. It was painfully apparent that I needed to learn more about Baldrige if this were indeed the right direction for ECMC.

Our consultant explained the principles and core values that serve as the driving force for excellence within the Baldrige program. We learned about the interrelatedness of the seven criteria identified in our feed-back report, especially the importance of measuring and reporting key organizational performance results. I began to realize that the problems with our QI program were a manifestation of our organizational design. If ECMC was to be successful in sustained improvement (the true performance excellence journey), we would need to begin by developing our systems and processes to address the Baldrige Criteria. It became apparent that we were in need of a paradigm shift in our organizational thinking from "doing and fixing things" to "building an organizational capacity" where excellence is the way of understanding our organization. If we aligned basic organizational structures and processes and incorporated the Baldrige core values and criteria into those structures and processes, our organizational performance would automatically improve. We came to understand that the Baldrige model is a long-term, organizationwide approach, as opposed to a rapid "quick fix and move on" concept. It made sense, and it just seemed like the right thing to do. The next question became, Where do we start?

* * * * *

 KEY POINT

Baldrige is not a magic potion for every health services ailment. However, it does have elements that the improvement initiatives in many healthcare organizations lack. For example, the Baldrige Criteria promote strategic alignment of the organization's goals and objectives at all levels.

ANOTHER MANAGEMENT FAD?

Is the Baldrige model of performance excellence just another management fad that will be quickly discounted or dropped back to very modest usage? Researchers who have studied management fads use a technique known as bibliometrics to determine how many articles have been devoted to a given concept over time. The rationale for this method is that bibliographic records are a relatively objective indicator for measuring discourse popularity. In other words, the higher the article counts, the

FIGURE 2.1 THE LIFE CYCLE OF TOTAL QUALITY MANAGEMENT,
1990-2001

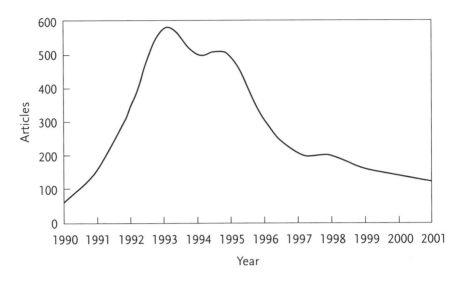

Source: Ponzi and Koenig (2002). Reprinted with permission.

larger is the volume of discussion. Ponzi and Koenig (2002) used this article-counting technique to analyze the life cycle of total quality management and business process reengineering. The life-cycle graphs for these two management models are displayed in Figures 2.1 and 2.2. The graphs strikingly illustrate the way in which these movements grew and fell in popularity.

From this analysis, it is reasonable to assume that management fads often begin to lose popularity in about five years.

 REFLECTION

What quality improvement "magic wands" has your organization implemented in the past ten years? What made some initiatives more successful than others? How can these lessons be applied to your journey toward performance excellence?

The criteria of the Baldrige quality program have not lost popularity. Why? Because the Baldrige Criteria do not represent a particular management model or business strategy. Instead, they provide a flexible umbrella with core principles that allow individual healthcare organizations

FIGURE 2.2 THE LIFE CYCLE OF BUSINESS PROCESS
REENGINEERING, 1990-2001

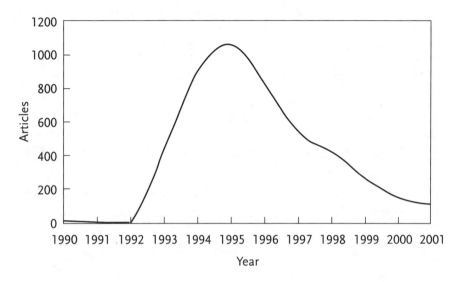

Source: Ponzi and Koenig (2002). Reprinted with permission.

the option to apply any of the various—and highly effective—process management philosophies and tools in the manner that best supports the needs of the organization. For example, the Baldrige Criteria ask, "How do you select, collect, align and integrate data and information for tracking overall organizational performance?" (NIST 2004a). An organization may choose to use Kaplan and Norton's (1996) balanced scorecard model or another approach for tracking organization performance. Six Sigma projects can assist organizations in meeting the Baldrige Criteria related to process management, but the Six Sigma methodology is not specifically recommended over other process improvement models.

The values and criteria that support the Baldrige award have become a beacon and blueprint for driving a wide variety of organizations to their highest levels of sustainable achievement. The criteria are now widely accepted as the de facto standard for performance excellence, and they are also the basis for many quality programs sponsored by professional organizations. An example is the American Health Care Association's Quality Award, which addresses the key requirements of performance excellence in long-term-care facilities. The criteria for the American Hospital Association's Quest for Quality Prize cover many of the concepts found in the Baldrige Criteria. "A good idea does not care who owns it" is an applicable phrase for what the Baldrige program is providing to businesses of all types and sizes. It is particularly rewarding to see these good ideas enjoying a growing adoption rate.

THE BALDRIGE CRITERIA

The Baldrige National Quality Program establishes the guidelines and the criteria that organizations can use to evaluate their performance or to apply for the Malcolm Baldrige National Quality Award. The program encourages performance improvement in all business sectors, including healthcare, by disseminating information about how superior organizations were able to achieve outstanding performance. The criteria for the Baldrige award have played a major role in the achievement of the goals established in 1988. Since they were first written, the award criteria have undergone several cycles of improvement. The NIST coordinates revisions to the standards.

The Baldrige Health Care Criteria for Performance Excellence are intended to help organizations use an integrated approach to organizational performance management that results in the following outcomes (NIST 2004b):

1. Delivery of ever-improving value to patients and other customers, thus contributing to improved healthcare quality
2. Improvement of overall organizational effectiveness and capabilities as a healthcare provider
3. Organizational and personal learning

The Baldrige framework for excellence is depicted in Figure 2.3. Leadership is the driving force for creating and sustaining the vision. Organizational capabilities necessary for supporting performance excellence include strategic planning; focus on patients, other customers, and markets; measurement, analysis, and knowledge management; staff focus; and process management. Optimal clinical and business results can be achieved when organizational strategic goals, objectives, and processes are linked and aligned to optimize the delivery and quality of services with a minimal expenditure of resources.

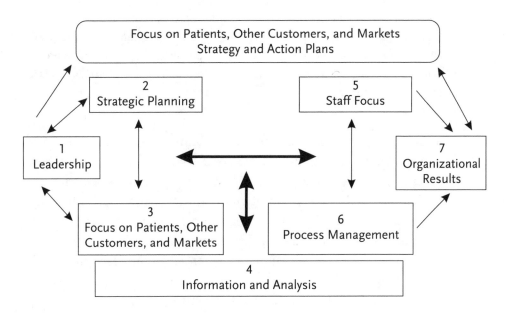

Source: NIST (2004, 5).

 KEY POINT

The Baldrige Criteria represent an integrated performance management approach for achieving performance excellence. The criteria comprise a framework that healthcare organizations can use to improve overall performance.

The comprehensive and nonprescriptive nature of the Baldrige Criteria makes them fundamentally different from the accreditation and regulatory standards that healthcare organizations have traditionally used to define quality. The Baldrige Criteria are presented as focused, open-ended questions resembling qualitative research questions. These questions, combined with the Baldrige core values, concepts, and scoring scale, provide organizations with a general road map for the performance excellence journey.

The difference between the Baldrige Health Care Criteria and the Joint Commission standards is illustrated in Figure 2.4. Rather than tell an organization what must be done, the Baldrige Criteria are posed as

2004 Baldrige Criteria	2004 Joint Commission Standard
How do you design processes to meet all key requirements, including patient safety, regulatory, accreditation, and payer requirements?	MM.2.10 Medications available for dispensing or administration are selected, listed, and procured based on criteria.

questions that are intended to encourage the development and implementation of the best plan for achieving excellence within the context of the organization's unique environment. The Baldrige Criteria are a platform for managing a healthcare organization toward achieving high performance while fulfilling accreditation and regulatory standards. Compliance with standards is a subset of the broader performance excellence journey.

Because the Baldrige Criteria are essentially nonprescriptive, an infinite variety of responses are possible. The nonprescriptive nature of the criteria allows for broad application across all types of healthcare organizations, but this flexibility can be troublesome to those looking for the one right answer. The Baldrige Criteria encourage organizations to understand, evaluate, and constantly improve the interrelated functions that are known to affect organizational excellence. Because of the complex nature of the healthcare industry, what might be the "right way" today will likely need adjusting tomorrow. Organizational excellence cannot be sustained by meeting minimum and sometimes outdated prescriptive standards.

Enablers of Excellence

The Baldrige Criteria allow senior leaders to take the role of diagnostic consultant for the organization to devise the best strategy for advancing performance excellence. Rather than mandating particular performance management techniques or models, the Baldrige Criteria prompt leaders to ask key questions about the organization, such as the following:

- What is high performance for us?
- How will we know if we are performing at our best?
- Why do we want to strive for excellence in the first place?

The key questions are grounded in numerous research studies of high-performing organizations. The Baldrige Criteria represent those enablers that, if present in an organization, increase its capacity for excellence.

Once you are familiar with all of the enablers of excellence, look inside your organization and ask, What are the "levers" that, if pulled correctly, will allow us to incorporate these enablers into our organization? Current organizational strategies, structures, and systems may need to be modified. The nature of leadership may need to change. Accountability systems may have to be strengthened. And so on. The questioning process helps you transform your organization into one that delivers high service quality, outstanding value, and sound financial performance.

In subsequent chapters, readers are introduced to many of the enablers of excellence that are embodied in the Baldrige Criteria.

Core Values and Concepts

The Baldrige award criteria for performance excellence are built on a set of core values and concepts that are the embedded beliefs and behaviors found in high-performing organizations. They are the foundation for integrating key business requirements within a results-oriented framework to create a basis for action and feedback, and they are described as follows:

- *Visionary leadership*: Senior leaders set directions and create a patient focus, clear and visible values, and high expectations. The directions, values, and expectations should balance the needs of all stakeholders. The leaders need to ensure the creation of strategies, systems, and methods for achieving excellence in healthcare, stimulating innovation, and building knowledge and capabilities.
- *Patient focus*: The delivery of healthcare services must be patient focused. All attitudes of patient care delivery (medical and nonmedical) factor into the judgment of satisfaction and value. Satisfaction and value are key considerations for other customers, too.
- *Organizational and personal learning*: Organizational learning refers to continuous improvement of existing approaches and processes

and adaptation to change, which leads to new goals and/or approaches. Learning is embedded in the operation of the organization.

- *Valuing staff and partners*: An organization's success depends increasingly on the knowledge, skills, creativity, and motivation of its staff and partners. Valuing staff means being committed to their satisfaction, development, and well-being.

- *Agility*: A capacity for rapid change and flexibility is a necessity for success. Healthcare providers face ever-shorter cycles for the introduction of new and improved healthcare services. Faster and more flexible response to patients and other customers is critical.

- *Focus on the future*: A strong future orientation includes a willingness to make long-term commitments to key stakeholders: patients and families, staff, communities, employers, payers, and health profession students. Important for an organization in the strategic planning process is the anticipation of changes in healthcare delivery, resource availability, patient and other stakeholder expectations, technological developments, new partnering opportunities, evolving regulatory requirements, community/societal expectations, and new threats by competitors.

- *Management for innovation*: Innovation means making meaningful change to improve an organization's services and processes and creating new value for the organization's stakeholders.

- *Management by fact*: Measurement and analysis of performance is needed for an effective healthcare and administrative management system. Measurements are derived from the organization's strategy and provide critical data and information about key processes, outputs, and results.

- *Public responsibility and community health*: Leaders need to emphasize the responsibility the organization has to the public, and they need to foster improved community health.

- *Focus on results and creating value*: An organization's performance measurements need to focus on key results. Results should focus on creating and balancing value for all stakeholders: patients, their families, staff, the community, payers, businesses, health profession students, suppliers and partners, stockholders, and the public.

- *Systems perspective*: Successful management of an organization requires synthesis and alignment. Synthesis means looking at the organization as a whole and focusing on what is important, while alignment means concentrating on key organizational linkages among the requirements in the Baldrige Criteria.

REFLECTION

To what extent do the Baldrige core values exist in your organization? What can you do to advance these core values?

Baldrige Criteria Categories

The Baldrige Health Care Criteria are designed as an interrelated system of items that address major areas of performance excellence. The 2004 criteria include 19 items organized into seven categories (or management disciplines) that cover the following elements:

1. Leadership
2. Strategic Planning
3. Focus on Patients, Other Customers, and Markets
4. Measurement, Analysis, and Knowledge Management
5. Staff Focus
6. Process Management
7. Organizational Results

KEY POINT

The Baldrige core values and the seven categories form the building blocks of an integrated system that requires both synthesis and alignment.

The *Leadership* category examines how senior leaders address values, directions, and performance expectations, as well as issues related to patients and other customers and market segments, empowerment, innovation, and learning. Also examined are how the organization addresses its responsibilities to the public and supports its key communities.

The *Strategic Planning* category examines how the organization develops strategic objectives and action plans. Also examined are how chosen strategic objectives and action plans are deployed and how progress is measured.

The *Focus on Patients, Other Customers, and Markets* category examines how the organization determines requirements, expectations, and preferences of users of its services. Also examined are how the organization builds relationships with customers and other stakeholders and determines the key factors that lead to public trust and confidence.

The *Measurement, Analysis, and Knowledge Management* category examines the organization's information management (i.e., databases, technology, equipment) and performance measurement systems and how performance data and information are analyzed. This refers to "how" the organization gathers information and measures performance; "what" is measured is examined in the Organizational Results category.

The *Staff Focus* category examines how leaders motivate and enable clinical and nonclinical staff to develop and realize their full potential in alignment with the organization's overall objectives and action plans. Also examined are the organization's efforts to build and maintain a work environment that supports performance excellence and personal and organizational growth.

The *Process Management* category examines the key aspects of the organization's processes, including patient-focused service design, service delivery, and other key clinical and support processes.

The *Organizational Results* category examines the organization's performance and improvement in key areas: healthcare results, satisfaction of patients and other customers, financial and market results, staff and work system results, operational performance, and governance/social responsibility. Identifying "what" key results are important for the organization and current levels of performance are also examined.

 KEY POINT

Use the complete set of Baldrige Criteria as a self-assessment tool to look at your organization through a new lens. This lens enables you to see the organization as a system of interrelated processes and practices designed to achieve customer satisfaction and, in turn, overall organization success.

Scoring System

Many healthcare organizations will never apply for the Baldrige award; however, an understanding of the system for scoring applicants is useful for self-assessment purposes. The scoring of responses to criteria items is based on three evaluation dimensions: approach, deployment, and results.

Approach refers to how the organization addresses the criteria requirements (i.e., the methods used). The factors used to evaluate approaches include the following:

- The appropriateness of the methods to the requirements
- The effectiveness of use of the methods and the degree to which the approach
  — is repeatable, integrated, and consistently applied;
  — embodies evaluation/improvement/learning cycles; and
  — is based on reliable information and data
- The alignment with the organization's needs
- The evidence of beneficial innovation and change

Deployment refers to the extent to which the organization's approach is applied to all appropriate areas or work units. The areas or work units considered when evaluating deployment vary depending on the criteria requirements. Deployment is evaluated on the basis of the breadth and depth of application of the approach to relevant processes and work units throughout the organization.

Results refer to outcomes achieved by the organization. The factors used to evaluate results include the following:

- The organization's current performance, especially as measured by the organization's performance goals
- Rate, breadth, and importance of the organization's performance improvements
- The organization's performance relative to appropriate comparisons and/or benchmarks
- The linkage of performance measures to key success factors defined by the organization

 KEY POINT

Many different factors influence how well healthcare organizations deliver services. The Malcolm Baldrige National Quality Award Criteria synthesize these factors into three areas: approach, deployment, and results.

Each year the Baldrige Criteria undergo slight revisions; for this reason, the full criteria set has not been reproduced in this book. The most current criteria manual can be obtained free of charge from the Baldrige National Quality Program at NIST. Call 301/975-2036, or go to the program's web site at www.quality.nist.gov. You will gain the most from the recommendations in this book if you also have the most current Baldrige Criteria set available for your reference.

BALDRIGE-BASED ORGANIZATIONAL ASSESSMENT

One of the best ways to gain organizationwide commitment to performance excellence is through participation in an actual assessment based on the full set of Baldrige Criteria. This assessment provides an opportunity for senior leaders and managers to reflect on the systems that support quality, think about things that need changing, and focus improvement efforts on the areas most relevant and important to the organization's goals. The assessment can help managers and staff members understand how they contribute to the principles of continuous improvement in a meaningful way. And it gives senior leaders a framework for looking at results from a systems perspective so that the organization can concentrate on improving performance in all key result areas and come up with metrics for monitoring that improvement.

Once completed, the assessment results provide a basis for developing a consensus on what needs to be done so that activities can be focused in a consistent direction. By using the Baldrige Criteria for periodical reassessments—ideally as part of the annual planning cycle—the organization can measure the progress of its performance excellence journey.

The assessment process needs to be as inclusive as possible if it is to have a significant impact. It is important to have the full commitment of the CEO and senior executive team. A project team of leaders coordinates and oversees the evidence-gathering part of the assessment, and subgroups are formed to gather information for each section of the criteria. One person should not be answering all of the Baldrige questions, as individual perceptions may sway the results. For most organizations, valid results are possible only if a team approach is used. If the goal is to actually improve the organization rather than merely obtain a high score, many people should participate in the assessment process. Moreover, those who participate gain a better understanding of what needs to be done to advance performance excellence and are more willing to support the improvement recommendations that come out of the assessment process.

Regular meetings (at least biweekly) should be held by the leadership team to ensure that information gathering is going smoothly and the assessment teams remain on target. Do not hurry the process. The Baldrige Criteria present penetrating questions that take time to think about and answer. Often teams must research the organization's practices to formulate intelligent answers. Much of the benefit of a Baldrige self-assessment lies in discovering gaps that leaders did not know about until people tried to respond to a particular item. Time spent thinking deeply about the Baldrige Criteria and how they apply to the organization is time well spent.

When all of the questions have been answered, the leadership team evaluates the results. A thorough Baldrige assessment typically highlights dozens of areas for improvement as well as organizational strengths. To advance performance excellence, the organization should concentrate on its weakest areas. Often it is useful to research how other organizations have solved similar problems. Many examples are found in this book. It may also be important to poll experts within the organization to collect their thoughts about how to best solve specific problems.

The Baldrige assessment provides a reproducible yardstick for tracking your organization's performance excellence journey. Often improvements in periodic Baldrige assessment scores will show up before performance measures indicate substantial improvement. Periodic reassessments provide an opportunity to celebrate successes as well as discover continued areas of weakness.

 KEY POINT

The Baldrige Criteria are built around cycles of learning. Periodic self-assessments provide leaders at all levels in the healthcare organization with the means to continually improve system performance.

Know Thyself

The Baldrige National Quality Award program describes the organizational profile as the starting point for self-assessment (NIST 2003). The profile provides a snapshot of the organization and includes the influences of how it operates and the key challenges it faces. At first glance, the profile appears to be merely a way to communicate information about the organization to the Baldrige award program examiners. However, the profile serves a much more important purpose in an organization's performance excellence journey. Some of the basic questions in the profile—Who are our key patient/customer groups and market segments? How are their requirements different? and What can we do to tailor our services to address those differences?—are fundamental questions that a lot of organizations think they can answer. But get your leadership group together and ask those questions. You will be amazed at how many different viewpoints come out. If the leadership team is not in agreement about the answers, the rest of your organization is not going to be aligned, either.

The organizational profile asks a number of questions about the environment in which you operate, the key relationships that your healthcare organization has, the challenges you face, and how you improve performance in your organization. The organizational profile is a very basic set of questions that sets a context for answering the following questions:

- Does your organization have a focus on what is important to it?
- Does your organization understand what its mission is?
- Does your organization understand the needs of patients and other customers and market segments?
- Does your organization understand what processes need to be in place to go about meeting those needs?

The questions in the organizational profile of the 2004 Baldrige Criteria for Health Care are found in Figure 2.5.

The self-assessment process begins with the development of an organizational profile that identifies what kind of an organization you represent, who your customers are, and what is most important to your organization. The profile provides a common lens for understanding and viewing your organization. It also helps to introduce senior leaders to the Baldrige model and identify key requirements to consider when looking at how the criteria translate into your environment.

The executive team alone can answer the questions in the profile; however, consider including key physician leaders to broaden the

FIGURE 2.5 ORGANIZATIONAL PROFILE QUESTIONS

Organizational Environment

1. What are your organization's main health services? What are the delivery mechanisms used to provide your healthcare services to your patients?
2. What is your organizational culture? What are your stated purpose, vision, mission, and values?
3. What is your staff profile? What are their educational levels? What are your organization's workforce and job diversity, organized bargaining units, use of contract and privileged staff, and special health and safety requirements?
4. What are your major technologies, equipment, and facilities?
5. What is the legal and regulatory environment under which your organization operates? What are the applicable occupational health and safety regulations; accreditation, certification, or registration requirements; and environmental and financial regulations relevant to health service delivery?

Organizational Relationships

1. What is your organizational structure and governance system? What are the reporting relationships among your board of trustees, senior leaders, and your parent organization, as appropriate?
2. What are your key patient and other customer groups and healthcare market segments, as appropriate? What are their key requirements and expectations for your healthcare services? What are the differences in these requirements and expectations among patient and other customer groups and market segments?
3. What role do suppliers and partners play in your key processes? What are your most important types of suppliers and partners? What are your most important supply chain requirements?
4. What are your key supplier and partnering relationships and communication mechanisms?

Competitive Environment

1. What is your competitive position? What is your relative size and growth in the healthcare industry or markets served? What are the numbers and types of competitors and key collaborators for your organization?
2. What are the principal factors that determine your success relative to your competitors and other organizations delivering similar services? What are any key changes taking place that affect your competitive situation or opportunities for collaborating?

FIGURE 2.5 *(continued)*

Strategic Challenges

1. What are your key healthcare service, operational, and human resource strategic challenges?

Performance Improvement System

1. What is the overall approach you use to maintain an organizational focus on performance improvement and to guide systematic evaluation and improvement of key processes?
2. What is your overall approach to organizational learning and sharing your knowledge assets within the organization?

Source: NIST (2004, 12–14).

experience. People can often come together in just one day to clarify the answers and come to a common understanding of the organization. Completion of the profile is the starting point for self-assessment. Often many gaps are identified just by that simple exercise. Once the results are communicated, people begin to talk about common needs and how to work on factors that are inhibiting performance excellence.

The organizational profile, along with answers to the questions in each Baldrige category, identify what your organization needs to work on first to have the greatest impact on results. The self-assessment is an excellent tool for gathering information from all levels within your organization to use when forming strategic plans for advancing performance excellence.

By comparing your organization with the values and concepts that are embedded as behaviors within high-performing organizations, you can identify where your organization has gaps in key characteristics. Figure 2.6 is an excerpt from one hospital's analysis of its Baldrige self-assessment results. The assessment identified gaps between where the hospital is now and where it wants to be. Detailed work plans are being developed, and managers and staff members throughout the organization will be involved in plan implementation. The leadership team will continue to monitor these efforts and provide direction for future system improvements.

Where We Are	Where We Want to Be	To Bridge this Gap, We Must
Organizational Results		
• Very low rate of staff turnover as noted by recent comparative report • Key indicators for clinical services: results have not been determined • No systematic way of gathering information, communicating, and using results	• All physicians and staff have a common understanding of what our key results are • Balanced scorecard measurements for key processes • Information used as a managerial tool for planning, program improvements, and resource allocation	• Identify key results by seeking input from physicians and staff • Identify ways to systematically gather and disseminate key result information to staff and public • Provide quarterly reporting to be used for staff empowerment, management decisions, and system improvement • Work with corporate headquarters to establish comparisons systemwide
Staff Satisfaction		
• Dedicated resources to building a strong human resources development program • No way of measuring the effectiveness of training and development efforts • Cultural gaps between physicians, managers, and staff members	• Extensive services provided to enhance employee and physician well-being, satisfaction, and motivation • Physicians, managers, and staff members work collaboratively to provide our services • These efforts are regularly evaluated	• Leadership will provide clear direction to managers and staff by identifying key results • A committee will be formed to identify and monitor the effectiveness of programs designed to increase communication, knowledge sharing, and collaboration

Assessment Resources

Numerous self-assessment resources are available from the Baldrige National Quality Program. Learn more about these free resources on the program's web site, www.quality.nist.gov. The National Baldrige Quality Program also sponsors regional conferences at which participants have an opportunity to learn directly from past award winners. These conferences include sessions designed to introduce people to the criteria and how to use them for self-assessment purposes.

Many of the state and regional Baldrige-based quality award programs have self-assessment resources available free of charge. In addition, many programs sponsor educational sessions. A list of these award programs, along with contact information, is found in the appendix at the end of this book. If your organization applies for a quality award, the evaluation process includes an assessment of your organization's strengths and weaknesses. The evaluation conducted by the award examiners can be an important source of feedback on your organization's progress toward excellence.

Below is a continuation of the case study from ECMC in Ellsworth, Kansas. Once the CEO became convinced that a systems approach was necessary for improving the hospital's performance, a commitment from the board was sought and organizational learning began. The case study, as related by ECMC's CEO, Roger Pearson, illustrates how the hospital partnered with the Kansas quality award program to learn more about the Baldrige model of organizational excellence.

ECMC CASE STUDY

ECMC's performance excellence journey included our participation in the state's quality award process. As the hospital administrator, I was interested in creating the opportunity for a significant paradigm shift in our organizational thinking and decided that we would be better served by actively participating in a Baldrige-based award program. Several states have developed state quality programs that use the Baldrige Criteria, and Kansas is one of those states. It is called the Kansas Award for Excellence (KAE), and it is administered by the KAE Foundation. The KAE criteria mirror the Baldrige National Quality Award Program, and the review process is similar. Award applications are reviewed and scored by a panel of examiners who write a feedback report identifying strengths and opportunities for improvements in the seven Baldrige Criteria. Recognition awards are issued to organizations that are successful at meeting the criteria. The KAE program has three levels of recognition:

1. Commitment to Quality—Level I
2. Performance in Quality—Level II
3. Kansas Excellence Award—Level III

A proposal was made to the ECMC board to adopt the Baldrige model as our basic structure for lasting performance excellence. This involved ECMC committing to a five-year plan, which would result in 75 percent of the management team becoming trained KAE examiners and achieving the Level III Kansas Excellence Award. The board approved the proposal, and the performance excellence journey at ECMC was on its way.

I believed that the most efficient and effective method of learning the Baldrige Criteria would be as a participant in the KAE award process. However, before ECMC submitted an award application, we needed a better understanding of how to apply the Baldrige principles. Therefore, in early summer 2000, the director of systems improvement and I attended a two-and-one-half-day KAE examiner training program. Following completion of the training, we were each assigned two applications to review and score. An examiner team usually comprises five to six members, whose responsibility it is to review one or two applications from Kansas businesses and provide a consensus feedback report on the strengths and opportunities for improvement for each of the seven categories of the Baldrige Criteria. Each examiner personally spends approximately 40 to 60 hours reviewing an application. Since the Baldrige approach applies to all types of business enterprises, an examiner team may be reviewing nonheathcare applications. My experience with the examiner process has shown me that the criteria are universal in application and that they can increase one's understanding of the approach, even when reviewing nonhealthcare organizations.

In 2001, three additional ECMC managers were trained as KAE examiners; in that same year, the hospital applied for and received the Level I KAE Award.

*　*　*　*　*

It is not necessary, but it may be desirable for an organization to engage a consultant to assist in the Baldrige-based assessment. Sponsors of quality award programs can recommend consultants with particular expertise in using the Baldrige Criteria to evaluate a healthcare organization. A search of the Internet will yield a large number of firms that offer Baldrige-based assessment tools (e.g., software, books) and on-site consultations.

Another option is to educate a core group of people in your organization in how to conduct a Baldrige-based assessment and use the results to advance performance excellence. Several companies and groups sponsor conferences or offer in-house training that is specific to the Baldrige Criteria. Two not-for-profit associations that sponsor Baldrige training are listed below.

American Society for Quality
www.asq.org
800/248-1946

The Association for Quality and
   Participation
www.aqp.org
800/733-3310

Several books are available on the topic of how to conduct a Baldrige-based self-assessment. A book specific to healthcare, *Insights to Performance Excellence in Health Care 2004: An Inside Look at the 2004 Baldrige Award Criteria for Health Care,* is published by ASQ (Blazey 2004). The book is updated annually to reflect any changes made to the healthcare criteria.

One of the best ways to learn how to apply the Baldrige Criteria in real-life situations is to volunteer to be an examiner for a quality award program. Examiners receive training in the criteria for performance excellence, the scoring systems, and the examination process. To learn more about the examiner application process, time-commitment requirements, and training opportunities, contact the quality award program in your state or region. A list of programs is found in the appendix at the end of this book. The Baldrige National Quality Program also relies on volunteer examiners; however, the prerequisite knowledge and skills for examiners are more stringent than required by local and state quality award programs. If your organization is just starting the performance excellence journey, it is more likely that your senior leaders and managers would qualify to be examiners at the state level.

The information in this book is also an excellent resource on the Baldrige Criteria. However, it is not intended to be a comprehensive source of information about how to conduct a self-assessment—that would be unnecessarily redundant given the availability of so many other resources on this topic. The purpose of this book is to describe the critical enablers of performance excellence (as defined by the Baldrige Criteria and to illustrate, through case studies and examples, how healthcare organizations can incorporate these enablers into daily practices.

REFERENCES

Blazey, M. 2004. *Insights to Performance Excellence in Health Care 2004: An Inside Look at the 2004 Baldrige Award Criteria for Health Care.* Milwaukee, WI: American Society for Quality.

Kaplan, R., and D. Norton. 1996. *The Balanced Scorecard: Translating Strategy into Action.* Boston: Harvard Business Press.

Kofman, F., and P. Senge. 1995. "Communities of Commitment: The Heart of Learning Organizations." In *Learning Organizations: Developing Cultures for Tomorrow's Workplace,* 18, edited by S. Chawla and J. Renesch. Portland, OR: Productivity Press.

National Institute of Standards and Technology (NIST). 2004a. *Malcolm Baldrige Criteria for Health Care 2004,* 22. Gaithersburg, MD: NIST.

————. 2004b. *Malcolm Baldrige Criteria for Health Care 2004,* 1. Gaithersburg, MD: NIST.

————. 2003. *Baldrige Self-Assessment and Action Planning: Using the Baldrige Organizational Profile for Health Care.* [Online document; retrieved 2/04.] http://patapsco.nist.gov/eBaldrige/HealthCare_Profile.cfm.

Ponzi, L. J., and M. Koenig. 2002. "Knowledge Management: Another Management Fad?" [Online article; retrieved 6/4/04.] *Information Research* 8 (1): paper no. 145. http://InformationR.net/ir/8-1/paper145.html.

CHAPTER THREE

Driver of Excellence: Leadership

NUMEROUS RESEARCH STUDIES of business management models have repeatedly substantiated the important role of leadership in achieving desired results. Studies of the Baldrige model of performance excellence suggest that leadership has the strongest relationship with business results, more than twice the effect of any other variable (Pannirselvam and Ferguson 2001; Wilson and Collier 2000; Flynn and Saladin 2001).

LEADERSHIP QUALITIES

Organizational excellence requires more than the right mission, motivation, ideas, planning, and funding. The CEO must lead the staff members, physicians, and other stakeholders in building a vision and maximizing resources to carry out the job. Exercising good leadership is an essential ingredient for developing and enforcing the ideals of excellence and building organizational capabilities. Leaders must create an environment in which the following occur:

- There is a clear focus on meeting the needs and expectations of patients and other stakeholders.
- Learning and innovation are embraced.
- The organization's direction is well defined and communicated.

- Physicians, managers, and staff members routinely address organizational priorities and performance expectations.

Mary-Frances Winters, president and founder of The Winters Group, Inc., a business consulting firm based in Landover, Maryland, believes that today's business leader needs to be audacious, be able to inspire and motivate others, possess strong character, and operate from values formed from deep conviction. The following are the leadership attributes that Winters (2003) suggests are very important:[*]

- *Slightly irreverent.* The leader must be willing to challenge the system even though on the surface it may appear that he or she is not being a team player.
- *Probing.* The leader must be someone who continually asks probing questions and is interested in getting to the root of an issue.
- *Willing to take action.* Many people in leadership positions become stymied by the complexities and paradoxes of business and procrastinate in making decisions because there is no easy or one right answer. Doing something for the good of the organization, even if it does not work, is almost always better than doing nothing.
- *Intuitive.* "Management by the facts" is a popular concept today, but facts may not always tell the whole story. Leaders must augment the facts with experiential gut feel.
- *Penchant for learning.* Leaders of the future will need to be well read (knowing a little bit about a lot of things), update their skills continuously, and encourage their people to do the same.
- *Painfully honest.* People have been conditioned to communicate in ways that sugarcoat the message. Those who are able to be forthright with compassion and empathy will make great leaders.
- *Relationship and network builder.* A leader knows the value of teamwork and building trusting relationships. Leaders seek out others to accomplish a task and know how to find the resources that they need through effective networking.

Building Trust

The ability to build a trusting and trustworthy organization is one of the most important characteristics of healthcare leaders. New leaders

---

[*]Portions of the article are reprinted here by permission of the author.

encouraging trust within the organization have achieved some of the most successful turnarounds of failing healthcare organizations. Trust takes a long time to establish and only seconds to destroy. If trust is abused in a high-trust organization, the impact can be serious. Trust needs to be accompanied by accountability.

Trust is about relationships—between the senior leaders and staff members and between the organization and its customers (e.g., independent physicians, patients and their families, the community).

A leader must operate from a set of high ethical beliefs and principles and also hold people in the organization to a similar standard. Anyone can be ethical when no pressure exists to be unethical. At times, however, such factors as personal ambition, convenience, greed, or prejudices get in the way of ethical behavior. Sometimes there is pressure to bend or break the rules a little. Leaders perceived as unethical can quickly lose the trust of people in the organization. The trustworthiness of senior leaders is at the heart of organizational performance excellence. Leaders have three ethical responsibilities that promote an environment of excellence:

1. Be a good role model.
2. Develop good ethical principles in others.
3. Lead in such a way that people in the organization are not put into ethical dilemmas.

If people in the organization are to place their trust in the senior leaders, then the leaders must be trustworthy and willing to place their trust in others. By and large, trust needs to be earned. Trust is the emotional glue of all relationships.

 SELF-ASSESSMENT

Read the questions and assign scores from 0 (never true) to 5 (always true). Add up your score to determine whether yours is a high-, medium-, or low-trust environment.

___ Our leaders are above reproach in their professional and personal lives.
___ My organization respects all individuals, groups, and companies that deal with it.
___ My organization empowers and expects people to do their best.
___ In my organization, people's responsibilities are matched with their authority and accountability.

___ People in my organization are inspired by its mission.

___ All decisions/actions within the organization are consistent with its mission.

___ In my organization, leaders communicate frequently, clearly, and broadly.

___ Budgets are shared and discussed in my organization.

___ People can comfortably disagree in my organization.

___ People in my organization understand its vulnerabilities.

___ Total Score

If you have assigned more than 40 points to your organization, yours is a trusting environment led by trustworthy and empowered leaders who have respect for others and who have established trust-building relationships. If you have awarded 15 or fewer total points, yours is a suspicious and trust-poor organization. With this score, it is unlikely that a common vision inspires your members. Do not even attempt to embark on the performance excellence journey until trust is restored. If your organization scored in the middle, there are aspects of trust that must be repaired if performance excellence is to thrive. Evaluating the trust level in your organization is vital. Understanding, repairing, and keeping trust are among the most important leadership duties.

Introspection

Leadership is the ability (or process) to influence, lead, or guide others to accomplish a goal in the manner desired by providing purpose, direction, and motivation. The skills and attributes necessary for effective leadership are not well understood. Some leaders influence, excite, and energize other people in the organization, while other leaders do not. Do you have the skills and attributes necessary for championing your organization's performance excellence journey? Complete the self-assessment at the end of this section to identify your strengths and weaknesses. The good news is that most leadership behaviors are learned. Use the questionnaire results to develop professional and personal growth strategies.

 REFLECTION

When you were influenced, excited, and energized by a leader to do something you thought impossible, what traits or skills did that person possess? Think about what created in you the desire to follow that leader. How can you incorporate some of these same attributes into your leadership style?

 SELF-ASSESSMENT

Leadership Attributes and Skills Questionnaire

This survey is designed to provide you with feedback about your level of comfort with leadership attributes and skills. Circle the number on the scale that you believe comes closest to your skill or task level. Be honest about your choices. There are no right or wrong answers; the results are only for your self-assessment and professional growth.

5 = very strong; 4 = moderately strong; 3 = adequate; 2 = moderately weak; 1 = very weak

1. I enjoy communicating with others.   5 4 3 2 1
2. I am honest and fair.   5 4 3 2 1
3. I make decisions with input from others.   5 4 3 2 1
4. My actions are consistent.   5 4 3 2 1
5. I give others the information they need to do their job.   5 4 3 2 1
6. I listen to feedback and ask questions.   5 4 3 2 1
7. I create an atmosphere of innovation.   5 4 3 2 1
8. I have wide visibility.   5 4 3 2 1
9. I give praise and recognition.   5 4 3 2 1
10. I criticize constructively and address problems.   5 4 3 2 1
11. I have a vision of where we are going and set long-term goals.   5 4 3 2 1
12. I set objectives and follow them through to completion.   5 4 3 2 1
13. I display tolerance and flexibility.   5 4 3 2 1
14. I can be assertive when needed.   5 4 3 2 1
15. I am a champion of excellence.   5 4 3 2 1
16. I treat others with respect and dignity.   5 4 3 2 1
17. I make myself available and accessible.   5 4 3 2 1
18. I accept ownership for senior leadership decisions.   5 4 3 2 1
19. I set guidelines for how people are to treat one another.   5 4 3 2 1
20. I am a good learner.   5 4 3 2 1
21. I know how to influence people and get support.   5 4 3 2 1
22. I admit my mistakes and take responsibility for my actions.   5 4 3 2 1
23. I am good at delegation.   5 4 3 2 1
24. I can separate the important issues from the inconsequential ones.   5 4 3 2 1
25. I have integrity and can be trusted.   5 4 3 2 1

By knowing themselves, leaders can take advantage of personal strengths and work to overcome weaknesses. Seeking self-improvement means continually strengthening your leadership skills, attributes, and behaviors. Some techniques for applying this principle follow:

- Use the above self-assessment to analyze yourself objectively to determine your weak and strong qualities.
- Ask for honest opinions from your senior leaders, managers, and staff members as to how you can improve your leadership abilities. The self-assessment tool could be reformatted into a survey tool for obtaining feedback about your leadership abilities from people in the organization.
- Study the causes for the success or failure of other business leaders, past and present.
- Strive to overcome your weaknesses and further strengthen those areas in which you are strong. Set definite goals, and plan to attain them.

The Baldrige Criteria are built on a set of interrelated core values that should be evident in all aspects of the organization, including leadership. Below are leadership enablers that demonstrate the Baldrige core values.

 LEADERSHIP ENABLER

Visionary Leadership
- ❏ Leaders have a keen understanding of how well the organization is performing and how it must perform in the future to meet and exceed expectations of patients and other stakeholders.
- ❏ Leaders set and communicate clear directions and high expectations throughout the organization.
- ❏ Leaders personally commit to continual improvement and visibly model continual improvement principles and practices.

Patient-Focused Excellence
- ❏ Leaders understand the desires and expectations of patients.
- ❏ Leaders consider the desires and expectations of patients when formulating short- and longer-term strategic objectives for the organization.
- ❏ Leaders focus the organization's activities on meeting patients' quality and performance needs.

Organizational and Personal Learning

❑ Leaders continually seek information about new and improved methods of healthcare delivery.

❑ Leaders engage physicians and staff members as full participants in learning and as contributors to improvement processes.

❑ Leaders provide opportunities for all staff members to learn and practice new skills.

Valuing Staff and Partners

❑ Leaders firmly believe that organizational success depends on the knowledge, skills, and motivation of the workforce, and all actions and decisions support this belief.

❑ Leaders avoid demotivating staff members and create conditions under which motivated employees flourish.

❑ Leaders build and manage strategic alliances with other providers and organizations to support and leverage resources and services.

Agility

❑ Leaders cultivate an organizational culture that can quickly respond to the needs of patients, staff members, and other stakeholders.

❑ Leaders emphasize process design quality, which means building quality into services and building efficiency into delivery processes.

❑ Leaders promote all aspects of timely performance to meet and exceed expectations of patients and other stakeholders.

Focus on the Future

❑ Leaders have a future orientation and a willingness to make long-term commitments to patients and all other stakeholders: the community, patients' families, insurers/third-party payers, employees, communities, employers, other healthcare providers, and so forth.

❑ Leaders anticipate changes in patient and other stakeholder expectations, new service opportunities, technological developments, regulatory requirements, and community/societal expectations.

❑ Leaders initiate plans, strategies, and resource allocations that reflect anticipated internal and external changes.

Managing for Innovation

❑ Leaders cultivate innovation for improving organizational effectiveness.

❑ Leaders manage the organization so that innovation becomes part of the culture and is integrated into daily work.

❑ Leaders encourage everyone to become innovative, questioning, suggestion producing, and boundary pushing to move the organization forward.

Management by Fact

❑ Leaders depend on measurement and analysis of performance to manage the organization.

❑ Leaders support the development of measures derived from the organization's strategy to provide critical data and information about key processes, outputs, and results.

❑ Leaders analyze many types of data—clinical performance, operations, market comparisons, patient/stakeholder feedback, staff related, and financial—to determine trends, projections, and cause and effect.

Social Responsibility and Community Health

❑ Leaders serve as role models to the organization, community members, and the public at large. They do not just talk about value statements, ethics, and social responsibilities; rather, all of their actions and decisions demonstrate the desired attitudes and behaviors.

❑ Leaders stress the organization's responsibilities to its patients, staff members, and community. This responsibility should be reflected in the values espoused by the organization, both internally and externally.

❑ Leaders create and sustain an organizational culture that promotes, internally and externally, the enduring values of integrity and quality.

Focus on Results and Creating Value

❑ Leaders understand the key results that patients and other stakeholders expect from the organization.

❑ Leaders focus the organization's attention on key results, guided and balanced by the interests of patients and other stakeholders.

❑ Leaders use a composite of performance measures to communicate short- and longer-term priorities, to monitor actual performance, and to marshal support for improving results.

Systems Perspective

❑ Leaders manage the whole organization, as well as its components, to achieve performance excellence.

❑ Leaders ensure that all elements of the business are integrated and aligned with the organization's mission, vision, and strategic objectives.

❑ Leaders promote a high degree of coherence between the individual elements of the organization's performance management system.

THE LEADERSHIP SYSTEM

The Baldrige Criteria that relate to leadership deal with what the senior leaders—those with the most responsibilities—actually do in the organization to advance performance excellence. The actions expected of senior leaders are found in the Leadership category as well as in other categories. Because leadership is considered the driver of performance excellence, the influence of leaders' actions would be expected in all areas. Leadership is exerted throughout the organization by way of the leadership system—the mission, vision, values, and operating systems—and the less tangible cultural elements related to "the way we do things around here." Each of these elements must support the organization's performance excellence aspirations. Take the vision statement, for example. Is it clear that your organization is striving for performance excellence? Does your vision statement reflect a steadfast desire to continually improve the quality of patient care and services? There is one universal rule of business excellence: an organization will never be greater than the vision that guides it.

Mission and Vision

The elements of excellence materialize within organizations as an offshoot of the leadership system. The mission and vision statements clearly express the reason for the existence of the organization and serve as focal points of commitment for the board, senior executive team, managers, and staff members. Decisions and actions taken at all levels should be consistent with the organization's mission and vision. The mission and vision statements must be broad enough to provide inspiration and specific enough to offer guidance to the organization both in setting broad policy and when making day-to-day decisions. Mechanisms should be in place to ensure that decisions are made in alignment with the mission and that decision makers are held accountable for adhering to the mission.

Consider the mission and vision statements from two past Baldrige quality award winners shown in Figure 3.1. Note how these statements inspire the organization's members to stretch their expectations, aspirations, and performance.

An organization's mission and vision statements should guide the implementation of all strategies. It should answer the question, "What will success look like?" It is the pursuit of this image of success that really motivates people to work together. The vision statement should be realistic and credible, well articulated and easily understood, appropriate,

ambitious, and responsive to change. It should focus the organization's
energies and serve as a guide to action. To make an impact, a vision
statement must rise above the mundane. It must grab the attention of
the organization and its stakeholders.

 REFLECTION

What is your organization's vision? Does it tell everyone in the organization what
success will look like? Does it capture the ideal of continual improvement?

Values

Values are beliefs that people in an organization hold in common and
endeavor to put into practice. The values guide everyone's work perfor-

mance. Examples of values in high-performing organizations include a commitment to excellent services, innovation, diversity, creativity, honesty, integrity, and so on. Ideally, an individual's personal values will align with the spoken and unspoken values of the organization. By developing a written statement of its values, the organization provides individuals with a chance to contribute to the articulation of these values as well as to evaluate how well their personal values and motivation match those of the organization.

Consider the value statements from two past Baldrige quality award winners shown in Figure 3.2. These values provide a behavioral framework for accomplishing the organizations' vision of excellence. Articulated values encourage common norms of behavior, which support the achievement of exceptional performance.

FIGURE 3.2 VALUES STATEMENTS OF PAST BALDRIGE AWARD WINNERS

SSM Health Care, St. Louis, MO (2002 winner of the Malcolm Baldrige National Quality Award, Health Care category)

Values
- Compassion. We reach out with openness, kindness, and concern.
- Respect. We honor the wonder of the human spirit.
- Excellence. We expect the best of ourselves and one another.
- Stewardship. We use our resources responsibly.
- Community. We cultivate relationships that inspire us to serve.

Pal's Sudden Service, a quick-service restaurant chain in northeast Tennessee and southwest Virginia (2001 winner of the Malcolm Baldrige National Quality Award, Small Business category)

Values
- Positive Energy. We will always nurture a positive, enthusiastic atmosphere, which will foster mutual trust and respect among employees, customers, and suppliers. Further, we will always operate with open agendas, positive interactions and genuine motives.
- Honesty and Truthfulness. We will always be honest and truthful in all relationships, respecting and relying on each other.
- Employee Well Being. We will always provide a safe, healthy, and desirable workplace.
- Citizenship. We will always provide community involvement through personal and company contributions of time, effort, and resources.

Through our best effort and consideration, we will always protect public health, safety, and the environment.

- Golden Rule. We will always do unto others, as we would have them do unto us.

Sources: SSM Health Care, www.ssmhc.com; Pal's Sudden Service, www.palsweb.com. Reprinted with permission.

It is one thing to have a written guide to an organization's values that remains on the wall or in a notebook; it is quite another thing to have living values that shape the culture—the way that things get done. High-performing healthcare organizations reinforce the values by doing the following:

- Constantly emphasizing the values in verbal and written communications
- Acknowledging and thanking people who achieve something that particularly reaffirms the values
- Communicating the organization's values to potential employees and medical staff members
- Providing new physicians and staff members with explicit information about the values
- Incorporating value statements into staff member competency statements and job requirements
- Confronting individuals who do not live up to the values of the organization
- Periodically asking people what they think of the values of the organization—not just staff members and physicians but also patients, suppliers, and other external stakeholders

 SELF-ASSESSMENT

Which of the statements below describes your process for setting, communicating, and deploying organizational values? (Check the statement that most closely describes your organization.)

❏ The organization's senior leaders do not set or communicate organizational values to employees. The majority of employees would not know the organizational values.

❑ A few senior leaders and managers set and communicate organizational values, but others do not. This gives mixed messages to employees about what is important.

❑ Some senior leaders and managers set, communicate, and use organizational values and performance expectations to manage some parts of the organization. These leaders model the values' importance through their actions.

❑ Many senior leaders and managers set, communicate, and use organizational values to provide direction for employees to help achieve values-driven goals. Leaders periodically ask for feedback to evaluate how well everyone understands the values and performance expectations.

❑ Most senior leaders and managers set, communicate, and use organizational values to provide direction for employees to help achieve values-driven goals. Leaders regularly get feedback on this process and have started making changes for improving values-driven performance.

Leadership Structure

To be a high-performing organization, the leadership structure must facilitate—not hinder—getting the work done. The Baldrige Criteria are silent on the subject of structure because there is no one perfect structure; all forms of structure have their strengths and weaknesses. Changing your organization's leadership structure may solve one set of problems only to create a different set of challenges. One of the main purposes of an organizational structure is to systematize communications and coordination within the organization.

No matter what structure is chosen, there is always potential for interdepartmental coordination problems and conflict. The rule of thumb is that the potential place for these problems is between the "boxes" in the organization chart. To effectively manage the structure, leaders must develop mechanisms to deal with coordination issues. These mechanisms can be both formal and informal. Some common formal mechanisms include periodic staff meetings, interdepartmental task forces, multidisciplinary committees, retreats, and policies and procedures. Informal mechanisms include the design and use of workspaces, conversations during work breaks, and staff parties.

Leaders must constantly work at identifying and eliminating practices and behaviors that get in the way of getting the work done. Mechanisms must be developed to assist and support the people within the organization in getting their work done. As an organization advances along the performance excellence journey, it will be important for its leaders to stop periodically and ask, "Does the structure of our organization assist the physicians and staff members to achieve the goals of the organization?" Use the self-assessment below to determine if adjustments need to be made in your structure to achieve ever-higher levels of performance.

✓ SELF-ASSESSMENT

The structure in my organization (check all that apply)
- ❏ Assists us in meeting our commitment to patients and other stakeholders.
- ❏ Allows us to effectively deal with key external stakeholders (e.g., regulators, suppliers, payers, community members).
- ❏ Assists us in securing needed materials and resources (e.g., supplies, physicians, staff, volunteers, funding).
- ❏ Allows senior leaders to recognize business opportunities and threats and rapidly adjust priorities and strategies.
- ❏ Effectively supports our core activities.
- ❏ Supports our culture, values, and management beliefs.
- ❏ Does not have excessive supervisory bodies or levels of supervision.
- ❏ Does not break up natural work units.
- ❏ Has clear lines of responsibility and accountability.
- ❏ Includes a defined leadership team consisting of key stakeholders (board, administrative, medical staff, nursing, clinical support).

Social Responsibility and Community Health

Leadership is the first step toward performance excellence; commitment to quality comes from the top, and the leadership then instills that commitment throughout the organization. Next, that commitment must be taken beyond the organization to the community. Organizational leadership requires an uncompromising dedication to social responsibilities and community health. This commitment covers areas that range from safety to ethics. The Baldrige Health Care Criteria state that "Public health services and supporting the general health of the community are important citizenship responsibilities of healthcare organizations" (NIST 2004). This typically includes efforts to support and strengthen—within the limits of organizational resources—key communities of strategic importance to the organization.

For strategic planning purposes, healthcare organizations must have formal mechanisms to obtain feedback about the needs of the community. For example, the Veterans Administration (VA) Healthcare Network in Upstate New York (known as Network 2), a healthcare organization committed to performance excellence, uses multiple feedback sources. Network 2 was the 2002 winner of the highest Veterans Health Administration award—the Kizer Quality Award—and in that same year reached Stage 2 (the Consensus Review Stage) in its application for the Malcolm Baldrige National Quality Award. To learn what patients and other key stakeholders need, Network 2 maintains local medical center consumer councils that provide an opportunity to identify community concerns and obtain predecisional input on planned network initiatives. Network 2 employees serve on a number of community and charitable projects and through these efforts gain valuable information about the social welfare and health services needs of the community. Involvement in these key activities provides Network 2 senior leaders with vital information that is used in the strategic planning process to set organizational goals (VA Network 2 2003).

 REFLECTION

What does your organization do very well with regard to obtaining feedback about the health services needs of your community? Describe one thing your organization could do better.

Ethical Behavior

The Baldrige award performance excellence criteria have long stressed that senior leaders should be ethical role models and that organizations have a responsibility to practice good citizenship. However, the criteria recently placed greater emphasis on ethical business practices by clearly stating that the responsibility for legal and ethical behavior starts with the organization's senior leaders and governing body. This emphasis is woven throughout all of the Baldrige Health Care Criteria. It is most visible in the Leadership category, which focuses on the role of governance in protecting stakeholder interests by ensuring fiscal accountability, ethical behavior, legal compliance, and organizational citizenship.

In 1997, the American College of Healthcare Executives (ACHE) began publishing its "Ethics Self-Assessment" each year in the March/

April issue of *Healthcare Executive* magazine. The self-assessment, which is also available online at the ACHE web site (www.ache.org), is designed to help senior leaders identify strengths and weaknesses in their ethical commitment and personal behavior (ACHE 2003).

It is no mystery why leadership is the first category in the Baldrige Criteria. Without a proper leadership system in place, business excellence and the appetite for the innovation required in a best practices organization would not exist. History has shown that almost every strength or weakness in a healthcare organization can be traced to the leadership system. Below is a continuation of the case study from Ellsworth County Medical Center (ECMC) in Ellsworth, Kansas. After using the Baldrige Criteria for an organizational self-assessment, CEO Roger Pearson, CHE, soon began to realize the importance of leadership, as he relates in the case study.

ECMC CASE STUDY

As ECMC began its performance excellence journey, I was struck (and somewhat humbled) by the fact that I was part of the problem. Our consultant introduced me to the Baldrige Criteria and the specific quality characteristics or functioning systems that are required for an organization to be effective. If ECMC wanted to improve its performance, it needed to improve its systems. And this is where the rubber meets the road for senior leadership. As CEO, I am responsible for the design and support of the systems currently in place. While attending a workshop in 2002 on patient safety improvement, I learned a new phrase: *latent system failure*. Such failures represent faults in the underlying system of a healthcare organization that on occasion contribute to adverse patient events. After mulling over what I had learned at the workshop, I realized that I owned a lot of responsibility for the latent system failures at ECMC that were affecting all aspects of performance. To begin improvements, I needed to ask a difficult question: Why have I allowed this system to be the way it is?

*   *   *   *   *

Each individual in the organization must practice leadership to produce best practice results. It is also incumbent on the senior leaders and managers to institute a culture of excellence and model organizational integrity. Below are leadership-system enablers that promote a high-performing organization.

LEADERSHIP-SYSTEM ENABLER

- [ ] A clear organizational vision is communicated to everyone in the organization and to key external stakeholders.
- [ ] A systematic process is in place to determine the future needs of patients and other stakeholders.
- [ ] Information regarding the health and service needs of patients and their families is regularly gathered and evaluated for strategic planning purposes.
- [ ] Senior leadership has an "open-door policy," whereby any staff member, at any level, can access senior staff.
- [ ] Staff members are empowered through encouragement of team participation and personal learning.
- [ ] The leadership structure allows for frequent interdepartmental interactions.
- [ ] The leadership structure allows for timely decision making.
- [ ] Senior leaders regularly evaluate compliance with standards of ethical behavior and public accountability.
- [ ] Compliance with all relevant regulations and accreditation standards is regularly monitored.
- [ ] A code of behavior for employees that provides a consistent, ethical framework for patient care and business operations has been developed and disseminated.
- [ ] The organization and its employees are actively involved in community projects that support the organization's mission and vision.
- [ ] The organization contributes to healthcare priorities established by the community.
- [ ] Standards of ethical behavior and a code of conduct are defined for the whole organization and communicated to all of its components.
- [ ] All elements of the organization's activities are integrated and aligned with the mission, vision, and strategic objectives.
- [ ] Key strategic objectives are aligned with the organization's mission and vision to ensure that all initiatives guide individual and collective work toward achieving the organization's purpose.

REFERENCES

American College of Healthcare Executives (ACHE). 2003. "Ethics Self-Assessment." [Online document; retrieved 12/04.] www.ache.org/newclub/CAREER/ethself.cfm.

Flynn, B. B., and B. Saladin. 2001. "Further Evidence on the Validity of the Theoretical Models Underlying the Baldrige Criteria." *Journal of Operations Management* 19 (6): 617–52.

National Institute of Standards and Technology (NIST). 2004. *Baldrige Health Care Criteria for Performance Excellence*, 4. Gaithersburg, MD: NIST.

Pannirselvam, G., and L. Ferguson. 2001. "A Study of the Relationships Between the Baldrige Categories." *International Journal of Quality and Reliability Management* 18 (1): 14–34.

VA Healthcare Network in Upstate New York (Network 2). Kenneth W. Kizer Quality Achievement Award Application. [Online document; retrieved 4/03.] www.va.gov/visns/visn02/vitalsigns/qualityachievement99.html.

Wilson, D., and D. A. Collier. 2000. "An Empirical Investigation of the Malcolm Baldrige National Quality Award Causal Model." *Decision Sciences* 31 (2): 361–90.

Winters, M. 2003. "Identifying Leaders for the New Economy." [Online article; retrieved 2/04.] www.ethoschannel.com/personalgrowth/new/4-mfw_growing.html.

CHAPTER FOUR

Getting from Here to There

HIGH-PERFORMING HEALTHCARE organizations have a disciplined strategic planning process to keep them focused and productive. The process raises a sequence of questions that helps planners examine experience, test assumptions, gather and incorporate information about the present, and anticipate the environment in which the organization will be working in the future. Organizations seeking performance excellence must anticipate and envision the future and use that knowledge to position them to be successful in the changing environment.

The Baldrige Criteria promote a systematic, thorough, and knowledge-driven strategic planning process that includes a review of the mission, vision, and goals of the organization. The *mission* provides the parameters—or limits—of the organization. The *vision* provides a view of how the organization seeks to differentiate itself from current and future competitors. The *goals* describe what the organization wants to achieve in terms of a variety of elements, such as market share, patient outcomes, and efficiency. Strategic goals focus on the vital few organization-level achievements that need to be reached. At the goal-setting stage, leaders are neither solving problems nor implementing strategies. Strategic goals are long-range change targets that guide the organization's efforts in moving toward a desired future state. Objectives define what the organization hopes to accomplish in support of strategic goals. In many ways, the goals and objectives are the heart of the strategic plan. The mission and vision answer the big questions about why the organization exists and how it seeks to benefit society, whereas the goals and objectives are the plan of action—what the organization intends to do over the next few years.

Leadership is the driver of performance excellence, and strategic planning is the linchpin of the leadership system. The process of strategic planning is closely aligned with other Baldrige categories. For example, feedback from patients and other customers is considered when establishing strategic goals. Particular attention should be paid to market or environmental changes. Previous years' performance results and process management activities are used in part to establish future objectives. Measurement data from other organizations are used to evaluate how an organization's performance compares so that stretch goals can be established. Identified human resource challenges are also addressed during the strategic planning process.

The end result—the strategic plan—feeds back into other organizational functions. For example, initiatives are undertaken to meet the critical needs of patients, other customers, and markets. Measures of strategic performance are defined, and these measures influence the measurements selected at the operational level. Action plans, including a human resource plan, are formulated to achieve strategic objectives. Specific process management activities are undertaken as part of the implementation plan.

Strategic planning is about the process of strategic thinking, not the publication of a document. The structured process is done to assist leaders and managers to become "strategists" so that they may create the organization's future. Unfortunately, this process is not always as worthwhile as it could be. Research in 2003 by the Financial Executives Research Foundation in Morristown, New Jersey, and the Buttonwood Group in Stamford, Connecticut, backs that up. Their survey found that only one-quarter of respondents think the annual planning process is time well spent. The survey also found that only 16 percent of planning time was spent developing strategic direction (Haugh 2004). When the majority of the strategic planning process is dedicated to budget discussions, it is no wonder that people view the process as a waste of time. Healthcare organizations must have a robust planning process that involves direction setting to ensure that resources—both financial and human—are focused on achieving organizational goals.

An organization can use numerous models to conduct strategic planning. The Baldrige Criteria do not suggest that one model is better than another; however, certain elements are necessary: assessment of internal strengths and weaknesses and external opportunities and threats; identification of values, mission, vision, and goals; and identification of strategies and performance measures.

✓ **SELF-ASSESSMENT**

Use the following checklist to evaluate the effectiveness of your organization's ongoing strategic planning. The checklist is based on the Healthcare Criteria for Performance Excellence from the 2004 Baldrige National Quality Program.

❑ Have you gathered and analyzed information on the needs and expectations of your patients and other groups for which you provide services?

❑ Have you analyzed external trends and opportunities (e.g., financial, market, technological, and societal factors)?

❑ Have you considered your staff capabilities and needs and identified additional requirements based on your goals and strategies?

❑ Have you considered your resource needs and availability? Have you allocated resources to ensure the accomplishment of your overall plan?

❑ Have you identified your key strategic/longer-term goals and your timetable for accomplishing them?

❑ Have you identified strategies to address your goals?

❑ Have you identified key performance measures for tracking the progress of your strategies and goals?

❑ Have you identified two- to five-year projections for key performance measures, including key performance targets and/or goals, as appropriate?

❑ Have you determined how your projected performance compares with your past performance and that of comparable organizations and competitors? Have you described the basis for these comparisons?

❑ Have you shared your organizational goals, strategies, and measures within the organization to ensure that all are aware and will be making decisions and taking actions that are consistent with those goals, strategies, and measures?

The organization's senior leadership team is responsible for completing, deploying, and developing implementation mechanisms for the strategic plan. They are responsible for involving medical staff leaders and employees in these steps and for committing the time and resources necessary to achieve success. To the extent possible, consensus on the organization's strategic goals should be reached. Failure to obtain consensus and commitment from all members of the executive team can lead to situations such as the one described in the case study below.

CASE STUDY

The CEO of a large urban hospital is championing a major change project intended to flatten the organization, further organizational learning, and more effectively integrate departments. The steering team for the change effort consists of the division directors whose departments will be most directly affected. In one of the first meetings of this group, the CEO says, "The project teams for our new initiatives will take 30 percent of each member's time." Division directors listen, and some nod their heads. "Since team members will include managers from departments in your division," the CEO continues, "you need to go back and negotiate priorities with your managers so their time can be freed up. As far as I'm concerned, this change effort is priority one." A lengthy conversation ensues about the amount of time needed to identify project team members and rearrange work priorities. Several of the division directors are thinking, "My managers will never go along with this. Everything is priority one around here. Freeing up 30 percent of someone's time is a joke!" However, only one director voices his concern about being "beaten up" by his managers. The division directors leave the room having overtly agreed to complete the assignment within two weeks. A month later, project team members have not yet been identified, and most managers have not freed up any time for the project.

*   *   *   *   *

 REFLECTION

Does your organization have strategic projects that are slow to get off the ground? Could the inertia be due to a lack of commitment and consensus by those most affected by the initiative? This can be especially problematic when achieving strategic objectives requires physician involvement. Medical staff leaders must be involved in the planning process at some level to ensure that physicians have a vested interest in the success or failure of the organization's mission.

Strategic planning goes beyond the development of a written plan. It includes the deployment and implementation of the strategic plan and the measurement and evaluation of the results. *Deployment* involves completing the plan and communicating it to all employees. *Implemen-*

tation involves resourcing the plan, putting it into action, and managing those actions. *Measurement and evaluation* consist not only of tracking implementation actions but also—and more importantly—assessing how the organization is changing as a result of those actions and using that information to update the plan.

DEVELOPING THE PLAN

Many books and articles describe how best to do strategic planning, so the process will not be discussed here in detail. What follows is a brief description of the four fundamental steps that are taken in the strategic planning process. Interspersed within the description are reflection and self-assessment points that can be used to contemplate your organization's planning process.

Step One: Get Ready

To get ready for strategic planning, an organization must first assess its readiness. While a number of issues must be addressed when assessing readiness, the determination essentially comes down to whether an organization's leaders are truly committed to the effort and whether they are able to devote the necessary attention to the big picture. Tasks to be completed during the preplanning step include the following:

1. Clarify roles (who does what in the process).
2. Identify the planning committee.
3. Develop an organizational profile (the questions in the Baldrige Criteria serve as an excellent framework for this profile).
4. Identify the information that must be collected to help make sound decisions.

The planning process is like any other process: it needs to be managed. Make sure that everyone is operating from the same set of expectations and knowledge base. A description of the flow of the planning process can be helpful for communicating expectations.

Do you have a description of your organization's overall strategic planning process, including the key steps and the key participants? Do you have a defined timetable for accomplishing the planning steps?

Step Two: Assess the Situation

An organization must take a clear-eyed look at its current situation. Part of strategic planning, thinking, and management is an awareness of resources and an eye to the future environment so that the organization can successfully respond to changes in the environment. The planning committee needs current information about the organization's strengths, weaknesses, and performance. This information helps to highlight the critical issues faced by the organization so that appropriate plans can be developed to address the gaps (i.e., the differences between the current and desired state). This cycle is illustrated in Figure 4.1.

The Baldrige Criteria suggest that the following key factors be analyzed during the gap analysis (NIST 2004):

- Your patient, other customer, and healthcare market needs, expectations, and opportunities
- Your competitive environment and/or your collaborative environment to conserve community resources and your capabilities relative to competitors
- Technological and other key innovations or changes that might affect your healthcare services and how you operate
- Your strengths and weaknesses, including staff and other resources
- Your opportunities to redirect resources to higher-priority healthcare services or other areas
- Financial, societal and ethical, regulatory, and other potential risks
- Changes in the local, regional, or national economic environment
- Factors unique to your organization, including partner and supply-chain needs, strengths, and weaknesses

An increasingly important part of strategic planning is projecting the competitive environment. The purposes of such projections are to detect

FIGURE 4.1 GAP ANALYSIS

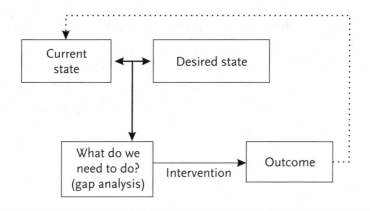

and reduce competitive threats, shorten reaction time, and identify op-portunities. Depending on the size and type of healthcare organization, a variety of modeling, scenario-based judgments, or other techniques can be used to project the competitive environment.

The products of step two include a database of information that can be used when making decisions and a list of critical challenges that demand a response from your organization.

 REFLECTION

During strategic planning, does your organization spend a sufficient amount of time trying to get a fix on driving forces, problems, issues, opportunities, impediments, and how it compares with other similar organizations? Does your organization compare its performance with others in key clinical, financial, and support processes? Does your organization benchmark performance against best-in-class organizations?

Step Three: Develop Strategies, Goals, and Objectives

Once the organization's critical challenges have been identified, it is time to figure out what to do about them. Now is the time to define the broad approaches to be taken (strategies) and the general and specific results to be sought (goals and objectives). Strategies, goals, and objectives may come from individual inspiration, group discussion, formal decision-making techniques, and so on—but the bottom line is that, in the end, the leadership team agrees on how to address the critical challenges.

Discussions at this stage frequently require additional information or a reevaluation of conclusions reached during the situation assessment. It is even possible that new insights will emerge that change the thrust of the organization's mission statement. The product of step three is an outline of the organization's strategic directions: the general strategies, long-range goals, and specific objectives that respond to critical challenges.

 SELF-ASSESSMENT

In the space provided below, list your organization's critical challenges in three categories: healthcare services, operations, and human resources. Next, list the specific objectives your organization has for addressing these challenges. Use additional paper if necessary.

Critical Challenges	Objectives to Address the Challenges
Healthcare Service Challenges	
Operational Challenges	
Human Resource Challenges	

The senior leadership team should ask for in-depth feedback from managers, physicians, and staff on the strategies and objectives. It is within the strategies and objectives—particularly the objectives—that changes required of the organization are explicitly expressed. Have each member of the senior leadership team share the draft plan with their respective midlevel managers, asking them to review the plan, get input from their employees, and provide feedback to the senior leadership team. A formal feedback process for medical staff members should also be in place. An important aspect of the feedback process is ensuring that everyone understands the organization's strategic objectives. It is the objectives that drive operational-level actions, and people must be clear on what is expected. What may be obvious to the senior leadership team may be vague or misleading to those people charged with meeting the objectives.

Figure 4.2 shows a strategic goal and corresponding objectives that were developed during the strategic planning process at a midsize community hospital in the Northwest. If you were a midlevel manager in this organization, would you know what the organization hoped to achieve in 2004? Are the strategic initiatives and expectations clearly understandable, or are they subject to interpretation?

The strategic plan should provide clear communication of the organization's priorities and directions and allow tracking of progress and performance. Compare the statements in Figure 4.2 with those found in Figure 4.3. Figure 4.3 is an excerpt from the 2003 strategic plan for Blake Medical Center in Bradenton, Florida. Midlevel managers in this hospital have a good idea of what the organization hoped to achieve in 2003. The strategic initiatives and expectations are understandable and not subject to a lot of interpretation.

FIGURE 4.2 ONE HOSPITAL'S STRATEGIC GOAL AND CORRESPONDING OBJECTIVES

Strategic Goal: Provide access to high-quality clinical care that distinguishes the hospital as a provider of choice in our region.

Objectives for 2004:
1. Improve access to health care services through continued development of cardiovascular services and women's health.
2. Provide a single standard of high-quality care across the organization through better integration of home care services and enhancement of medical management and case management services.
3. Continuously enhance the quality of care by implementing a patient safety plan and by instituting a hospitalist model of care for inpatients.

FIGURE 4.3 PARTIAL LIST OF BLAKE MEDICAL CENTER
(BRADENTON, FL) 2003 STRATEGIC GOALS AND
CORRESPONDING OBJECTIVES

Strategic Goal: Quality Healthcare

2003 Objectives:
1. Reduce incidence of skin breakdown in patients.
2. Improve accuracy of patient identification.
3. Improve effectiveness of communication among caregivers.
4. Improve safety of using high-alert drugs.
5. Eliminate wrong-site, wrong-patient, wrong-procedure surgery.
6. Improve safety of using infusion pumps.
7. Improve effectiveness of clinical alarm systems.
8. Improve or maintain 2002 outcome measures for patients with acute myocardial infarction and congestive heart failure.
9. Improve prevention of surgical infections through timely administration of first dose of prophylactic antibiotics, use of appropriate antibiotics, and discontinuance of prophylactic antibiotics within 24 hours after the end of surgery.

Strategic Goal: Customer Satisfaction

2003 Objectives:
1. Meet or exceed overall patient satisfaction scores as established by the HCA Tampa Bay Division.
2. Continue to exceed HCA company-wide physician satisfaction scores.
3. Continue to exceed HCA company-wide employee satisfaction scores.

Strategic Goal: Community Impact

2003 Objectives:
1. Continue to offer patient support groups for all main service lines and provide community education programs.
2. Provide a minimum of two community health screenings and healthcare patient education.
3. Demonstrate community involvement at all levels of the organization.

Source: Blake Medical Center, Bradenton, FL. Reprinted with permission.

Your organization's strategic plan must adequately communicate strategic goals and objectives to all levels of staff. If the plan is vague or subject to interpretation, several things can happen, including the following:

- Improvement projects at the operational level have little or no relationship with the organization's strategic priorities.
- Strategic initiatives are slow to get off the ground because the desired endpoint is unclear.
- Strategic initiatives do not achieve the senior leaders' intended goals.
- Operating plans are unrealistic or based on weak assumptions.
- Organizational resources are not directed at strategic priorities.
- Staff development and human resource needs cannot be adequately planned for.
- Misunderstandings occur about what key measures must be tracked to determine organizational success.
- Alignment and consistency of purpose throughout the organization cannot be achieved.
- Operational-level confusion occurs that could lead to cynicism about any improvement efforts.

Strategic planning is basically about deciding what you want and can reasonably expect to have. It makes no sense to go through the time, money, and emotion of strategic planning if the end result is not articulated clearly to everyone. Done right, strategic planning unites an organization and gives it a powerful motivation for moving ahead on the performance excellence journey.

 SELF-ASSESSMENT

Here is a question your senior leaders and managers should be asked about each of your organization's strategic objectives: How will we measure our success? If no one can come up with an answer to that question or if people cannot agree on an answer, chances are that the objective is too vague or subject to interpretation. If that is the case, rewrite the objective until consensus can be reached on how to measure success. Unclear objectives will diminish your plan's credibility and divert precious energy and focus.

Objectives must be precise and measurable. Otherwise, the organization's leaders will not be able to determine whether operational initiatives have actually achieved the intended purpose. It is important to set target levels of performance: tangible, measurable objectives with which actual performance can be compared.

Step Four: Complete the Written Plan

This step essentially involves putting all of the strategic planning decisions down on paper. This is also the time to consult with the executive team and managers to determine whether the document can be translated into operating plans (the subsequent detailed action plans for accomplishing the goals proposed by the strategic plan) and to ensure that the plan answers key questions about priorities and directions in sufficient detail to serve as a guide. Revisions should not be dragged out for months, but action should be taken to answer any important questions that are raised at this step. The end product of step four is a strategic plan.

The Baldrige Criteria do not dictate a certain format for the written plan. There are many ways to go about the task of plan documentation. What you want is the best possible explanation of your organization's plan for the future, and the format should serve the message.

STRATEGIC PLAN DEVELOPMENT ENABLERS

- ❏ A consistent process is used for strategic planning that guides organizational decision making and resource allocation.
- ❏ A defined strategic planning process, key steps, key participants, and timelines are used.
- ❏ Needs and expectations of patients and other customers are considered during strategic planning.
- ❏ Market and competitive position information is considered during strategic planning.
- ❏ Financial, societal, and competitive risk information are considered when setting strategic goals and objectives.
- ❏ Organizational performance in key clinical and business activities as compared with other organizations is considered during strategic planning.
- ❏ Technological and other key changes affecting services or how the organization operates are considered during strategic planning.

- ❏ Strategic goals and objectives balance the needs of all key stakeholders: patients and other customers, markets, employees, and the community.
- ❏ Key strategic goals, objectives, timetables, and targets are addressed by the plan.
- ❏ The organization's competitive position, success factors, strategic challenges, and performance improvement priorities are addressed by the plan.
- ❏ Managers understand the strategic goals and objectives and their department's roles and responsibilities.
- ❏ Physician leadership understands the strategic goals and the medical staff's specific roles and responsibilities.

STRATEGY DEPLOYMENT

Deploying the strategic plan involves several activities: communication, implementation, resourcing, and measuring success. Think about Deming's (1986) Plan-Do-Study-Act (PDSA) cycle. Actions taken to deploy the strategic plan are the last three steps in the cycle. The strategic plan is developed during *Plan*, and *Do* encompasses both the deployment and implementation of the plan. During *Study*, progress is tracked and results are measured. *Act* involves adjusting or standardizing the systems of patient care based on feedback from the measurement step. The important elements of deployment follow.

Communicate the Plan

The senior leadership team needs to have formal communication methods for sharing the strategic plan and implementation initiatives. Some organizations use general meetings and newsletters to share information with physicians and employees. In large organizations, leaders may use video or electronic communications. By communicating strategic objectives and the initiatives underway to achieve these objectives, senior leaders convey that everyone in the organization has a role in the achievement of success. Some organizations include the strategic plan in the new employee orientation process as well as in materials provided to new medical staff members. If senior leaders address new employees in their orientation, a discussion about the strategic plan should be included. Managers should be able to explain to staff members how daily work activities affect the success of the organization as reflected in the plan.

Ongoing communication is crucial for success. It is extremely important for the senior leadership team to share lessons learned and successes and to show that work is being accomplished. The fact that senior leaders are paying attention to strategic goal accomplishment helps to focus everyone's attention on the plan.

Implement the Plan

On completion of the strategic plan, an implementation plan is prepared. This is a schedule of events and responsibilities that details the actions to be taken to accomplish the goals and objectives laid out in the strategic plan. The implementation plan may be prepared by the original planning committee, by a different and larger group, or by a series of task groups. The strategic plan tells *what* your organization wants to do; the implementation plan tells you *how* it will be done, step by step. Both are critical. A good implementation plan has several important characteristics, including the following:

- An appropriate level of detail—enough to guide the work that needs to be done but not so much that it becomes overwhelming or confusing or unnecessarily constrains creativity
- A format that allows for periodic reports on progress toward the specific goals and objectives
- A structure that coincides with the strategic plan—the goal statements and objectives in the strategic plan and the implementation plan are one and the same
- Specification of who will implement what part of the plan and when
- Reporting mechanisms (e.g., evaluation meetings, monthly progress reports to keep senior leaders informed)

Implementation is a critically important step. Use it to translate all of the objectives into clear, realistic, and implementable plans. Explain the major decision points, time scale, milestones, and actions required by management and others to progress with the plan. Explain contingency plans to cover shortfalls. Be realistic about the likely rate of progress, and make provision for slippages. Summarize the key elements in a project management chart or table (Figure 4.4).

FIGURE 4.4 EXCERPT FROM A STRATEGY IMPLEMENTATION
PLAN

Strategic Goal 2:	Increase Organizational Learning			
Objective 8:	By December 2004, one group instructional space will be equipped as a multimedia self-learning training center.			
Action/Task Description	Target Completion Date	Champion/ Process Owner	Resources Required	Status/ Comments
Identify location of instructional space	03/04	S. Pickard, staff development director	Staff time	
Acquire and install equipment	10/04	S. Pickard, staff development director	$5K for site preparation and purchase of computers and other equipment	Medical foundation contribution is expected to cover costs
Train managers to use equipment	12/04	S. Pickard, staff development director	Staff time, education time from existing budget	

Resource Plan

Resourcing is a component of strategic plan implementation. It involves providing the people, money, and materials to ensure successful implementation. Many organizations link the strategic plan with the budgeting process at the initial strategic planning session or soon afterward, when they create implementation teams. Some choose to have implementation teams identify resources and present them to the senior leadership team for approval. This helps the senior leadership team prioritize implementation actions and allot resources to move the organization toward achieving its strategic goals. Many aspects of plan resourcing are found in Baldrige category 5, Staff Focus. This category addresses how the organization links the strategic plan with work system needs, staff development needs, and related human resource factors. If the human resource and staff development directors are not involved in the development of the strategic plan, they should become involved as soon as possible during the deployment phase. More about the link between human resources and the strategic planning process is found in Chapter 7.

Measure Success

Two types of measurement systems are necessary to give a complete picture of strategy implementation. One type involves tracking the progress of initiatives; the other involves collecting data to measure the effectiveness of initiatives. Because two types of measurement systems are necessary, different forms of evaluation occur. One form is the evaluation of activities, which involves looking at the progress of implementation plans. For example, referring to the example in Figure 4.4, leaders would want for know if the organization is on target for purchasing equipment for the multimedia training center. It is important for the senior leadership team to keep up to date on implementation actions at regular review sessions, make appropriate adjustments, and remove organizational impediments.

The other form of evaluation analyzes the measurement data resulting from the strategic measurement system. These data are targeted at measuring outcomes of mission effectiveness now and into the future. For example, has staff member performance improved now that the multimedia training center is available? This form of measurement may be new for healthcare organizations that have typically measured performance at the process level (e.g., the number of staff members participating in self-learning activities). Process-level measures are important for managing day-to-day activities, but strategic measures are also needed to get a picture of the organization's overall effectiveness.

The Baldrige Criteria address strategic and operational-level measurement in the Measurement, Analysis, and Knowledge Management category. This is covered in greater detail in Chapter 6, but it is important to point out here that a critical link exists between strategic planning and measurement. The organization's strategic plan influences the choice of operational-level or process-level measures as well as key high-level measures.

The senior leadership team decides which key high-level performance indicators will be used to measure progress toward goal attainment. When objectives have been expressed as tangible, factual targets, these can be transformed into measures that are used to evaluate actual performance. Figure 4.5 shows examples of the 2003 high-level performance measures established at FHN, an integrated healthcare delivery system in Freeport, Illinois. FHN is composed of FHN Memorial Hospital, Family Healthcare Center–Stephenson Street, the Leonard C. Ferguson Cancer Center, home health care and hospice, occupational and chiropractic care, family dental care, Jane Addams outpatient mental health services, Northern Illinois Health Plan, and individual physician offices. Objectives in six strategic categories have been turned into high-level measures for which targets are set. The executive team receives the results of all measures, while only a subset is reported to the health system board.

The Baldrige Criteria emphasize the importance of establishing performance targets for both short- and longer-term planning horizons. In addition, targets should be based in part on the following factors:

- The organization's past performance and stretch goals
- The projected performance of similar organizations and/or competitors
- Industry standards and best practices benchmarks

Measures of organizational effectiveness express the intent of your strategic plan and provide a vital means for connecting the plan to operations. This connection is described in greater detail in Chapter 6. To provide the motivation necessary for executing the strategic plan, the

Strategic Category: People

Measures Reported to the Board	Target	Desired Direction
% patients satisfied with services	96.4	⇧
No. days from call-in to clinic appointment	1	⇩
% RN vacancy	10.2	⇩
Overall score on staff survey	3.90	⇧
Average rating on staff survey (5-point scale)	4.0	⇧

Additional Measures Reported to Executive Team	Target	Desired Direction
Average rating of all questions on leadership survey (5-point scale)	4.00	⇧
% dollars spent by FHN employers at Freeport-area providers	75.0	⇧
% patients satisfied with inpatient services	97.5	⇧
% patients satisfied with outpatient services	98.5	⇧
% patients satisfied with skilled-nursing-unit services	95.2	⇧
% patients satisfied with ambulatory care services	98.0	⇧
% patients satisfied with home care/hospice services	99.5	⇧
% patients satisfied with physician office services	97.7	⇧
% patients satisfied with occupational and chiropractic services	90.0	⇧
% patients satisfied with emergency services	89.5	⇧
% people who would recommend Lena Nursing Home to others	93.3	⇧

Strategic Category: Finance

Measures Reported to the Board	Target	Desired Direction
Total margin %	2.9	⇧
Accounts receivable (A/R) days	60.0	⇩
Days cash on hand	45.0 Y/E	⇧
Debt service ratio	>2.50	⇧
Total hospital net operating revenue/adjusted patient days	$1,260	⇧
Total physician net operating revenue/patient visit	$101	⇧

Additional Measures Reported to Executive Team	Target	Desired Direction
Hospital: % A/R >90 days	25	⇩
Hospital: Net A/R days (A/R — contractuals and bad debt / 6-month average net daily revenue)	57.0	⇩

FIGURE 4.5 *(continued)*

Hospital: Discharged unbilled days (discharged unbilled $/average daily gross revenue)	7.0	⇩
Physician: % A/R >90 days	31.0	⇩
Physician: Net A/R days (A/R — contractuals and bad debt/6-month average net daily revenue)	67.0	⇩

Strategic Category: Clinical/Quality

Measures Reported to the Board	*Target*	*Desired Direction*
Mean LDL results for diabetic patients' tests	<100	⇩
No. flu shots administered to FHN employees/community	15,000	⇧
% inpatient mortality	≤2.0	⇩
% cases with guidelines in which guidelines were used	>80	⇧
Medication error rate (errors/patient days)	0.58	⇩
Rate of ventilator-assisted pneumonias (per 1,000 ventilator days)	5.3	⇩

Additional Measures Reported to Executive Team	*Target*	*Desired Direction*
% medication errors due to transcription	33.5	⇩
% rate of inpatient falls (falls/patient days)	0.35	⇩
% inpatient restraint use (no. restrained/patient days)	0.99	⇩
% inpatients with documentation of pain reassessments	100	⇧
% other patients with documentation of initial pain assessment	100	⇧
% unplanned returns to surgery (no. returns/total surgeries)	<0.9	⇩
% returns to ED within 48 hours of visit	≤1.2	⇩
% hospital readmits with same/similar diagnosis	≤4.00	⇩

Strategic Category: Operations/Efficiency

Measures Reported to the Board	*Target*	*Desired Direction*
% network operating margin	2.5	⇧
Hospital efficiency (operating expenses/adjusted patient days)	$1,030	⇩
Physician efficiency (expenses/physician visit)	$140	⇩
% contractuals (contr. expenses/gross revenue)	46.2	⇩
Hospital productivity (adjusted patient days/FTE)	8.13	⇧
Physician productivity (patient visits/FTE)	81.95	⇧

FIGURE 4.5 *(continued)*

Physician contractual ratio (margin/total physician FTES)	($232,633)	⇩
Operations improvement (nonbudgeted savings through multiple budget cycles)	$300,000	⇧

Additional Measures Reported to Executive Team	Target	Desired Direction
FTE per adjusted occupied bed (inpatient/outpatient)	<4.00	⇩
Skilled nursing unit: worked hours/patient day	7.50	⇧
Home care: worked hours/patient visit	3.10	⇧
Hospice: worked hours/patient visit	3.50	⇧
Physician: physician visits/FTE	84.23	⇧
Cancer center: paid nursing hours/patient visit	1.29	⇧
Nursing home: worked hours/patient day	5.63	⇧
Revenue per paid FTE in occupational and chiropractic services	$84,190	⇧
Revenue per paid FTE in TPA employer services	$5,292	⇧
Gross revenue per paid FTE in dental employer services	$90,221	⇧
FHN per member per month claims cost	$236.81	⇩
New program review: total no. network counseling sessions	262/mo 3,150/yr	⇧
New program review: MRI volume	226/mo 2,712/yr	⇧
No. potentially avoidable acute care days	≤15 days/mo 216/yr	⇩
No. inpatient days saved due to discharge facilitation	>80 days/mo 960/yr	⇧

Strategic Category: Growth		Desired
Measures Reported to the Board	Target	Direction
Total physician patient encounters	235,623	⇧
Net collectable revenue	$111,134,114	⇧
No. physician visits primary care—regional	16,727	⇧
No. physician visits primary care—central	7,783	⇧
No. patient visits for specialty care	21,618	⇧
Employer services: number of covered lives	4,724	⇧
Employer services: number of patient encounters	11,783	⇧
Volume: hospital outpatient visits	158,333	⇧
Volume: hospital acute care admissions	5,043	⇧
Hospital case mix index	≥1.0800	⇧

FIGURE 4.5 *(continued)*

Strategic Category: Community

Measures Reported to the Board	Target	Desired Direction
Direct contributions to Trust	$416,667	⇧
Charges written off to charity care	$2,754,270	⇩

Additional Measures Reported to Executive Team	Target	Desired Direction
Hospital inpatient: Charges written off to charity care	$1,267,815	⇩
Hospital outpatient: Charges written off to charity care	$895,083	⇩
Physician office: Charges written off to charity care	$591,372	⇩
Cancer center: Charges written off to charity care	$0	⇩
Dental/ME: Charges written off to charity care	$0	⇩

Source: FHN, Freeport, IL (2003). Reprinted with permission.

measures also need to be linked with the organization's reward system, whether financial or professional. Techniques for creating a consistent reward system tied to strategy execution are covered in Chapter 7. Lastly, strategic planning decisions drive process management initiatives. This connection is covered in Chapter 8.

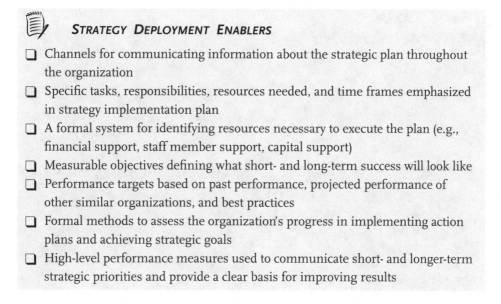

STRATEGY DEPLOYMENT ENABLERS

☐ Channels for communicating information about the strategic plan throughout the organization

☐ Specific tasks, responsibilities, resources needed, and time frames emphasized in strategy implementation plan

☐ A formal system for identifying resources necessary to execute the plan (e.g., financial support, staff member support, capital support)

☐ Measurable objectives defining what short- and long-term success will look like

☐ Performance targets based on past performance, projected performance of other similar organizations, and best practices

☐ Formal methods to assess the organization's progress in implementing action plans and achieving strategic goals

☐ High-level performance measures used to communicate short- and longer-term strategic priorities and provide a clear basis for improving results

REFERENCES

Deming, W. E. 1986. *Out of the Crisis*. Cambridge, MA: Massachusetts Institute of Technology Center for Advanced Engineering Study.

Haugh, R. 2004. "Plan. Replan. Plan Again." *Hospital and Health Networks* 78 (2): 24–26.

National Institute of Standards and Technology (NIST). 2004. *Malcolm Baldrige Criteria for Health Care 2004*, 18. Gaithersburg, MD: NIST.

CHAPTER FIVE

Know Thy Customers

KNOWING YOUR PATIENTS, other customers, and other markets is key to growing your healthcare business. Customer satisfaction is essential for long-term success. You want your customers to be happy with the healthcare services the organization provides, and you want them to stick with the organization as their health needs grow and change. The Baldrige category Focus on Patients, Other Customers, and Markets addresses how the organization determines requirements, expectations, and preferences of customers. There is a focus on the measurement of customer satisfaction and how leadership uses this information in the strategic planning process. Some of the key excellence indicators in this category include the following:

- A systematic method for determining longer-term patient, other customer, and other market requirements
- Several active mechanisms for learning from its various customers—patients, physicians, payers, and other purchasers of healthcare services
- Levels of customer satisfaction determined for all groups and actionable information obtained
- An effective system for prompt resolution of customer complaints
- High priority placed on improving customer relationships and loyalty

The importance of focusing on customers is evident in all industries, and these initiatives have spawned a management discipline known as customer relationship management (CRM). Elements of CRM include the following (Cap Gemini Ernst & Young 2002):

- Identifying and profiling today's and tomorrow's customers
- Allowing customers a choice in how they interact with the organization (e.g., in person; by phone, fax, or e-mail)
- Developing mechanisms that minimize customer irritation, such as long wait times, multiple handoffs, and insufficient information
- Developing the capability to satisfy customer requests at first contact
- Treating customers as valued individuals by learning about their preferences, interests, concerns, and desires

 KEY POINT

Customer relationship management is simply about how your organization interacts with its customers. To be successful, healthcare organizations must find out what the customer wants and then deliver it in the manner that the customer wants.

High-performing healthcare organizations understand, embrace, reach out to, and value their current and future customers. Understanding customers and working hard to develop and manage lifelong relationships with those customers is a strategic imperative for an organization. This is especially important now that patients are assuming more financial accountability for their own care and will be making personal health service buying decisions. Creating a focus on patients, other customers, and other markets requires that healthcare organizations have diverse listening and learning strategies to gain an in-depth knowledge of their customers and market. Customer satisfaction must be a high-priority strategic objective with organizationwide emphasis on customer relationship building. This includes effective complaint management, creation of feedback mechanisms to determine customer satisfaction, and use of that feedback to improve services.

The first step in improving the organization's focus on patients, other customers, and other markets is to identify key customers. This involves answering the following questions:

- What services do we provide?
- Who are our internal customers?
- Who are our external customers?
- Who are our partners?

These questions may already have been addressed during the strategic planning process. If not, they need to be answered now. Also, customers are not homogeneous. It is important to understand patient patterns and diversity so that the organization designs appropriate listening and relationship-building strategies with each customer group. Otherwise, organizational decision making may be swayed by the needs of one vocal or visible group and the notion that by answering their demands you are satisfying all customers. Once customer segments are clearly identified, it is time to initiate listening and learning strategies and relationship-building practices.

LISTENING AND LEARNING

Customers are an organization's best source of business information, whether you are working on improvements to an existing service or planning to launch something new. Customer data allow senior leaders to open up the lines of communication, align resources, and make changes or launch services more quickly. Talking to customers directly increases the odds of achieving organizational success by focusing on what really matters. When a healthcare organization routinely asks its customers for feedback and involves them in business decisions, they in turn become committed to the success of the organization. The goal is to determine what influences customers' health service buying decisions, how important each influencing factor is, and how the organization measures up to the competition in the most important areas.

 KEY POINT

A fundamental concept of performance excellence: Customers are likely to judge the service as excellent when performance exceeds their expectations. Unfortunately, organizations often have misperceptions about customer expectations, unless they have explicitly asked their customers what they want through surveys or other means.

Information Sources

Healthcare organizations must use many different avenues for listening to and learning about customer requirements. Tactics may include direct, face-to-face feedback; written correspondence; analysis of complaints and compliments; and surveys. Do not overlook physicians and frontline staff members as sources of information about customers. They interact with patients, families, and other stakeholders constantly and probably know a great deal about customers' likes and dislikes. Physicians and staff members usually know what is going well, what needs fine tuning, and what needs a major overhaul. Start the search for customer information in-house. Most likely, senior leaders will uncover some processes that can be fixed immediately, which will make customers happy and get the organization started on the right track.

Complaints and Inquiries

An important source of information is customer complaints and inquiries. Ideally, employees can handle problems without involving other people in the organization. For example, if a physician's office calls the health information management department to complain that a patient report has not yet been received, the employee taking the call should be able to find the report and quickly fax it to the person on the phone. But if the report is missing or is not yet transcribed, someone else needs to get involved. In this situation, the problem is handed off to a supervisor or manager.

Some organizations do not use the term "complaint," preferring instead to call such an occurrence a "problem" or an "opportunity." Whatever term is used, it is important for people to know to what the term refers. Generally a customer complaint is defined as any indication that the service or product does not meet the customer's expectations. High-performing organizations use approaches such as the following to handle complaints (Federal Benchmarking Consortium 1996):

- Train and empower frontline employees to resolve most complaints during the first contact.
- Make it easy for customers to complain through the extensive use of centralized customer help lines, 1-800 numbers, complaint/comment cards at the point of service, and easy-to-use customer appeal processes.
- Enter complaint data in fully automated and integrated information systems for analysis purposes. Use the data to identify and fix root causes of dissatisfaction and to determine future directions for product and service improvements. By centrally collecting the data, this valuable information can be incorporated into the strategic planning process, thus ensuring future competitiveness.
- Consider complaints to be customer feedback and opportunities to improve alongside other measures of customer satisfaction.
- Dedicate a cross-functional team to collect and analyze data and report complaint information to top management.

Healthcare organizations are beginning to recognize that it makes good business sense to empower frontline staff to do whatever it takes to satisfy customers. To achieve this goal, staff members must have the authority, training, and responsibility for service recovery. Service recovery takes a lot of different forms. At one hospital, staff members can offer cafeteria discount coupons that range in value from $5 to $20. At another hospital, patient advocates can speed up payment refunds or waive late-fee penalties. Sometimes a careful explanation of the reason for a decision or empathetic listening along with an apology is all that is needed.

If your organization does not have a systematic way of collecting information about complaints, one should be developed. Ask staff to use a form like the one shown in Figure 5.1 to create a record of the complaint or inquiry and the subsequent actions taken. This customer service action form helps prevent problems from falling through the cracks while at the same time providing a source document for information about customer complaints and inquires. When a customer lodges a complaint that cannot be resolved by the employee receiving the complaint, the top portion of the form is filled out and sent on to the appropriate person.

Make it clear to employees that this form is not just window dressing; rather, it is an important part of their job responsibility to satisfy customers. Every employee should have a supply of these forms to get the ball rolling when faced with a situation that he or she cannot resolve. And everyone must be aware of the priority that these reports should be afforded and the turnaround time expected for resolution. If your organization has a secure computerized information system, consider creating an easy-to-complete electronic form. It may be helpful for staff to code the root cause of any problem or question for analysis purposes.

 SELF-ASSESSMENT

Does your organization

- ❏ Make it easy for customers to complain?
- ❏ Encourage resolution of customer complaints by the frontline person receiving the complaint?
- ❏ Seek to delight customers who have problems?
- ❏ Train and prepare employees to respond appropriately to customer complaints?
- ❏ Gather and analyze information about customer complaints?
- ❏ Provide customer satisfaction information to staff members?
- ❏ Use customer complaints and inquires for planning purposes?

Customer Needs Assessment

Do not limit listening and learning strategies to just complaints and inquiries. Studies show that only 2 to 4 percent of dissatisfied customers ever complain, so you will be missing the 96 to 98 percent of people who

FIGURE 5.1 CUSTOMER SERVICE ACTION FORM

Customer	Time and Date
	Originator
Telephone	Department
	Telephone

Situation requiring action

ROUTING

To		Department	

Time received	

Action taken

Recommended next steps

To		Department	

Time received	

Action taken

Recommended next steps

To	(Last)

have opinions about your services. Surveys and focus groups are two popular methods for gathering information about customer needs. Be sure that the objectives are clear and specific if either of these techniques is used. A broad questionnaire or focus group session may provide lots of information, but often the results are too general to be acted on.

Surveys are relatively easy to conduct and can be used to reach a large number of patients and other customers; however, the one-way transfer of information can be limiting. Focus groups take more time and effort, tend to cost more, and do not reach as many of the organization's customers, but they may produce clearer feedback because of the opportunity for two-way exchange. The organization will learn the most about customer requirements and expectations from a combination of surveys and focus groups. Shown in Figure 5.2 is a patient survey intended to gather information about what customers view as important as well as their level of satisfaction.

In addition to surveys, comment cards are a common method for gathering feedback from patients, families, and other customers. Both tools provide some of the same information, but each is intended for a specific purpose. A survey is used to gather aggregate information from a target population. This allows the organization to know with a degree of certainty the extent to which various services or attributes are important to customers so that strategic decisions can be made. Comment cards only provide broad opinions, which are often valid but which cannot be used for analysis purposes, because the information is not considered statistically valid or representative of the customer base. Since anyone can complete a comment card, in many cases they are only completed after a negative experience and have thus been referred to as "complaint cards." The primary purpose of the comment card is to provide information to managers and staff members quickly so that operational problems can be corrected as soon as possible. In addition, comment cards emphasize open-ended questions for broader comments on the health service experience. Comment cards, as such, serve to supplement rather than replace surveys of customer expectations.

 Key Point

When patients and other customers of healthcare services are given the opportunity, they will suggest innovations that the organization has not even considered.

FIGURE 5.2 SAMPLE CUSTOMER SATISFACTION AND EXPECTATION SURVEY

Instructions

This survey asks about how well we measure up to your expectations. Being an outstanding healthcare organization is important to us, and we appreciate the advice of our patients as we seek continuous improvement.

Please mark the questions below according to the following satisfaction scale: 1 for poor, 3 for average, and 5 for outstanding.

In the last column indicate how important you feel this attribute or service is to you. Please circle H for highly important, L for low importance, and M for medium importance.

If you wish to add information or provide examples that describe your opinions, please do so in the space provided at the bottom of the page. Your comments are valuable to our understanding of your needs, and we appreciate hearing from you.

	Satisfaction Level	*Importance*
1. Employees are sincerely interested in caring for me.	1 2 3 4 5	H M L
2. The organization has convenient service hours.	1 2 3 4 5	H M L
3. Employees understand my special needs.	1 2 3 4 5	H M L
4. The services and equipment are modern and up-to-date.	1 2 3 4 5	H M L
5. The physical facility is visually appealing.	1 2 3 4 5	H M L
6. I am kept informed about what services will be performed.	1 2 3 4 5	H M L
7. Employees are never too busy to answer my questions.	1 2 3 4 5	H M L
8. The behavior of professional staff instills confidence in me.	1 2 3 4 5	H M L
9. I feel safe while I am receiving healthcare services.	1 2 3 4 5	H M L
10. Employees have the knowledge to answer my questions.	1 2 3 4 5	H M L
11. If I have a problem, it is resolved quickly and satisfactorily.	1 2 3 4 5	H M L
12. My healthcare experience is error free.	1 2 3 4 5	H M L
13. Employees give me prompt service.	1 2 3 4 5	H M L
14. Services are done right the first time.	1 2 3 4 5	H M L

Comments:

More information about customer requirements is not necessarily better, but getting the right kind of data is critical. The key characteristics of good customer data are as follows:

- *Ongoing*—Change is going to happen. Your customers may change, their needs may change, the healthcare environment may change, and the organization will most certainly change. As the organization advances along the performance excellence journey, customers' expectations will likely rise, too. To respond to these changing needs, a healthcare organization needs to constantly assess its customers.
- *Specific*—To make the kind of improvements customers want, the organization needs detailed feedback. While general satisfaction surveys may provide an overall view of expectations, senior leaders can only respond to specific feedback.
- *Timely*—If the organization is using outdated information, it may be obsolete and no longer relevant.
- *Focused*—Because most healthcare organizations have limited resources, often only high-priority customer requirements can be met. During the strategic planning process, use information gained through surveys, focus groups, and other feedback mechanisms to identify the problems that can be realistically fixed.

Satisfaction Surveys

Getting feedback about customers' expectations and requirements is not exactly the same as surveying for satisfaction. Satisfaction questionnaires generally provide information about how pleased customers are with existing services, not what their requirements are for those services or what services are needed but not currently available. This difference may appear subtle, but it is important. If your organization only relies on satisfaction survey results for customer feedback, you will not have all the information you need to respond to customer expectations and changing market demands. High-performance organizations seek out information from customers by asking two distinctly different types of questions:

1. How are we performing?
2. What services or performance do you expect from us?

The first question is the one most often asked in satisfaction surveys. Many healthcare organizations already have some type of satisfaction survey that is periodically used to gather customer feedback about performance. In an attempt to create apples-to-apples comparisons of health plans and providers, the Centers for Medicare and Medicaid Services (CMS) is working collaboratively with the Agency for Healthcare Research and Quality (AHRQ) to develop standardized patient satisfaction survey instruments. Since 1995, AHRQ has taken the lead in developing assessment tools to measure patients' experience of care in health plans, nursing homes, physician group practices, and end-stage renal disease services. In 2003, CMS teamed up with AHRQ to launch the Hospital Quality Initiative, which includes a patient satisfaction survey. The survey covers the following eight domains (CMS 2004):

1. Nurse communication
2. Nursing services
3. Doctor communication
4. Physical environment
5. Pain control
6. Communication about medicines
7. Discharge information
8. Overall rating of care/recommendation of hospital to others

For more information about this initiative, visit the CAHPS Survey Users Network web site at www.cahps-sun.org and the CMS Hospital Quality Initiative web site at www.cms.hhs.gov/quality/hospital.

While it may be theoretically possible to extrapolate customer expectations from satisfaction survey results, the questions are not intended for that purpose. That is why healthcare organizations should not rely solely on satisfaction surveys to learn from their customers.

 SELF-ASSESSMENT

Answer these questions to see if there is anything you could be doing to know your customers better.

1. Does your organization have a strong customer relations program in place?
2. Do you receive feedback from customers on a regular basis?
3. Has your organization made changes or implemented ideas at the request of customers?

4. Do you contact customers just to see how satisfied they are with your services?
5. Do you have an idea about what healthcare products or services your customers will need in the next two to five years?
6. Do you send out satisfaction and needs assessment surveys on a regular basis to solicit input from your customers?
7. Can you quantify the level of customer satisfaction with your services?
8. Do you know who your best and most loyal customer groups are?

Establish a Continuous Feedback Strategy

Asking customers how the organization is doing and what needs are not being met and listening to the answers should be an ongoing process. Most healthcare organizations already have some methods to obtain customer feedback. These may include the following:

- Postal, telephone, or electronic surveys
- Focus groups
- Comment cards
- Complaints procedures
- Open houses and town hall–style meetings with customer groups
- Healthcare support groups
- Regular meetings with managers and staff members for input

While valuable, some of these methods are episodic and can be biased because the people willing to take the time to fill out comment cards or attend meetings may not be representative of the majority of the organization's customers. Episodic feedback mechanisms may capture the comments of people vocal enough to complain, but they may not capture the comments of others equally (or even more) dissatisfied but less vocal. Therefore, the feedback strategy should be balanced with methods that accurately reflect (from a statistical perspective) patient and other customer satisfaction tools, such as postal, telephone, or electronic surveys. Both routine and episodic feedback should be gathered at regular intervals and linked with the organization's performance measurement and improvement framework. Figure 5.3 is a sample customer feedback plan developed during a hospital's strategic planning process. The plan is revisited annually to determine if changes need to be made to ensure that the organization is effectively listening to and learning from its customers.

FIGURE 5.3 CONTINUOUS CUSTOMER FEEDBACK PLAN

Data Required	Method	Frequency	Responsibility
Patient expectations and needs	Focus groups	–Annually for outpatient areas –At six-month intervals for inpatient areas	Director, customer relations
Patient satisfaction	–Exit survey (outpatient) –Postal survey (all)	–Continuous –One month each quarter	Frontline staff Director, customer relations
Patient/family priorities for improvement	–Exit survey (outpatient) –Postal survey (all)	–Continuous –One month each quarter	Frontline staff Director, customer relations
Patient/family complaints	Complaint management system	Continuous	Director, customer relations
Physician satisfaction	Postal survey	Annual	Director, medical staff services
Physician priorities for improvement	Focus groups	Annual	Director, medical staff services
Employee ideas for improving patient/family relations	Survey at staff meetings	Annual	Division vice presidents
Community health services needs assessment	Focus groups	Annual	Director, customer relations

- ❏ Clear understanding of the organization's important customer groups
- ❏ A systematic, continuous process for listening to and learning from various customer groups
- ❏ Varied mechanisms for obtaining information about customer requirements, expectations, and preferences
- ❏ Varied mechanisms for obtaining information about customer satisfaction
- ❏ Information provided by staff members about how well the organization is meeting customer expectations and where improvements are needed
- ❏ Customer input considered during the strategic planning process
- ❏ Customer feedback used to redesign and/or add new services
- ❏ Knowledge of how the organization measures up to competitors in the areas considered most important to customers
- ❏ Decisions made by frontline staff to resolve customer problems
- ❏ A complaints mechanism, including resolution process, process for making change in response to complaints, recording of complaints, and reporting of complaints and changes made

RELATIONSHIP BUILDING

Successful healthcare organizations do not just communicate with patients and other customers through satisfaction or needs assessment surveys. They also seek out opportunities to increase customer participation in all aspects of healthcare delivery. Users of healthcare services may be patients, their families, or potential customers. They can be individuals or a group of people with a collective interest (e.g., a disease-oriented group or special interest group). Participation can be at different levels of the organization, such as in the areas of strategic planning, service and facilities planning, policy development, service delivery and care processes, and review and evaluation of care and services. Also, the degree of participation can range from low (information giving and information seeking) to high (consultation and partnership).

Healthcare organizations can use various methods and models to build relationships with customers. There is no right way of enabling people to participate. What is most important is that the organization clearly identifies who its customers are and what the purpose and mechanisms are for involving them. For maximum benefit, relationship building with customers should be part of an overall organizational strategy rather than sporadic projects.

Figure 5.4 is an audit tool for evaluating a healthcare organization's dedication to customer and community participation. Use this self-assessment to rate your organization's level of commitment to and activity in the areas of customer and community involvement. The results can be used to identify organizational strengths as well as gaps and limitations. In those areas in which your organization's scores are low, establish priorities for building better relationships with patients, other customers, and the community.

FIGURE 5.4 ORGANIZATIONAL SELF-ASSESSMENT OF CUSTOMER AND COMMUNITY PARTICIPATION

Rating Scale: 5 = Outstanding achievement
              4 = Extensive achievement
              3 = Moderate achievement
              2 = Some achievement
              1 = Little achievement

Circle Your Level of Achievement

1. Patient, other customer, and community participation has been incorporated into the organization's vision, values, and any philosophical statements.   1 2 3 4 5

2. The organization has clearly identified its patients, other customers, and community served.   1 2 3 4 5

3. The organization has clearly defined the purpose and mechanisms for involving patients, other customers, and community members at different levels.   1 2 3 4 5

4. The organization involves patients, other customers, and community members in assessments of health service needs.   1 2 3 4 5

5. The strategic directions of the organization respond to the needs expressed by patients, other customers, and community members.   1 2 3 4 5

6. The leaders, champions, or staff members delegated with the responsibility for patient and other customer participation are clearly defined and identifiable within the organization.   1 2 3 4 5

FIGURE 5.4 *(continued)*

7. The organization has key customer policies in place, such as 1 2 3 4 5
    –Patient/other customer rights and responsibilities
    –Complaints
    –Patient/other customer access to information
    –Patient/other customer participation
8. The organization has well-functioning mechanisms to 1 2 3 4 5
    ensure that patients and other customers find out about
    –Their rights and responsibilities
    –How to make a complaint or commendation
    –How to access information
    –How they can participate in decision making
9. Staff education programs are in place to support the 1 2 3 4 5
    implementation and maintenance of customer-service
    policies.
10. Organizational resources have been allocated to support the 1 2 3 4 5
    incorporation of patient, other customer, and community
    input into strategic planning.
11. Patient and other customer participation is an element in 1 2 3 4 5
    everyone's job description.
12. Patient and other customer participation efforts and 1 2 3 4 5
    achievements are a component of employee performance
    management and staff recognition activities.
13. Patient, other customer, and community input is a key part 1 2 3 4 5
    of organizational decision making.
14. The organization has methods for recognizing the 1 2 3 4 5
    contribution of patients, other customers, and community
    members.

Source: Adapted from the National Resource Centre for Consumer Participation in Health (Australia), "Draft Community and Consumer Participation Audit Tool for Hospitals," 2000.

Relationship building not only creates opportunities for customer feedback but it also helps to make the healthcare organization indispensable to patients and the community. It is a terrific way to add value and enhance your market position. Following are six relationship-building strategies that can help transform your organization into a valuable resource for customers.

1. *Communicate frequently.* How often do you reach out to customers? Do the bulk of your communications focus on your healthcare services? For best results, it is important to communicate frequently and vary the types of messages you send. Instead of a constant barrage of service promotions, send customers helpful health-related newsletters or softer-sell messages.

2. *Hold special health-related events.* Any event that allows your staff to interact with patients and potential users of healthcare services is a good relationship builder. High-performing organizations have extensive community outreach and education programs. For example, Royal Oak (Michigan) Beaumont Hospital, a 2003 finalist for the American Hospital Quest for Quality Award, has an outreach program called the School of Community Education, in which 81 courses are offered multiple times throughout each year. The number of community members participating in the courses ranges from 15,000 to 25,000 annually (Beauregard and Winokur 2004).

3. *Build two-way communication.* When it comes to relationships with patients and other customers, listening can be every bit as important as telling. Use every tool and opportunity to create interaction, including asking for feedback through your web site. Customers who know they are heard instantly feel a rapport and a relationship with the organization.

4. *Enhance your customer service.* Do you have a dedicated staff or channel for resolving customer problems quickly and effectively? How about online assistance? One of the best ways to add value and stand out from your competitors is to have superior customer service. People often make healthcare purchasing decisions between parity services based on their perception of the patient experience.

5. *Launch multicultural programs.* It is probably time to add a multilingual component to your patient/customer relationships. For example, you might offer a Spanish-language translation of your web site or use ethnic print media for health education materials. Ethnic audiences will appreciate communications in their own language, and bilingual programs will go a long way toward helping your organization build positive relationships with minority customers.

6. *Visit the trenches.* It is important to go beyond standard satisfaction surveys to build relationships with patients and other customers.

When was the last time senior leaders attended a community health education class or talked with families while they waited for a loved one to come out of surgery? There is no better way to really understand the challenges your patients and other customers face and the ways your organization can help meet them than to occasionally get out in the trenches.

 KEY POINT

Participation of patients, other customers, and the community in the decision making of a healthcare organization leads to change. These changes are not only about improving processes in response to customer feedback but they are also about changes to systemic practices in the organization that enable and support customer relationships.

The Baldrige Criteria identify customer relationship building as an important attribute of high-performing healthcare organizations. Enablers of success are detailed below. The purpose of relationship building is to ensure that customers' needs are met, which in turn will increase customer loyalty and help to expand market share. Relationship building is not a one-time project. It must be a continuous effort that incorporates the needs and expectations of patients, other customers, and the community into organizational decision making. Customer participation in service planning, delivery, and evaluation are key elements in the advancement of performance excellence.

 RELATIONSHIP-BUILDING ENABLERS

☐ Organizational commitment to customer relationship building
☐ Active learning environments in which the organization learns new things from patients, other customers, and the community
☐ Opportunities for all patients and other customers to participate in organizational decision making at whichever level people self-select to using whichever mechanisms people feel most comfortable with
☐ Training received by staff members in customer service and effective relationship building, for which they are then held accountable
☐ Customer input used to design services that are appropriate and that meet both patient and community needs

REFERENCES

Beauregard, K., and S. Winokur. 2004. "Royal Oak Beaumont Hospital: Putting the Patient in Patient Safety." In *Partnering with Patients to Reduce Medical Errors,* edited by P. Spath, ch. 7. Chicago: AHA Press.

Cap Gemini Ernst & Young. 2002. *Customer Relationship Management in Healthcare.* McLean, VA: Cap Gemini Ernst & Young.

Centers for Medicare & Medicaid Services (CMS). 2004. "Hospital Quality Initiative (HQI)." [Online information; retrieved 6/18/04.] www.cms.hhs.gov/quality/ hospital/.

Federal Benchmarking Consortium. 1996. "Serving the American People: Best Practices in Resolving Customer Complaints." [Online article; retrieved 2/04.] http://govinfo.library.unt.edu/npr/library/papers/benchmrk/bstprac.html.

CHAPTER SIX

From Data to Knowledge

THE CONTEMPORARY OPERATING environment in healthcare organizations is challenging. To survive, everyone needs to be well informed. To lead the organization, the senior executive team needs information about the organization's current state and the direction in which it is heading. Managers need to know how their departments are performing. Staff members and physicians need information that allows them to do their job well.

Advancing performance excellence requires that a healthcare organization manage its information assets. In studies of the relationship of the Baldrige Criteria to organizational results, information and analysis together have been found to be the second most important driver of performance excellence (Pannirselvam and Ferguson 2001; Flynn and Saladin 2001). The effect of leadership is indirect, driving the system that causes the results. Information and analysis have a more direct effect, influencing the systems and procedures that lead to organizational excellence. In the simplest terms, information and analysis are the brain center for alignment of the organization's operations and its strategic directions. Collection and analysis of the right information and data are critical. Knowledge is how the organization determines where it is, if it is going in the direction defined in its strategic plan, and how it compares with competitors or providers of like services.

To advance performance excellence, an organization must place major strategic emphasis on information and knowledge—the lifeblood of all healthcare activities. To accomplish strategic aims, high-performance organizations develop and maintain effectiveness in the following segments:

- Information systems and infrastructure
- Information management
- Information analysis
- Internal information flow

Information system and infrastructure covers areas such as computerized information systems and the establishment of a competent infrastructure to enable the achievement of strategic goals. High-performing organizations have data systems that allow for universal access to information and enhance decision making. Ideally, information systems, processes, and resources are consolidated under one umbrella, with a multidisciplinary group of users setting expectations and providing strategic direction.

Information management refers to information quality. For instance, the accuracy and timeliness of information processed and provided by internal data systems is key to top management's decision making. The organization's information system must also have the ability to acquire external information for market analysis and competitive benchmarking (both financial and clinical).

Information analysis refers to the process of analyzing data that support senior leaders' knowledge of organizational performance and organizational planning. Evaluation of information is necessary for measuring the overall health of the organization as well as making progress toward achieving key performance results and strategic objectives. Information derived from organizational analyses should be linked to departmental operations to support decision making and daily operations of key patient care and support processes at all levels. Measures of departmental success should be aligned with the organization's key performance goals.

Internal information flow refers to the information transfer process within the organization that allows people to obtain needed information in a timely manner. Transfer of information also covers the sharing of knowledge. Communication barriers must be broken down to allow for the freer flow of knowledge and lessons learned within the organization. What does ineffective knowledge transfer look like? Consider this: In a multihospital system, a protocol for trauma care was developed at one hospital for a cost of approximately $2,500. Three other hospitals in the system developed similar protocols, each costing approximately the same in terms of clinical and support staff time. Poor knowledge transfer between hospitals in the system resulted in wasted resources.

The Baldrige Criteria found in the Information, Analysis and Knowledge Management category cover three elements of performance excellence: business intelligence, performance measurement, and knowledge management. Business intelligence deals with the implementation of the organization's strategy. Performance measurement involves gathering and analyzing the vast amount of information in and around the organization. Knowledge management addresses how the organization manages information and staff competencies. (Each of these components is discussed below.) Despite the different viewpoints of these elements, they share one connective factor: information.

Figure 6.1 illustrates how these key elements interact. During the performance excellence journey, an organization must learn how the elements are related to each other and how they overlap. To advance performance excellence, it is important to pay close attention to how and for what purposes the three elements are being used in the organization.

The trio of business intelligence, performance measurement, and knowledge management provides a framework for strategic performance improvement. As some overlapping occurs, coordination between the three elements is needed. The performance excellence journey requires foresight, a knowledge of history, and active involvement. Not a single component of the integrated circles should be underrated, because each plays a vital role in the organization's operations as well as strategy development and deployment. Table 6.1 illustrates the differing purposes for using each component. As the table shows, the level of use differentiates between operational (short term) and strategic (long term) levels.

In an ideal situation, an organization uses all three components simultaneously to manage and improve performance. For example, effective knowledge management needs performance measurement to determine the current situation of staff member competencies. Where major competency gaps are identified, an improvement plan is put in place and target levels of competence are defined. Measurement is used for continuous improvement as the organization sets and resets target levels as it advances along the journey to excellence. There is also a connection between measurement and business intelligence. Performance measure-

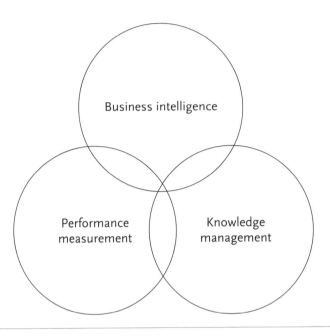

ment is used to generate data for strategic planning. The information allows senior leaders to identify performance gaps based on internally defined targets and performance at comparable organizations. When business intelligence is efficiently used, it generates vast masses of data, which need to be converted into information and intelligence. An efficient knowledge management system can assist the organization by attaching meaning to this information. The use of knowledge management leverages the value of using business intelligence and vice versa.

Every healthcare organization has a mission and vision that are somewhat permanent. Strategy is an explicit, periodically updated plan for reaching specific goals. Strategic planning takes into account both the external environment and the internal status of the organization. In high-performing organizations, business intelligence, performance measurement, and knowledge management connect with one another and with the strategic planning process. Figure 6.2 illustrates these connections.

The Baldrige Criteria address both the approach to gathering information and its deployment. *Approach* refers to how the organization

		Primary Use
Operational Level	Business intelligence	Gain knowledge about important matters within and around the organization to provide better information for decision makers. Motivate, control, and guide staff members, performance management, etc.
	Performance measurement	Motivate, control, and guide staff members, performance management, etc.
	Knowledge management	Effectively share knowledge among staff members. Provide management with an understanding of the organization's knowledge level.
Strategic Level	Business intelligence	Gain knowledge about important matters within and around the organization to make emergent strategies possible or determine if current strategies are valid.
	Performance measurement	Implement strategies and receive feedback for strategy development and deployment.
	Knowledge management	Develop staff member competencies according to strategic goals.

ensures that necessary information is available for decision making. *Deployment* refers to how all levels in the organization use the information for advancing performance excellence. Details of these elements are described throughout the reminder of this chapter. Although each component is covered separately, there is significant overlap between them, which should not be overlooked.

BUSINESS INTELLIGENCE

Business intelligence is the process of gathering and analyzing internal and external information relevant to the organization's performance.

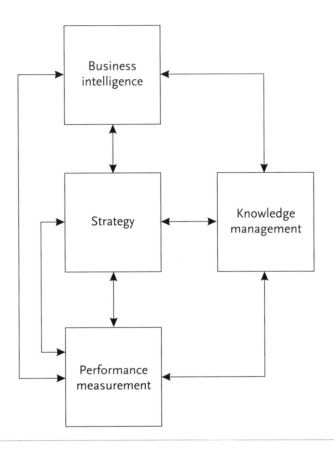

This activity supports operational and tactical business decision making. In recent years, business intelligence has become synonymous with information technology (IT) and decision-support applications such as data mining, forecasting, and online analytical processing. Yet business intelligence is much more than IT applications; it is about making sound business decisions based on accurate and current information, whether the data are computer generated or gathered manually. Computerized decision-support tools facilitate business intelligence, but in the end it is people who conduct the analyses and make the final choices.

To enhance business intelligence, high-performing healthcare organizations set up systems and services designed to acquire, share, and disseminate information of all kinds, from the data derived from patient encounters to events in the marketplace. However, information also reaches the organization by all kinds of routes that are not initially set up as information acquisition mechanisms. For example, while communicating with other facilities, case managers may learn of payer contracts and the discounts provided by competing organizations. The nursing director may find out about the financial difficulties of a competitor while at an informal dinner with colleagues. In other words, business intelligence embraces not only the formal systems set up to manage internal information flow and the systems designed to access external information but also the organizational and personal communication systems through which information reaches the organization and is disseminated.

The Baldrige Criteria address the concept of business intelligence with questions such as the following:

- How do you select information that is used to support operational and strategic decision making?
- How do you make needed data available?
- How do you use data and information to support organizational decision making and innovation?
- What analyses do you perform to support your organization's strategic planning?

The ability to gather and effectively analyze internal and external information relevant to the organization is a major step in the journey toward performance excellence. A fundamental concept is that of "intelligence," which is different from "information." *Intelligence* is actionable information—data turned into knowledge that is actually used for something. The U.S. Central Intelligence Agency gives the following illuminating definition of intelligence in this context: it is " . . . knowledge and foreknowledge of the world . . . [that is] the prelude to . . . decision and action" (U.S. CIA 1999). The term *foreknowledge* refers to the future and its evaluation relative to the present. The phrase *prelude to decision and action* focuses on the need to have some kind of system in place whose aim is to capture the value of the data gathered, the analysis of which will lead to a business response. For a healthcare organization, effective anticipation and proactive response to future developments is a critical component of success.

High-performing healthcare organizations have access to business knowledge that allows senior leaders to make intelligent or information-based decisions in the following areas:

- *Marketing*—Determine from the results of marketing activities who is likely to use healthcare services, what services are used, and when.
- *Forecasts*—Identify demands for a service, and use the information to forecast the pattern of demand for upcoming weeks and months.
- *Customer loyalty*—Discover the characteristics of patient groups that are now using another healthcare provider. Determine which groups the organization wishes to recapture. Identify patient groups at risk of defecting to another provider to plan preemptive offerings to keep market share.
- *Resource management*—Compare expected versus actual costs of treatment and length of stay for patients admitted for a particular condition or treatment. Forecast expected costs and reimbursement for upcoming weeks and months.
- *Outcome management*—Compare outcomes of care for select patient populations with the outcomes achieved by other healthcare providers. Determine the cost/benefit ratio of various treatment options. Evaluate the impact of staffing strategies on patient outcomes.

Senior leaders can evaluate these issues—and a host of others—provided the relevant data have been collected, are available, and are reasonably accurate. It is more than a matter of data generation; healthcare organizations have plenty of data. It is estimated that the amount of information in the world doubles every 20 months. This flood of raw data must be carefully managed. The ability of senior leaders and other people in the organization to make knowledge-based decisions is dependent on the richness, accuracy, and completeness of the available data. For example, a hospital that has been admitting patients for many years has information that senior leaders can use to estimate the overall average cost of treatment and length of stay for groups of patients. If this data were also used by clinicians to better understand the details of care provided to individual patients, it would be helpful for clinical decision making.

Fact-Based Decisions

Fact-based decisions by definition require information. For strategic purposes, an organization should have a system for gathering and analyzing patient/customer, operational, financial, and market-related performance data. The types of information in these categories are detailed in Table 6.2.

As mentioned earlier, these data are not used as the sole input for making decisions, nor do they directly supply what is considered to be business intelligence. Decisions are made and business intelligence is garnered only with the combination of factual information, human judgment and intuition, and the ability to interpret the information within the context of the organization's mission, vision, and values.

 REFLECTION

Does your organization have the means to systematically collect, analyze, and disseminate information as intelligence to the users who need to make decisions? What critical pieces of information are unavailable?

Up to this point, the discussion has focused on information about an organization and how it supports business intelligence. Another component of business intelligence is how the organization compares with others. It is not just a matter of whether you believe you have a quality organization; rather, the question is, what do you compare it with? Healthcare organizations focused on quality and improving performance actively seek out opportunities to compare results from key processes and services with organizations from within and outside of the healthcare community. Do you know how your performance compares with your competition? With similar healthcare organizations? With other service industries? Does your organization have a formal way to identify comparative or competitive information?

Without a comparison or benchmarking process, senior leaders may not be accurately gauging organizational performance and may be limiting learning opportunities. Use of competitive and comparative information is important to all healthcare organizations. It helps alert senior leaders to competitive threats and situations in which consumer expectations are not being met. The organization needs to know where it stands relative to competitors and to best practices. Recent research

TABLE 6.2 EXAMPLES OF INFORMATION NEEDED TO SUPPORT BUSINESS INTELLIGENCE

Patient/Customer Information
- Service satisfaction trends
- Needs and expectations
- Complaint trends
- Community health needs

Operational Information
- Trends in key operational outcomes
- Trends in key clinical outcomes
- Staff member satisfaction trends
- Staff turnover rates

Financial Information
- Cost per patient trends
- Resource allocation
- Debt service trends
- Charitable contribution trends

Market-Related Information
- Trends in numbers of patients seen
- Market penetration changes
- Demographic composition of customer base and service usage

found that making comparative performance information available to healthcare organizations appears to stimulate improvement activities in those organizations in which performance is reported to be low (Hibbard, Stockard, and Tusler 2003). Making these comparative data available to the public provides an even greater stimulus for organizational improvement activities.

Comparative performance data are also important for establishing improvement priorities during the strategic planning process. Comparative analyses of both financial and nonfinancial results and outcomes allow an organization to more accurately assess current and future performance. Without such information, senior leaders are missing opportunities to move organizational performance to the next level. Leaders in high-performing healthcare organizations use the knowledge gained through comparative and benchmarking information to create the impetus for significant—or "breakthrough"—improvement or change.

Effective selection and use of competitive comparisons and benchmarking information and data require (1) the determination of needs and priorities; (2) criteria for seeking appropriate sources for comparisons, from both within and outside of the healthcare industry; and (3) the use of comparative data and benchmarking information to set stretch targets and to promote major improvements in the areas that are most critical to your organization's vision and business strategy.

1. Does your organization support business intelligence by gathering and analyzing information for key
   - ❏ Customer-focused results?
   - ❏ Financial- and market-data results?
   - ❏ Human resource results?
   - ❏ Organizational effectiveness results?

2. Does your organization actively seek out opportunities to compare your performance for key
   - ❏ Customer-focused results?
   - ❏ Financial and market data results?
   - ❏ Human resource results?
   - ❏ Organizational effectiveness results?

3. Does your organization have systems to
   - ❏ Collect information about your environment, competitors, patient and other customer needs, and payer/employer expectations?
   - ❏ Collect information about best practices or best performing organizations?
   - ❏ Conduct gap analyses to determine where you are and where you want to be in key areas of performance?

Business intelligence supports a variety of purposes, such as planning, reviewing overall performance, improving operations, and comparing performance with similar organizations or with best practices benchmarks. To adequately support these information requirements, high-performing organizations develop an information infrastructure that meets the needs of varied users. Many types of data and information are needed for performance measurement and improvement. Performance areas include patients, other customers, markets, operations, competitive comparisons, services, employees, costs, and financials. Senior leaders must be able to extract larger meaning from data and information to support evaluation, decision making, and operational improvements within the organization. This entails using data to determine trends, projections, and cause and effect.

A major consideration involves the selection and use of performance measures. The measures chosen should best represent the factors that lead to improved customer, operational, and financial performance. A comprehensive set of measures tied to the organization's strategic goals and objectives is the foundation for aligning improvement activities at the operational level.

![] BUSINESS INTELLIGENCE ENABLERS

❏ Information analysis guides performance toward key results and toward attaining strategic objectives.

❏ Actions intended to improve performance are based on an understanding of the cause/effect connection among and between processes and performance results.

❏ A close connection exists between performance analysis and organizational planning.

❏ The performance measurement system is periodically reevaluated and updated to meet changing information needs.

❏ Competitive comparisons, from both within and outside of the healthcare industry, are used to set stretch targets and promote major improvements in those areas that are most critical to the organization's success.

❏ Information and analyses are readily available to managers and staff to enable effective support for decision making and daily operations.

PERFORMANCE MEASUREMENT

Performance measurement is the process of quantifying the efficiency and effectiveness of purposeful actions. The actions may be at the operational level, or they may be one of many initiatives designed to achieve strategic goals. The main rationale for measuring an organization's performance is to be able to manage it. Measurement is a dynamic process in which (1) measures are constructed based on strategically important success factors, (2) those measures are used to help implement planned strategies, and (3) the analysis of the measurement provides feedback for new strategy formulations. Performance measurement, of course, also has several operative uses. However, to keep from being overpowered by performance data that do not add to the organization's business intelligence, measurement should be aligned as closely as possible with strategy. Performance measurement can be used to do the following:

- Translate the organization's strategy into concrete objectives
- Communicate the objectives to physicians and staff members
- Guide and focus physician and staff member efforts so that objectives are achieved

- Control whether or not the strategic objectives are reached
- Visualize how the efforts of individuals contribute to the overall strategic goals

Four main phases are related to the performance measurement process.

1. The measures are chosen.
2. The measurement system is implemented. The implementation step includes determining how data for the measures are collected, how the measurement results are reported, and how the measures are used.
3. The information is used.
4. The measures are updated, thus closing the loop on the process.

Every time the organization's strategic goals or objectives change, the measurement system must be redesigned accordingly. If the loop is not closed, performance data may no longer provide strategically important information.

 KEY POINT

Simply gathering data for its own sake is of very little use to anyone, unless it helps people determine some kind of action or response.

To advance performance excellence, healthcare organizations must have a measurement system that tracks overall organizational performance and daily operations. Overall organizational performance is monitored using high-level measures derived from strategic goals and objectives. Measures of operational- or department-level performance are used to determine how daily operations are affecting the organization's ability to achieve strategic goals and objectives. The organization's performance measurement system should facilitate knowledge-based decisions and the alignment of organizational directions and resource use.

Measurement System

Organizational measures of success have traditionally been a mixture of regulatory or accreditation requirements, error corrections, leaders' information needs, and data on process performance. While these measures are valid and useful, many are not high-level or strategic measures. In general, organizational measures have been used to control present activities. By contrast, a high-level measurement system communicates to all echelons of an organization what is vital to achieving its vision of excellence. High-level—or "30,000 foot"–level—measures of performance and targets are chosen during the strategic planning process. That process, which was described in Chapter 4, is summarized in Figure 6.3. As you see, measurement is step four in the cycle.

There are many frameworks for constructing a high-level measurement system. A commonly used model is the balanced scorecard (Kaplan and Norton 1996). Others include the performance prism (Neely, Adams, and Kennerly 2003) and the performance pyramid (Wedman et al. 1998). The Baldrige Criteria do not promote a particular measurement system model, but organizations are expected to employ a systematic approach that is aligned throughout the organization. A typical problem for the executive team is that it becomes inundated with information that is difficult to apply. Evidence suggests that the use of a balanced scorecard or some other systematic measurement model can assist organizations in confronting their information problems to improve business intelligence.

High-level performance measures are used to evaluate success factors from different points of view, such as those of the customer, staff members, clinical processes, and financial success, as well as from the point of view of past, current, and future performance. This way, different aspects of the organization's performance can be measured and managed. The following six aspects of performance used at FHN in Freeport, Illinois—called "strategic themes"—helped the organization categorize its 2003 high-level measures (see discussion in Chapter 4):

1. People
2. Finance
3. Clinical/Quality
4. Operations/Efficiency
5. Growth
6. Community

The University Health Network in Toronto, Canada, uses a balanced scorecard to measure critical aspects of that organization. This scorecard

FIGURE 6.3 STRATEGIC PLANNING CYCLE

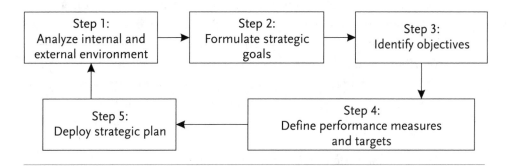

is broken down into the following five key areas (University Health Network 2004):

1. *Client and community focus*—how patients and the community view the performance at the network hospitals. This is measured primarily through inpatient, emergency, and outpatient satisfaction surveys.
2. *System competency*—whether appropriate outcomes are being produced. This section includes a variety of measures, such as mortality rates, infection rates, length-of-stay measures, alternative-level-of-care days, and readmission rates.
3. *Financial performance and condition*—efficiency and effectiveness of resource use. The primary measure for this is the cost per weighted case.
4. *Responsiveness*—timeliness of patient access to care. This is measured using various wait-time measures across the network.
5. *Work life*—staff view of the performance of the network hospitals. This is measured using employee opinion surveys, staff turnover rates, sick hours, and overtime hours.

The number of high-level performance measures from which to choose is virtually unlimited. Typically organizations select 15 to 30 for the governing board to keep tabs on (The Governance Institute 2000). The senior leadership team and managers may choose to monitor several additional high-level measurements.

High-level performance scorecards are populated during the strategic planning process, at which time performance goals and objectives are defined. Next, the organizationwide measures of success are selected and performance targets established. The high-level performance measures and targets, as well as the strategic plan, are communicated throughout the organization. At this point, measures of departmental performance are selected. These measures evaluate the operational-level contribution to achieving strategic goals and objectives. Measurement results are reported and acted on. The details of the measurement development steps are discussed in the following section.

Step 1: Define Performance Goals and Objectives

Create consensus for the need to measure performance within the context of organizational strategy and objectives. Using a scorecard approach, categorize your key areas of strategic performance. For simplicity's sake, say an organization has identified four strategic themes: customer satisfaction, clinical quality/safety, workforce excellence, and financial performance. In each of these categories, the senior leaders have established specific objectives, such as the following:

- *Customer satisfaction*—Objective: Improve patient satisfaction.
- *Clinical quality/safety*—Objective: Reduce unintended patient injuries.
- *Workforce excellence*—Objective: Reduce staff turnover rates.
- *Financial performance*—Objective: Reduce operating costs.

Step 2: Create the High-Level Scorecard

The scorecard will include relevant high-level measures sorted into performance categories or strategic themes. Do not force required measurements onto the scorecard. Start by taking inventory of existing performance measures throughout the organization and getting input from managers and physician groups. Use the inventory to determine the types of measures people are already collecting data for, sources of information for the measures, timing of reports, and whether or not the measurement is required by an external organization. Managers and physician groups can provide insight into the key issues (both internal and external) affecting their department or profession. For example, in 2004, appropriate management of patients' pain was a key accreditation issue of the Joint Commission on Accreditation of Healthcare Organizations, so senior leaders may have wanted at least one high-level measure related to this topic. Involving managers and physicians in defining high-level measures increases their interest in and ownership of the scorecard results. Use the measurement inventory and manager/physician input to identify at least one measurement for each strategic objective. Listed in Figure 6.4 are examples of high-level performance measures for the objectives described in step 1.

Notice how the measures in Figure 6.4 add clarity to the strategic objectives. Now everyone knows exactly how the organization will measure success. When measurements are clearly understood, senior leaders can push decision making down to a level at which the actions necessary to achieve objectives can be initiated. Five to seven strategic measures for each performance category are recommended. Too many measures can lead to collecting data that are meaningless.

 KEY POINT

The senior leadership team needs to ensure that everyone knows how the organization will evaluate the success of strategic objectives. This is accomplished by defining high-level performance measures for each objective.

With so many requirements for data collection coming from accrediting groups, payers, and regulatory agencies, information shortage is not an issue for most healthcare organizations. However, it is important to keep in mind that just because an external entity requires a particular measurement does not make that measurement strategically important to the organization. Be careful to separate externally defined data gathering requirements from your strategic scorecard development. Some organizations create a scorecard category entitled "Monitored Elements of Performance" (or something similar) for reporting externally defined measures that are not strategically important to the organization. While these measures can be incorporated into your scorecard, remember that they are not tied directly to your organization's strategy.

Step 3: Define Performance Targets

Performance targets are important: they clarify what the organization hopes to achieve and when. To advance performance excellence, targets

FIGURE 6.4 HIGH-LEVEL MEASURES FOR STRATEGIC OBJECTIVES

Objective: Improve patient satisfaction

Measures
- Inpatient loyalty index
- Patient perception of safety
- Patient perception of overall care

Objective: Reduce unintended patient injuries

Measures
- Total medication errors that cause patient harm
- Total other adverse events that cause patient harm
- Average score on staff safety culture survey

Objective: Reduce staff turnover rates

Measures
- Average overall employee satisfaction score
- Average staff retention rate in nursing department
- Average staff retention rate in nonnursing departments

Objective: Reduce operating costs

Measures
- Hospital operating margin
- Patient revenue per adjusted patient day
- Profit versus estimated profit

should be stretch goals based on past performance, what best performing organizations can accomplish, and internally or externally defined expectations.

There are two common misconceptions about performance targets. First is the idea that only the highest targets should be selected. In fact, an organization is much more likely to make incremental improvements in programs or services if realistic criteria for success are established. The other misconception is that failure to reach performance targets is a sign of poor-quality services. This fallacy causes people to set unrealistically low performance targets to guarantee "success." In reality, the goal of assessment is to learn where adjustments are needed so that the organization can continually improve. In an environment dedicated to performance excellence, people are not punished for missing targets.

Found in Table 6.3 are examples of high-level performance measures that support business intelligence at a health system in the southwest United States. Note that, for many of the measures, the system targets are based on best practices or performance expectations established by external sources.

TABLE 6.3 EXAMPLES OF HIGH-LEVEL PERFORMANCE
MEASURES, TARGETS, AND EXTERNAL SOURCES CONSULTED
WHEN SETTING TARGETS

High-Level Performance Measures	Target	Source of Comparative Data
1. Patient falls with injuries per 1,000 patient days	0	None available
2. Total reported medication errors	0	None available
3. Evidence-based hospital referral volume: coronary artery bypass—12 months	$\geq$500	Leapfrog Group
4. Evidence-based hospital referral volume: coronary angioplasty—12 months	$\geq$400	Leapfrog Group
5. Evidence-based hospital referral volume: abdominal aortic aneurysm repair—12 months	$\geq$30	Leapfrog Group
6. Evidence-based hospital referral volume: carotid endarterectomy	$\geq$100	Leapfrog Group
7. Evidence-based hospital referral volume: esophageal cancer surgery	$\geq$7	Leapfrog Group
8. Clean surgical site infection rate	$\leq$1.5%	Centers for Disease Control and Prevention (SENIC study)
9. Percent obstetrical patients receiving care in first trimester	90%	Healthy People 2010 goal (proportion of women who receive prenatal care beginning in first trimester): 90%
10. Percent home health care patients seen within 24 hours of referral	100%	Goal established by home health agency
11. First dose of antibiotics given within 8 hours of patient's admission for pneumonia	100%	State quality improvement organization (2001) study— best performing hospital: 98%

TABLE 6.3 *(continued)*

High-Level Performance Measures	Target	Source of Comparative Data
12. Blood cultures prior to first antibiotic dose for patients admitted with pneumonia	95%	State quality improvement organization (2001) study— best performing hospital: 100%
13. Pneumococcal vaccine screen/administration for patients admitted with pneumonia	90%	State quality improvement organization (2001) study— best performing hospital: 67%
14. Oxygenation assessment within 24 hours of patient's admission with pneumonia	90%	None available
15. Assessment of left ventricular ejection fraction for patients admitted with congestive heart failure	90%	State quality improvement organization (2001) study— best performing hospital: 96%
16. ACE inhibitor at discharge with ejection fraction <40% for patients admitted with congestive heart failure	80%	State quality improvement organization (2001) study— best performing hospital: 100%
17. Discharge instructions regarding diet/weight/meds/ appointment/symptoms for patients admitted with congestive heart failure	90%	None available
18. Annual foot exams and microalbumin tests for clinic patients with diabetes	80%	Healthy People 2010 (adults with diabetes who have at least an annual foot exam): 75%
19. Percent patients who report they "would recommend" our hospital	95%	National Research Corporation top 10% comparative data
20. Percent hospital patients who rate overall quality of care as good or excellent	90%	National Research Corporation top 10% comparative data

Step 4: Communicate and Institutionalize the Measures

High-level performance measures must be more than just a report that is completed periodically and then forgotten until the next due date rolls around. It is impossible for an organization to advance performance excellence—not to mention the Baldrige values—if strategic performance measures are not communicated and institutionalized. The idea of high-level performance measurement is to create a strategy-focused organization. This is accomplished by cascading the measures throughout the organization to create a link between operational measures and high-level measures. The performance scorecard in each department should include measures that are relevant to the organization's strategic objectives. At the operational level, people need to be evaluating the inputs, processes, and outputs that directly contribute to the organization's success (as defined by the high-level measures). For example, if the hospital were seeking to reduce the overall rate of nosocomial infections, department-level measures would be used to evaluate tasks or activities that have a clear relationship with that outcome.

Measurement at the senior level in an organization should link to measurement at the next lower level. To help managers select strategy-relevant operational measures for their department/unit, have them answer the following questions:

- What tasks or activities must people in my department/unit do right every time (or most of the time) to achieve the organization's strategic objectives?
- What tasks or activities must people in my department/unit stop doing to achieve the organization's strategic objectives?

- What new tasks or activities must be added in my department/unit to achieve the organization's strategic objectives?

Use a similar questioning technique with medical staff committees or groups. Measurements used by the medical staff to evaluate physician performance should provide information about their personal and professional contribution toward achieving organizational goals.

Figure 6.5 shows examples of operational-level measures for the following four strategic objectives: improve patient satisfaction, reduce unintended patient injuries, reduce staff turnover rates, and reduce operating costs. Departments and medical staff groups choose performance measures only for relevant objectives. For example, in the sample shown, the medical staff pediatric department does not have a performance measure for the objective related to staff turnover. Just like high-level measures, performance targets are established for operational measures.

Each department should build a performance scorecard that is based in part on the high-level organizational scorecard. In some situations a department may have additional measures that are of particular service-specific or discipline-specific interest. For example, the quality control measures of diagnostic testing performance found on the laboratory scorecard may not "fit" into any of the organization's strategic performance categories. However, all departments and medical staff groups should have at least one performance measure for each relevant organizational objective.

 KEY POINT

No part of your organization's performance can be measured effectively if it is evaluated independently of your strategic goals and objectives. Operational measures link priorities at the department level with organizational goals.

What performance measures are being tracked in your organization? Customer satisfaction? Profit margin? Clinical outcomes? All of the above? Whatever your focus, the measurements should advance performance excellence by supporting the organization's strategy. High-performing organizations focus on "where we are going," not just "where we have been," and performance measures are used to ensure that the organization is going in the right direction. Use the self-

Figure 6.5 Operational-Level Measures of Performance and Targets Categorized by Strategic Objectives

Nursing Services—General Surgical Unit

Strategic Objectives	Relevant Performance Measures	Target
Improve patient satisfaction with services	• Percentage of shifts in which RN:patient ratio meets hospital staffing standards	90%
	• Percentage of patients reportedly "very satisfied" with discharge instructions	95%
Reduce unintended patient injuries	• Percentage of patients with PCA pump monitored in accordance with nursing procedures	100%
	• Number of missed medication doses for high-alert medications	≤10 per month
Reduce staff turnover rate	• Staff turnover rate	≤7%
Reduce operating costs	• Productive nursing staff hours per patient day	≤4.5

Pediatric Department—Medical Staff

Strategic Objectives	Relevant Performance Measures	Target
Improve patient satisfaction with services	• Percentage of parents reportedly "very satisfied" with their involvement in the care of their child	85%
Reduce unintended patient injuries	• Percentage of medication orders with inappropriate pediatric dosing	0%
	• Percentage of pediatric patients who are restrained for more than one hour without physician evaluation	0%
Reduce operating costs	• Percentage of medication orders for "off formulary" medications	≤10%

Note: PCA = patient-controlled analgesia.

assessment below to see if your organization's performance measurement system measures up.

1. Are your organization's strategic goals clearly understood by the senior executive team, medical staff leaders, and managers?

   ❏ Yes ❏ No

   If your answer is no, this is your starting point for improving the performance measurement system. Get people together and make sure everyone understands your strategic goals.

2. Do you have a set of objectives to execute the strategic goals?

   ❏ Yes ❏ No

   If not, this is your next step. Develop a set of objectives for each strategy to take you in the direction you want to go. Generally, four to eight objectives per strategy are the most that a small to medium-size healthcare organization can manage while maintaining other operations.

3. For each strategic objective, do you have high-level performance measures that communicate what you will be tracking to evaluate success?

   ❏ Yes ❏ No

   For instance, if training is a key component for achieving an objective, you would want to track how many staff members have been through the required classes.

4. Are your high-level performance measures valid? Do they truly measure their accomplishment of the objectives?

   ❏ Yes ❏ No

5. Do your high-level measures clearly communicate what your organization is trying to accomplish?

   ❏ Yes ❏ No

6. Is the information available for your high-level measurements? Do the data already exist, or will added effort and expense be required to gather the information?

   ❏ Yes ❏ No

   If it is too difficult to gather the information needed for some measures, it may be counterproductive to include the measurement in your performance scorecard.

7. Do you have a sufficient number of high-level measures to track each objective?

   ❏ Yes ❏ No

   For example, if you are tracking employee satisfaction and you use a once-a-year survey that only a small number of staff members return, you may not have sufficient information for evaluating satisfaction. Consider adding measures such as feedback from focus groups or results from exist interviews. Some objectives may be well served with only one measure.

8. Do you have performance targets set for each high-level measure?

   ❏ Yes ❏ No

   Time frames should be set for performance targets so that people know when the expected levels are to be reached.

9. Are high-level performance targets challenging yet attainable?

   ❏ Yes ❏ No

10. Have departments/units identified performance measures and targets for all relevant organizational objectives?

    ❏ Yes ❏ No

Step 5: Report the Results

Step 5 is the point at which performance measurement intersects with business knowledge. To enable senior leaders to gain knowledge about important matters within and around the organization, a comprehensive yet concise measurement report format should be used. A few of the common report formats are highlighted in this section.

A balanced scorecard approach is often used to get the full picture of the health of an organization. An advantage of this approach over the single aggregate measure is that individual measurement results can be seen. The balanced scorecard has been likened to an airplane cockpit: rather than giving pilots just one "trouble light" (the plane is either okay or not okay), a bank of gauges is supplied so that the pilot may see trends and any trouble that is developing. Certain alarm values exist to draw the pilot's attention when problems arise. Similarly, the balanced scorecard provides an overview of organization performance. Alarm levels can be built in through established targets or statistically defined control limits.

A table format is the simplest and least graphic of all data displays. Information is arranged in rows and columns. An excerpt from a table format report of high-level performance measures at a home health agency is found in Table 6.4. Some balanced scorecard reports use a table format.

Many types of graphic data displays can be used to present performance measurement results, and a few universal rules dictate which type of graph best portrays any given set of data. You are likely to find that, in many cases, the same data set can be shown many different ways.

TABLE 6.4 EXECUTIVE TEAM PERFORMANCE REPORT—HOME
HEALTH AGENCY

		Results		
	Target	First Quarter	Second Quarter	Third Quarter
Strategic Category: Clinical Performance				
• Percentage of nonhospice patients with adequate pain control	≥90%	94%	95%	90%
• Percentage of hospice patients with adequate pain control	≥85%	91%	86%	82%
• Surgical wound infection rate	0%	0%	.05%	0%
• Timely physician notification of significant changes in patient's status	100%	100%	98%	100%
Strategic Category: Operational Efficiency				
• On-time delivery of home health services	≥95%	90%	89%	92%
• Average length of stay for nonhospice patients	≤15 days	12	16	22

The hard part is determining which type of graph best supports business intelligence in the organization.

Some organizations use a combination of graphic and statistical reports of high-level measures. Figure 6.6 is a one-page performance measurement report that provides significant detail about the measurement (including the relevant strategic category), a definition of the measurement, the rationale for monitoring this topic, the organization's target performance, its strategic domain, the formula used to create the measure, the data source, and the frequency of reporting. A line graph is used to report the actual results.

This one-page-per-measurement format can be especially useful when an organization first begins to report high-level measures to the governing board, senior leadership, and physician groups. Because a full or half page is devoted to each measure, many of the common questions can be addressed upfront. As people become more familiar with the measures, some of the explanatory notes can be eliminated and the

FIGURE 6.6 ONE-PAGE HIGH-LEVEL PERFORMANCE
MEASUREMENT REPORT

Measurement: Employee Retention Rate

Strategic Category: Staff Focus

Measurement Definition: Retention of regular and part-time employees during fiscal year 2003

Rationale: Employee retention is a cost-effective recruitment strategy. The cost of replacing an employee is estimated to be a minimum of one-third of the annual salary for that position. Failure to retain employees in appropriate numbers may erode the experience/knowledge level of staff members and may be disruptive to the quality and continuity of services.

Target: 85.5%

Measurement Formula: 100% minus (annual number of full- and part-time employee separations divided by annual average number of full- and part-time employees)

Data Source: Human resources information system

Reporting Frequency: Quarterly actual used to project annual experience on a quarterly basis. Annual experience calculated at conclusion of fiscal year.

Results

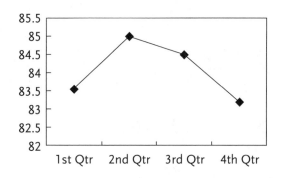

format condensed. However, be careful not to abbreviate the report so much that it no longer contributes to the business intelligence of the organization.

Dashboards are another commonly used format for reporting high-level performance measures. They serve the same function as reports presented in a table format; however, symbols and/or colors are used to draw people's attention to performance concerns.

QUALITY

Measures	Actual 2002	Goals 2003
Clinical Indicators:		
Infection Control		
Hospital-wide	****	****
Surgical Site Infections	****	****
Mortalities	******	******
Blood Product Transfusion		
Criteria Met	******	******
Transfusion Reactions	******	******
Cross-X to Transfuse Ratio	******	******
Pathological Tissue Review	******	******
QIO External Project		
Congestive Heart Failure	***	****
Acute Myocardial Infarction	****	****
Peer Review Summary		
Level 0	*****	******
Level I	****	*****
Level II	***	*****
Level III	***	***

CUSTOMER SERVICE

Measures	Actual 2002	Goals 2003
Overall Inpatient	****	****
Admissions	******	******
Billing	***	*****
Environment	******	*****
Expectations	****	*****
General Care	****	****
General Reputation	***	*****
Getting Around	****	*****
Key Results	****	****
Leaving the Hospital	****	*****
Meals	***	*****
Nursing Care	*****	*****
Pain Management	**	****
Physician Care	****	*****
Problem Resolution	****	*****
Visitors/Family	****	****

FINANCIAL

Measures	Actual 2002	Goals 2003
Financial Ratios:		
Profitability		
Operating Margin	******	*****
Total Margin	****	****
Return on Equity	******	******
Return on Total Assets	****	****
Liquidity		
Current Ratio	******	******
Days in Accounts Receivable Net	**	*****
Average Payment Period	***	****
Days Cash on Hand	*	****
Capital Structure		
Long-term Debt to Equity	******	******
Cash Flow to Total Debt	******	******
Debt Service Coverage	******	*****
Long-term Debt to Total	****	*****
Capitalization		

OPERATIONAL

Patient Safety:

Measures	Actual 2002	Goals 2003
Restraints		
Emergency Department	*	****
Inpatient	*	****
Incident Reports		
Falls	***	****
Medication Errors	***	****
Sentinel Events	**	***
Documentation Compliance		
History & Physical	***	****
Discharge Summary	***	****
Operative Report	***	****
Overdue Records	***	***
Telephone/Verbal Orders	*	***

Measures	Actual 2002	Goals 2003
Overall Emergency	***	***
Attendees	***	****
Billing	**	***
Entering	*****	******
Environment	******	******
Expectations	N/A	N/A
General Care	***	****
Getting to the ED	***	***
Key Results	**	***
Leaving the ED	****	****
Nursing Care	****	****
Pain Management	**	***
Physician Care	***	***
Problem Resolution	***	***
Waiting for Care	***	*****

Measures	Actual 2002	Goals 2003
Operational Indicators:		
Salaries & Benefits as % N/R	***	****
FTE/Adjusted Bed	*****	*****
Cost per Adjusted Bed	*****	******
Total Admission/Observation	*	***
Average Length of Stay	**	***
Average Daily Census	*	***
Average Case Mix	****	****
Employee Satisfaction	*****	*****
Employee Turnover	******	****
W/C Experience Mod	*****	****

Key   Exceptional = ***** (Blue)
       Below Normal = ** (Red)
       Above Normal = **** (Blue)
       Marginal = * (Red)
       Normal = *** (Yellow)

Source: Sebasticook Valley Hospital, Pittsfield, Maine. Reprinted with permission.

In 2002, Sebasticook Valley Hospital (SVH) in Pittsfield, Maine, began using a dashboard-style format to report high-level performance measures to its governing board and senior leaders. The information is presented in a trifold report card similar to the type used in grade schools. Stars and colors are used to signify the hospital's actual performance in four strategic categories: quality, customer service, financial, and operational. Figure 6.7 is the dashboard report SVH developed at the start of 2003, which shows the performance measures used in 2002, the actual results from 2002, and the performance targets for 2003. A key to understanding the meaning of the stars used to report results is provided at the bottom of the report. The actual report is printed in color, with the stars appearing in different colors. Not only can governing board members and senior leaders quickly see how well the organization is doing by counting the stars but they can also judge results by the color coding. Actual results from 2003 are reported to board members and senior leaders using the same format as that shown in Figure 6.7.

Creating a scorecard that relies on symbols and/or color to denote performance results requires some behind-the-scenes decisions. People must decide on the numeric levels that equate to the performance ratings. For example, what is an "exceptional" nosocomial infection rate versus one that falls into the "normal" category? This decision must be made on a measurement-by-measurement basis with input from appropriate departments and physician groups.

Each year the leadership team at SVH reviews the high-level performance measures to determine continued relevance to strategic goals. During this review, the numeric values that correspond with the performance ratings are revisited and revised as necessary. To illustrate these decisions, Figure 6.8 shows one measure from each of the four strategic performance categories at SVH. The measurement definition is shown, along with the numeric results that correspond with the performance ratings.

Whenever possible, report comparative data along with your organization's actual performance results. This adds another dimension to the report, which in turn adds to the business intelligence of the organization. Figure 6.9 is an excerpt from a high-level performance measurement report used at a healthcare organization in the Mid-Atlantic states (XYZ Health, a fictitious name). Comparative data from a variety of sources are displayed along with the organization's actual results.

The complexity of managing healthcare services requires that leaders

FIGURE 6.8 PERFORMANCE RATING DECISIONS

Strategic Performance Category: Quality

Measure: Restraints—inpatient

Definition: State licensing regulations/Medicare conditions of participation require that patients placed in restraints (any type) will have certain elements documented within their record. A 100% compliance with all requirements is expected.

Performance Rating/Numeric Values

Exceptional = ******	(100% compliance)
Above Normal = ****	(98–99%)
Normal = ***	(97%)
Below Normal = **	(96%)
Marginal = *	(95%)

Strategic Performance Category: Customer Service

Measure: Pain management

Definition: The extent to which staff members assess, treat, and educate patients about pain

Performance Rating/Numeric Values

Exceptional = ******	(2 or more standard deviations [S.D.] above the mean)
Above Normal = ****	(1–2 S.D. above the mean)
Normal = ***	(+ or – 1 S.D. from the mean)
Below Normal = **	(1–2 S.D. below the mean)
Marginal = *	(2 S.D. below the mean)

Strategic Performance Category: Financial

Measure: Days cash on hand

Definition: The number of days the organization could pay its cash operations and expenses if none of the accounts receivable were collected

Performance Rating/Numeric Values

Exceptional = ******	(72.0 days)
Above Normal = ****	(60.0 days)
Normal = ***	(52.0 days)
Below Normal = **	(51.0 days)
Marginal = *	(40.0 days)

FIGURE 6.8 *(continued)*

Strategic Performance Category: Operational

Measure: Salaries and benefits as a percentage of net revenue

Definition: The cost of salaries, wages, fringe benefits, and contract labor as a percentage of net revenue

Performance Rating/Numeric Values

Exceptional = ******	(48%)
Above Normal = ****	(50%)
Normal = ***	(52%)
Below Normal = **	(55%)
Marginal = *	(58%)

Source: Sebasticook Valley Hospital, Pittsfield, Maine. Reprinted with permission.

be able to simultaneously view performance in several areas. A useful tool for this purpose is the spider diagram. Also know as a radar chart or gap analysis tool, the spider diagram can help people visualize the gaps between the current and desired performance for a diverse set of measurements. High-level performance measurement data presented in a graphic spider diagram can

- minimize information overload through the succinct presentation of multiple measurements,
- illustrate relationships between strategic performance goals, and
- allow senior leaders to determine whether improvements in one area may have been achieved at the expense of performance in another area.

What makes this particular reporting format unique is that a diverse set of measurements can be displayed using one tool. All high-level performance measures can be displayed on the diagram, or separate diagrams can be created for each strategic performance category. Figure 6.10 is a spider diagram illustrating two sets of high-level measures described earlier in this chapter (see Figure 6.4). The report is divided in half to display measurement data for two of the strategic objectives: improve patient satisfaction and reduce staff turnover. The outer circle

Cesarean Section Rate

Goal = Below peer mean

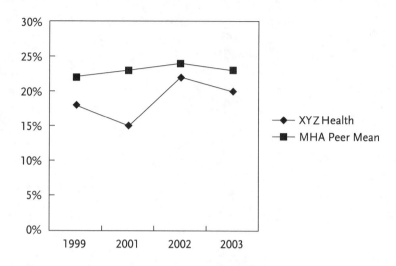

Source: Comparative data provided by the Maryland Hospital Association (MHA 2003).

Warfarin Given to Stroke Patients with Atrial Fibrillation

Goal = ⇧

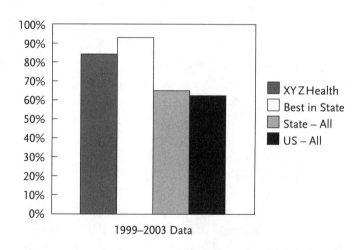

Source: Comparative data provided by the State Quality Improvement Organization contracted by CMS to oversee quality and utilization for Medicare beneficiaries and data from all states.

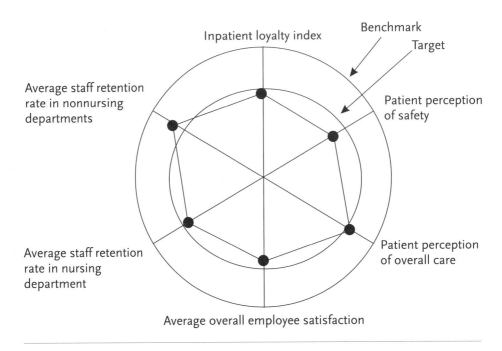

represents the benchmark target (best practices), and the inner circle
represents the organization's performance target. The actual results for
each measure are plotted and connected with a line. The completed
graph looks a bit like a spider's web, hence its name.

Spider diagrams illustrate interrelationships between performance
measurement data for one period of time. However, this diagram must
be supplemented with other types of reports to show performance
trends.

Step 6: Analyze and Act on the Results

Performance measurement data must be more than a report distributed
to leadership; they must become part of an organization's performance
excellence journey. Measuring performance is about knowing how the
organization is performing, comparing that performance with expectations, and then taking action if the actual performance differs significantly from expectations. A healthcare organization will only move along

in the performance excellence journey when measurement is tied to the priority areas for improvement identified during strategic planning.

Measurement helps focus organizational attention on those aspects of performance that are not going as planned so that actions can be taken to correct the trend. Some strategies devised to achieve objectives might not work. In this situation, measures will show that the relationship between the strategy and the expected outcome does not exist. Further investigation must be undertaken to reveal the causes. Corrective actions should have a positive impact on the relevant measures of performance without having a significant negative effect on any others.

Feedback from high-level and operational measures is also used to validate or adjust (when appropriate) the strategic direction of the organization. Sometimes the data may reveal areas in which goals, strategies, or objectives are inadequate. In that instance, the goal, strategy, or objective may need to be adjusted. It may also show that the attainment of the goal, strategy, or objective is complete. The senior leadership team must adjust the plan as needed. Formally revisiting the strategic plan on a periodic basis (e.g., annually) is necessary to ensure that strategic priorities continue to drive the organization. This relationship between performance measurement and the strategic planning process is illustrated in Figure 6.11.

Alignment and integration are key concepts for successful implementation of an organization's performance measurement system. They include (1) how the measures are aligned throughout the organization, (2) how the measures are integrated to yield organizationwide results, and (3) how performance measurement requirements are deployed within the organization. Senior leaders should be able to effectively track high-level measures as well as departmental/operational performance in key areas that affect the organization's strategic objectives. High-performing organizations use a systematic process to align and integrate the performance measurement system.

PERFORMANCE MEASUREMENT ENABLERS

- ☐ High-level and operational measures of performance focus on the key areas of business and clinical performance as defined in the strategic plan.
- ☐ Performance targets reflect stretch goals based on past performance and the performance of competitors and other organizations that provide similar healthcare services.

- ❑ Sufficiently detailed high-level performance measures are needed so that deployment throughout the organization is possible.
- ❑ Performance measures at the department/operational level are aligned with the organization's strategic objectives and high-level measures.
- ❑ Performance measurement data improve the organization's understanding of the relationship between processes and results.
- ❑ Fact-based decisions are supported by the collection and analysis of performance measurement information.
- ❑ When performance does not meet expectations, specific action agendas are developed and deployed.
- ❑ Performance measurement data are used to evaluate the effectiveness of actions intended to improve performance.
- ❑ High-level and departmental performance measurement results support strategic planning and operational decision making.

KNOWLEDGE MANAGEMENT

Knowledge management is an organizational process used to achieve better performance through effective knowledge sharing and organizational learning. Often people equate knowledge management with information technology tools; however, these tools are merely facilitators and not the essence of knowledge management. The goal of knowledge management is to deliver the intellectual capacity of the organization to the people who make the day-to-day decisions that in aggregate determine the success or failure of the organization. This involves knowing where knowledge resides (e.g., databases, printed matter, people's heads) and distributing it to the right people at the right time.

Every healthcare organization has some form of knowledge management. Some are very effective at managing their knowledge resources; however, many are not. Ask yourself these questions: How long does it take people in my organization to learn something new? How fast does a new employee or medical staff member get up to speed on how the organization works? Do personalities often get in the way of open, constructive, clear communication and knowledge sharing? Is there an infrastructure for keeping knowledge updated and accessible? Are there means of effective communication within the organization and with suppliers/customers? The organization that is adept at creating and using knowledge has a clear advantage over those that are not.

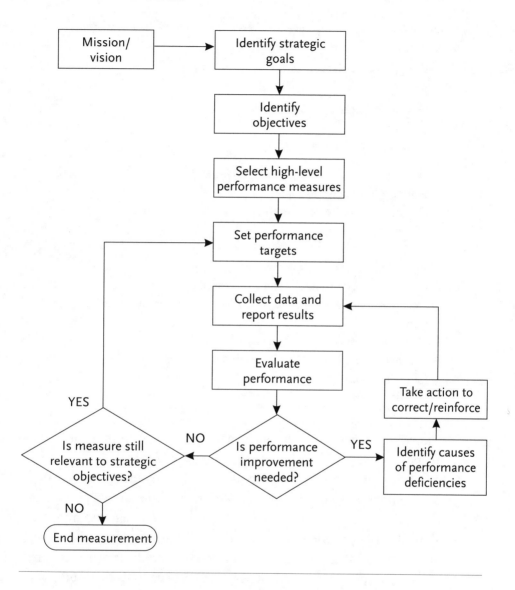

High-performing organizations have efficient methods for knowledge sharing, interaction, and organizational learning. These involve the use of information technology tools, but more importantly, efficient methods are achieved through a supportive organizational culture. This culture is best portrayed by the survey statements found in Figure 6.12. How would staff members in your organization rate these statements?

Would the answers vary by department, position, or profession? Would managers and senior leaders have different opinions?

Overcoming cultural barriers requires an organization to create an atmosphere in which sharing knowledge and innovating is valued and rewarded. Knowledge management needs to be integrated into everything that everyone does; it needs to become part of the way people work. By using knowledge management principles, better performance can be achieved through improved interactions between individuals or groups. Moreover, to be efficient, knowledge must be accessible; thus, there is a storage component to the process. People in the organization need ready access to critical information necessary for their job as well as to best practices information. The greatest benefit gained from effective knowledge management is that it does not waste a most important asset: people's time.

High-performing organizations have data systems that allow for universal access to information for enhanced decision making. Managers and staff members need the following:

- Knowledge that is context filtered
- Knowledge that is easily accessed
- Knowledge that is valid, with some authenticity behind it
- Access to knowledge through training and education
- Access to what has been learned by others
- Tools to effectively capture and transfer knowledge

 KEY POINT

It is important for organizations to "know what they know" and be able to make maximum use of that knowledge.

Technology Enablers

Information technology is an important enabler of knowledge sharing. This technology can range from something as elementary as electronic mail and messaging to something as sophisticated as electronic document management. Some of the common tools for managing knowledge in an organization are described below.

- Electronic mail and messaging, group calendars, and scheduling technologies allow for the rapid exchange of knowledge based on common document formats and directories. This increases the likelihood that a significant exchange of information can take place.
- Skills inventories and subject-expert databases contain information about who's who and who knows what in the organization. When maintained online (i.e., on an intranet), these databases can be extremely useful if designed and managed correctly.
- Electronic meeting systems provide instant communication support for a group of people, no matter where they are and when they need to exchange information. Software applications allow people to brainstorm about issues, categorize responses, create surveys, and vote on decisions. Intrafacility improvement teams as

well as people located at different sites can use this technology. Meeting sessions can be in real time or not (e.g., bulletin board system, groupware discussion database).

- Virtual communities in an Internet environment provide people with a way to share or gather knowledge.
- Document management systems are available to maintain explicit knowledge. A wide range of software is available to aid in capturing, storing, retrieving, and filtering the knowledge stored in documents. Coupled with workflow systems such as process diagramming and electronic forms routing products, document management technologies are fast becoming the engines for corporatewide content management.
- Workgroup and groupware development tools are software utilities designed to support group working and allow for remote access to computers. These utilities provide the initial framework for many knowledge management applications.
- Information distribution and "push" products allow users to search for and place up-to-date information on a web browser according to predetermined categories.
- Data visualization and knowledge mapping applications provide a graphic view of concepts related to a user query. By delivering information graphically, the software allows users to view query results in context and find relevant data quickly and easily. When a collection of information changes, the software dynamically reflects the change in its concept map.

 KEY POINT

Technology can enable people's knowledge-sharing activities by delivering relevant information to users from every possible source.

High-performing organizations seek to ensure that employees are making the best use of available information technology to perform their work and to gather and share knowledge. Employees are provided opportunities, incentives, support, and training to make appropriate use of technology to do their work and to acquire and share knowledge. Personal learning as it relates to staff development and human resources is addressed in Chapter 7.

Organizations that fail to invest in knowledge management lessen their ability to innovate, invent, or adapt to a changing environment. Performance excellence cannot be advanced unless people learn something new, even as they unlearn the old. High-performing organizations do not leave knowledge management and organizational learning to chance. These organizations have a strategy, a process, and the wherewithall to invest in knowledge management.

KNOWLEDGE MANAGEMENT ENABLERS

❏ An enabling environment for knowledge sharing and learning
❏ Provision of staff training in the skills needed for information sharing
❏ Expanded information access through investments in information technology applications and the information infrastructure
❏ Generation and sharing of knowledge among people in the organization and with patients and other customers, suppliers, and partners

REFERENCES

Flynn, B., and B. Saladin. 2001. "Further Evidence on the Validity of the Theoretical Models Underlying the Baldrige Criteria." *Journal of Operations Management* 19 (6): 617–52.

Hibbard, J., J. Stockard, and M. Tusler. 2003. "Does Publicizing Hospital Performance Stimulate Quality Improvement Efforts?" *Health Affairs* 22 (2): 84–94.

Kaplan, R., and D. Norton. 1996. *Translating Strategy into Action: The Balanced Scorecard.* Boston: Harvard Business School Press.

Maryland Hospital Association. 2003. *Quality Indicator Project.* Elkridge, MD: The Association of Maryland Hospitals & Health Systems.

Neely, A., C. Adams, and M. Kennerley. 2003. *Performance Prism: The Scorecard for Measuring and Managing Stakeholder Relationships.* New York: Financial Times Prentice Hall.

Pannirselvam, G., and L. Ferguson. 2001. "A Study of the Relationships Between the Baldrige Categories." *International Journal of Quality and Reliability Management* 18 (1): 14–34.

The Governance Institute. 2000. *The Board's Role in Monitoring Quality*, 12. Washington, DC: The Governance Institute.

University Health Network, Office of Planning and Performance Measurement. 2004. "OPPM—Performance Measurement." [Online information; retrieved 01/04.] www.uhn.ca/uhn/corporate/oppm/site/corporate/corporate.asp.

U.S. Central Intelligence Agency (CIA) Office of Public Affairs. 1999. *A Consumer's Guide to Intelligence,* vii. Washington, DC: CIA.

Wedman, J., J. Laffey, R. Andrews, D. Musser, L. Diggs, and L. Diel. 1998. "Building Technology Infrastructure and Enterprises: Increasing Performance Capacity." *Educational Technology Magazine* 38 (5): 12–19.

CHAPTER SEVEN

Bottom-Up Excellence

I N HEALTHCARE ORGANIZATIONS, the largest share of operating expenses is devoted to the workforce. To advance performance excellence, this investment must be maximized. High-performing organizations recognize that human capital—the workforce—largely determines their capacity to perform. The degree of excellence that can be achieved by the organization is dependent on its people.

Two principles are central to the human side of performance excellence. First, people are an investment, and, as with any investment, the goal is to maximize value while managing risk. As the value of the workforce increases, so does the performance capacity of the healthcare organization. Second, an organization's human resource policies and practices must be aligned to support the mission, vision for the future, core values, strategic goals, and objectives. The workforce management systems—from the organizational level down to individual staff members—must link with the organization's strategic and operational planning.

Workforce issues are covered in the Baldrige category of Staff Focus. This section addresses all key human resource practices directed toward creating an environment with a strong focus on performance excellence. The Staff Focus category examines how the organization's work systems and staff learning and motivation efforts enable everyone to develop and use their full potential in alignment with the organization's overall objectives and action plans. Also examined are the organization's efforts to build and maintain a work environment and staff support climate that is conducive to performance excellence and to personal and organizational growth. The emphasis in this Baldrige category is to ensure that staff resources support objectives set in strategic planning. Representative areas in the Staff Focus category include the following:

- How staff development aligns with strategic direction
- How the organization addresses both individual and organizational learning
- How the organization assesses and uses cross-training, work layout, decision making, and innovation
- How the organization maintains effective communication
- How the organization aligns incentives for the achievement of organizational objectives
- How the organization contributes to staff well-being, satisfaction, motivation, and retention

As the CEO and managers at Ellsworth County (Kansas) Medical Center (ECMC) became more familiar with the Baldrige Criteria—especially the Staff Focus category—they were able to create a new organizational viewpoint. This awakening is described in the case study below, as related by Roger Pearson, CHE, CEO of ECMC.

ECMC CASE STUDY

Like many healthcare organizations, the priority at ECMC had always been to satisfy the needs of patients and their families. However, the Baldrige Criteria also identify excellent organizations as satisfying the needs of staff: their work systems, education, and well-being. When we considered the relationship between patient satisfaction and staff satisfaction, a new thought began to emerge, and that was that *all* results are accomplished by staff. Therefore, patient satisfaction—or performance excellence—occurs consistently only after employees are satisfied. The performance excellence journey must begin with employee satisfaction—it is the engine that drives all external customer satisfaction. Employees are just as much customers of ECMC as are patients and the community and as such should command the same strategic investment of organizational time and energy.

FIGURE 7.1 VISION 20:20 MODEL, ELLSWORTH COUNTY
MEDICAL CENTER

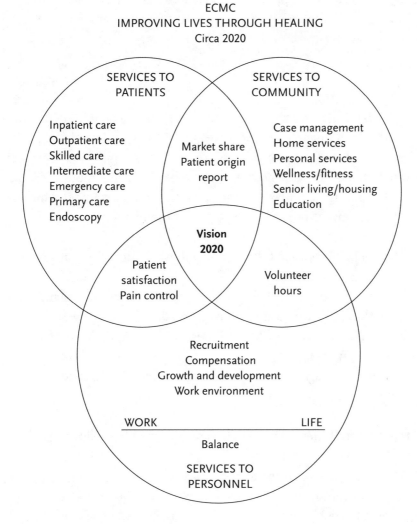

ECMC
IMPROVING LIVES THROUGH HEALING
Circa 2020

SERVICES TO PATIENTS

Inpatient care
Outpatient care
Skilled care
Intermediate care
Emergency care
Primary care
Endoscopy

SERVICES TO COMMUNITY

Case management
Home services
Personal services
Wellness/fitness
Senior living/housing
Education

Market share
Patient origin
report

Vision 2020

Patient
satisfaction
Pain control

Volunteer
hours

Recruitment
Compensation
Growth and development
Work environment

WORK   LIFE

Balance

SERVICES TO
PERSONNEL

Source: Ellsworth County Medical Center, Ellsworth, Kansas. Reprinted with permission.

The organization's future survival would increasingly be determined by its ability to meet and exceed, equally well, the expectations and requirements of three customer groups: patients, employees, and the community. This realization, which was applied to the ECMC strategic planning process in 2001, resulted in the development of our Vision 20:20 model. The model, illustrated in Figure 7.1, combines the dual concept of perfect vision and a defined future date. It articulates the four key strategic initiatives ECMC must emphasize to achieve our mission. The model visually represents the equality of organizational attention and effort that must be applied to each customer group if ECMC is to create a strategic differentiation between ECMC and competitors in the minds of our three key customers.

*   *   *   *   *

The Baldrige Criteria support the belief that to be high performing, organizations must create processes that enable and reinforce positive workforce attitudes and behaviors. This process begins with hiring motivated employees, and it continues not so much by motivating them but by avoiding demotivation and creating conditions under which motivated employees flourish. How are staff members demotivated?

- By not being trained fully, not only in work functions but also in attitudes and values
- By being micromanaged and their managers not understanding that they are trustworthy and concerned with doing a good job
- By not being praised when it is deserved (when their extra efforts are not noticed)
- By their managers being ill-tempered, impolite, inconsiderate, or nonappreciative

Motivated staff members seem to flourish when the following occur:

- Expectations are clearly stated by leaders.
- Leaders communicate with openness and are able to listen.
- Desirable behaviors and attitudes are rewarded.
- There is a general sense of fairness.
- Constraints are removed, and fewer controls are in place.

Senior leaders must demonstrate a real commitment to the achievement of success through people. There is a need to see the organization as a balance between its technical systems (the way services are produced) and its social systems (the way people are organized, managed, trained, and consulted). Performance excellence is advanced when employees become innovative, questioning, suggestion producing, and boundary pushing. Motivated staff members move the organization forward with the force of their own creativity and expertise. When an organization is able to achieve "bottom-up" excellence, there is a general sense of excitement about reaching goals, improved cooperation occurs, and a greater willingness to be accountable is evident. To create bottom-up excellence, the following three broad areas of staff management and improvement must be addressed:

1. Work systems
2. Staff education, training, and development
3. Staff well-being and satisfaction

High-performing organizations have a well-developed strategy for creating a valuable workforce. This includes organizing and managing work and jobs to promote cooperation and empowerment. Procedures support effective communication and skill sharing across healthcare professions and work units. The characteristics and skills needed for particular jobs are well defined and serve as the basis for evaluating potential hires and current employees. Staff education and training programs are designed specifically to contribute to the achievement of the organization's strategic goals and objectives. And the organization has established plans to promote workplace health, safety, security, and ergonomics. The components of an effective staff management and improvement strategy are covered in this chapter.

WORK SYSTEMS

Work system refers to the manner in which work is structured, organized, and carried out so as to accomplish the desired output in an efficient manner to meet or surpass customer expectations. The system itself encompasses work processes, job structure, compensation, career progression, and work practices. The degree to which employees are empowered to participate in the planning process and day-to-day operations and share in the organization's successes determines the achievement of a high-performance work system. Studies of the organization factors that contribute to the retention of nursing staff have repeatedly found that the work system affects staff turnover rates (IOM 2003; Bauman et al. 2001). The work systems in organizations that have received Magnet designation by the American Nurses Credentialing Center have the following characteristics (Aiken 2001):

- There is an administrative priority on quality of care and support of clinicians.
- Management gives clinicians—nurses and physicians—authority for designing work and staffing patterns.
- The organization invests in staff continuing education.
- Administration listens and responds to the concerns of caregivers who are closest to patients.
- There is more flexibility in policies, schedules, and job changes within the organization.
- Senior leaders promote decentralized decision making, greater staff autonomy, and accountability.

High-performance organizations have a holistic view of employees as key stakeholders, realizing that excellence is not possible without a satisfied workforce. Incentives are particularly important in creating a results-oriented workforce. Employees' performance expectations should be aligned with the organization's mission. Personal accountability for performance must be reinforced by both rewards and consequences.

Workforce Values and Culture

People must be viewed as assets capable of contributing skills, knowledge, experience, and commitment rather than as costs that are merely a budgetary consideration. Encouraging employee involvement and providing an environment in which it can flourish produce tangible rewards for individuals and the organization. An effective work system has the following characteristics:

- It is rooted in the involvement and participation of people at all levels in the organization.
- It recognizes that labor unions are partners that have a stake in the process.

- It is aimed at the joint interests of both the people and the organization.
- It recognizes that management and staff members have a joint interest and a joint role in creating an organization that meets both customer and employee needs.
- It involves a set of best principles and practices designed to release the potential of people at all levels in the organization.
- It supports the organization's mission, values, and strategic objectives.
- It is more than just one tactic, such as empowered work teams or job enrichment.

 REFLECTION

Does your organization have a clearly expressed statement of how people are to be viewed by the organization and how they are to be managed? Do your work system values support excellence or the outmoded concept of workforce control that inhibits performance improvement?

As with most factors that affect organizational excellence, the culture in the organization greatly affects the work system. Progression from a culture of workforce control to workforce empowerment and involvement will take some time. Supporting this long-term change requires leadership commitment and perseverance.

Healthcare organizations tend to be hierarchical, where relationships between doctors, nurses, and other health professionals and among the various levels of power have typically been authoritarian in nature. This hierarchy does not facilitate a culture of participation and trust. For example, one study found that hierarchical nursing teams reported lower levels of information sharing (Cott 1997). Teamwork has been seen as a mechanism to encourage a more collegial working environment among health professionals (McConnell 2000).

In a culture that supports workforce excellence, the manager's role becomes that of initiator, counselor, and facilitator. This is accomplished by doing the following:

- Providing a vision and communicating it
- Encouraging effective staff member teamwork and cooperation
- Encouraging the free flow of ideas and initiative

- Developing staff members rather than rigidly controlling them
- Overseeing more flexible work structures and ensuring that objectives are met

Management styles may need to change to support a new workforce culture. Revisions to the work system intended to support performance excellence will not be effective unless the practices and beliefs of management actively support the new environment.

 REFLECTION

Does your leadership team create a culture in which people at all levels talk to each other? What can you do better to keep dialog flowing throughout the organization?

Structure and Job Design

Achieving workforce excellence has implications for organizational structure. It is assisted by flatter structures that push decision making down to the appropriate level within the organization to capitalize on individual skills and experience. The aim is to get staff members to identify with and own the services they provide. This organizational approach eliminates the need for extensive, hierarchical control systems and ensures the delivery of healthcare services that meet the needs of patients and other customers.

The way work is structured and designed also affects the work system. Jobs should form a coherent whole, either independently or with related jobs. The activities should make a significant contribution to the delivery of health services, and this should be visible to the employee performing the job. While it may not be possible to achieve all of the ideal characteristics, consider the following factors when structuring and designing jobs:

- Provide some variety of pace, method, location, and skill.
- Provide feedback on performance, both directly and through other people.
- Allow for some discretion and control in the timing, sequence, and pace of work efforts.
- Include some responsibility for outcome.

- Provide some opportunity for learning and problem solving (within the individual's competence).
- Provide opportunities for development in ways that the individual finds relevant.

 SELF-ASSESSMENT

Does the structure and design of jobs in your organization support workforce performance excellence? Or do the jobs create a controlling environment that inhibits the success of your work systems?

Job Design in a Controlling Environment

❑ Work is broken down into single tasks requiring narrow skills. There is fragmentation among related tasks.
❑ Rules and external controls are used to manage staff members.
❑ Job responsibilities focus on doing, not thinking. Staff members are expected to work; managers are the thinkers.
❑ Quality is inspected through some type of audit process.
❑ Job responsibilities are closely controlled, and staff members have no authority.

Job Design in an Environment that Supports Workforce Excellence

❑ Tasks are grouped and require multiple, broad skills. Emphasis is placed on the whole process.
❑ Staff members (individually or in groups) are afforded a degree of self-determination.
❑ Job responsibilities are a combination of doing and thinking. Everyone's ideas are viewed as valuable.
❑ Quality is built into the job, and it is everyone's responsibility.
❑ Staff members (individually or in groups) are encouraged to make decisions and solve problems.

To support performance excellence, the contribution and commitment of every employee must be maximized. The approach demands that considerable attention be given to communications. It requires more than the top-down passing of information. There is a need to provide necessary information for decision making at all levels in the organization and to encourage speedy feedback about work situations and performance. Commonly used communication vehicles include newsletters, briefings, bulletins, staff meetings, videos, and management by walking around. Computer networks provide a channel for immediate organizationwide communication.

Joint problem solving is an enabler of performance excellence. It provides the opportunity for a much higher level of staff involvement in a wide range of issues. To address particular problems, form project teams composed of a cross-section of people from within the organization representing all relevant levels and functions. Other approaches aimed at enhancing staff involvement and capitalizing on their experience, talents, and abilities include meetings concerned with continuous improvement, quality circles, staff surveys with feedback, and other suggestion schemes.

Performance Expectations

Is your organization's performance management system aligned with your vision and strategic goals? Alignment must begin at the level of job performance expectations. Expectations enable and motivate performance toward achieving organizational goals while ensuring accountability among employees.

To advance performance excellence, some organizations have clearly defined performance expectations that are drawn in part from an understanding of the human capital competencies needed to support the organization's vision. For example, the Veterans Health Administration (2003) has identified eight core competencies that address the skills and attitudes most needed by employees to meet the challenges of the twenty-first century. These core competencies are as follows:

1. Personal Mastery (Dealing With Yourself)
2. Technical Skills (Dealing With Yourself)
3. Interpersonal Effectiveness (Dealing With Others)
4. Customer Service (Becoming "Other" Oriented)
5. Flexibility/Adaptability (Becoming Comfortable With The Unpredictable)
6. Creative Thinking (Reaching Outside "The Box")
7. Systems Thinking (Putting It "Together")
8. Organizational Stewardship (Accepting Accountability)

More detailed descriptions of these core competencies are found in Figure 7.2. The competencies serve as a foundation for the development of job descriptions and performance expectations at all levels

Personal Mastery (Dealing With Yourself)
- Assume responsibility for your own personal development and career goals
- Maintain a balance between your work and your personal life
- Take time to reflect on what satisfies you
- Manage yourself realistically, including time and physical/emotional health
- Seek opportunities for continuous learning
- Always be aware of how you are perceived by others
- Improve your skills, knowledge and behavior as a result of evaluation and feedback
- Learn from setbacks or failures as well as from successful efforts

Technical Skills (Dealing With Yourself)
- Seek and use knowledge and skills that are necessary to perform your job
- Understand the processes, methods and technologies related to any assignment
- Demonstrate practical and technical information
- Evaluate the outcome of your work
- Keep current on new developments in your field or area of expertise
- Use available technology effectively (voice mail, automation, software)

Interpersonal Effectiveness (Dealing With Others)
- Build and maintain positive relationships
- Handle conflicts and negotiations effectively
- Develop trust and respect
- Collaborate and work well with others
- Show sensitivity and compassion for others
- Be sensitive to people from different cultures
- Encourage staff input in making decisions
- Recognize and use ideas from others
- Communicate clearly when speaking and writing
- Actively listen to others
- Honor your commitments and promises

Customer Service (Becoming "Other" Oriented)
- Understand that customer service is fundamental to our work
- Be a model of commitment to customer service
- Understand and meet the needs of internal customers
- Manage customer complaints and concerns efficiently and promptly
- Plan your work so that it is responsive to your customer's needs

- Use customer feedback data in planning and providing products and services
- Identify and reward behaviors that strengthen customer satisfaction

Flexibility/Adaptability (Becoming Comfortable With The Unpredictable)
- Respond positively to new or changing situations
- Be comfortable with ongoing change
- Be aware of how you handle change
- Handle multiple tasks simultaneously
- Seek and welcome other people's ideas
- Remain calm in high-pressure situations
- Make the most of available resources

Creative Thinking (Reaching Outside "The Box")
- Consider new ideas and approaches
- Be willing to suggest and try new ideas
- Look beyond the "VA way" and the "way we've always done it"
- Be willing to take risks (trying a new way)
- Challenge assumptions
- Solve problems creatively
- Demonstrate resourcefulness
- Value and support others who are willing to go out of "the box"

Systems Thinking (Putting It "Together")
- Understand the complexities of VA healthcare and how it is delivered
- Recognize the results that specific actions have on other parts of the system
- Think of context
- Know how your role relates to the "big picture"
- Demonstrate an awareness of the purpose, process, procedures, and outcomes of your work

Organizational Stewardship (Accepting Accountability)
- Demonstrate commitment to people
- Empower others
- Trust others
- Support life long learning
- Accept accountability—for yourself, others, and the organizations' development

Source: Veterans Health Administration (2003). Reprinted with permission.

in the organization. Employees receive ongoing feedback about areas of strength and opportunities for growth, and they are given a more intensive assessment of their performance in these core competencies at the time of annual performance evaluation. Figure 7.3 provides the definition of the core competency of flexibility/adaptability, along with a description of the qualities that would be found in an individual who has mastered this competency and examples of this competency in practice. The job practices/responsibilities related to the core competency of flexibility/adaptability are hierarchical: the more responsibilities an employee has, the more highly developed are the expectations for this core competency.

Performance expectations aligned with the organization's vision and strategy are especially important for senior leaders and managers. High-performing organizations know what kinds of leaders are needed (i.e., their roles, responsibilities, attributes, and competencies) to achieve business objectives. Leaders' performance standards are explicitly aligned with the organization's mission, goals, and strategies.

Central DuPage Health, a healthcare system located in the western suburbs of Chicago, began creating a link between managerial competencies and strategies in 1996. As part of an organizationwide cultural transition to a learning organization, important leadership competencies were identified. Similar to the competency definition process at the Veterans Health Administration, senior leaders and the management team at Central DuPage Health asked themselves, "What skills and behaviors must our leaders have to support our mission, vision, and business strategy?" The human resources director also researched a considerable amount of literature to identify leadership competencies that are prevalent in high-performing organizations. The final list of leadership skills was categorized into the four areas that are considered to be strategically important to the organization's success: serving others, strategic thinking and action, quality and performance improvement, and continuous learning. These categories and their corresponding skills are shown in Figure 7.4.

The competency requirements are being phased in at Central DuPage Health, where existing managers are encouraged to gain necessary skills that they currently lack. The leadership skills are also considered when new leaders are recruited and hired. The ultimate goal is to ensure that individuals in leadership positions at Central DuPage Health have the competencies necessary to support the organization's mission and

Flexibility/Adaptability is the ability to quickly adapt to change, handle multiple demands simultaneously, and accommodate new situations and realities. The successful employee works well with all levels and types of people, welcomes divergent ideas, and maximizes limited resources.

Qualities Which Demonstrate Flexibility/Adaptability:
• Responds appropriately to new or changing situations
• Handles multiple inputs and tasks simultaneously
• Seeks and welcomes others' ideas
• Works well with all levels and types of people
• Accommodates new situations and realities
• Remains calm in high-pressure situations
• Makes the most of limited resources
• Demonstrates resilience in the face of setbacks
• Understands change management

Examples of Flexibility/Adaptability in Practice:
All Employees
• Willing to learn new procedures and technology
• Open to ideas different from one's own
• Looks for better alternatives to "the way we've always done it"
Work Unit or Team Leader
• Adapts supervisory style to individual needs of employees
• Handles multiple projects and duties simultaneously, prioritizing as needed
• Respects and deals effectively with others' fears of change
• Fosters flexibility through cross-training and developmental work assignments
Care/Service Line Leaders, Other Managers
• Applies leadership and management skills to newly-assigned positions and duties
• Responds to decreases in staffing or increases in workload by involving all parties in restructuring the work
• Understands and applies change management principles
Senior Executives
• Responds to changing priorities and resources with optimism, encouraging staff to respond positively and proactively
• Stays abreast of, and educates staff about, changing conditions in the healthcare market
• Teaches application of change management principles

Source: Veterans Health Administration (2003). Reprinted with permission.

Competency Category: Serving Others
Skills:

- Integrates Patient Focused philosophy and customer focus in all aspects of work.
- Demonstrates respect for each individual in all encounters.
- Encourages expression of diverse opinions, ideas and questions.
- Provides timely information, expectations and feedback.
- Addresses conflicts in timely, skillful manner.
- Builds partnerships within teams, organization and beyond.
- Actions and behaviors are consistent with expressed beliefs and values.
- Eliminates barriers to staff input and access to leaders.
- Acknowledges and honors the contributions of others.
- Proactively offers service and assistance.

Competency Category: Strategic Thinking and Action
Skills:

- Stays current in health care trends, Central DuPage Health's marketplace, and specific area of expertise.
- Describes structure, functions and inter-relationships of areas of the organization/health system.
- Demonstrates skill in interpersonal and team dynamics.
- Conveys mission, vision and priorities of this healthcare organization.
- Balances focus on future with addressing current priorities.
- Makes timely decisions.
- Forwards action, results and adaptation to shifting priorities.
- Completes projects and assignments on time.
- Manages time in a way that balances personal and professional objectives.

Competency Category: Quality and Performance Improvement
Skills:

- Employs multiple methods of seeking customer knowledge and feedback.
- Shares and posts customer and trend data.
- Identifies and accesses appropriate benchmark resources.
- Uses comparative data in developing improvement plans/goals.
- Uses systematic improvement tools and methodology
- Establishes and communicates clear improvement goals with individuals and teams.
- Challenges the status quo.

FIGURE 7.4 *(continued)*

- Supports development and testing of new ideas and initiatives.
- Assists every member of team in identifying how their role/work is connected to the experience of our patients and customers.

Competency Category: Continuous Learning
Skills:
- Pursues clear, learning and development goals for personal performance and career relevance.
- Requests and learns from feedback.
- Seeks and takes on new challenges.
- Makes effective hiring decisions.
- Focuses individuals and team attention on opportunities for learning in daily work and team debriefs.
- Assigns work and projects that prepare staff for next level of career achievement and development.
- Advises and enrolls staff in educational opportunities in support of current and future performance.
- Encourages use and integration of new technology within the workplace.
- Coaches and mentors others.
- Demonstrates personal agility in response to change.

Source: Central DuPage Health, Winfield, IL, March 2003. Reprinted with permission.

business goals. The organization's focus on continuous learning enables managers—as well as staff members—to expand their competencies to meet current and future strategic needs (Sibery and Boynton 2002).

Reward Systems

The organization's reward system must support performance excellence. It needs to reflect that individuals are being encouraged to participate in meeting the organization's strategic goals and continually support improvement. This can be accomplished in a number of ways. For example, SSM Health Care (SSMHC), a private, not-for-profit healthcare system based in St. Louis, Missouri, uses a systemwide tool called Passport.[1] Passport creates a line of sight from the personal goals set between the manager and employee during a performance appraisal and the organization's goals. Employees are expected to develop personal goals that support the short- and long-term objectives of the facility, the overall organizational goals of ssmhc, and department performance expectations. Passport contains the ssmhc mission and values; the characteristics of exceptional healthcare services; spaces for entity, departmental, and personal goals and measures; and a place for the employee and manager to sign and date the document. The ssmhc employee reward system is based in part on achievement of these personal goals.

Becoming a high-performance organization requires that senior leaders help managers and staff shift from an individual mind-set to thinking and operating as part of the organization. The good news is that the majority of people sincerely want to be part of something significant. When employees are rewarded for their commitment to the overall success and vision of the organization, any other issues generally resolve themselves. It is also important to hold nonperformers accountable. Employees need frank and constructive feedback on performance, and actions must be taken when warranted. Failure to act on individual performance problems is a demotivator for work teams striving for continual improvement.

Blake Medical Center in Bradenton, Florida, has embraced the Baldrige concepts as a way of advancing performance excellence. By linking the performance management system with the organization's vision and strategic goals, senior leaders at Blake have been able to create unity and tremendous commitment among managers and staff. This linkage provides all individuals in the organization with a frame of reference by which they perform their jobs, thus reducing the need for management control, criticism, or intercession. The relationship between three of the organization's 2003 strategic goals and the performance expectations at the department and employee level are illustrated in Figure 7.5. This example is from the medical imaging department at Blake.

Hiring and Recruiting

High-performing organizations have a recruiting and hiring strategy that is targeted to fill short- and long-term human capital needs and, specifically, to fill gaps identified through its strategic planning process. This requires an explicit link between the organization's recruiting efforts and the skills identified as being necessary to meet strategic objec-

Strategic Goal: Reduce Incidence of Patient Skin Breakdowns

Medical Imaging Department Performance Expectation: Achieve a 95% or higher documentation rate on patient assessment evaluation.

Employee Performance Expectation: Assess each patient for skin condition and document completion on each requisition.

Strategic Goal: Improve Accuracy of Patient Identification

Medical Imaging Department Performance Expectation: Reduce the potential of radiating the incorrect patient.

Employee Performance Expectation: Check for arm band identification on each patient, match it to the patient chart and indicate on the requisition that the check has been completed.

Strategic Goal: Continue to Exceed Company-Wide Physician Satisfaction Scores

Medical Imaging Department Performance Expectation: Exceed the physician satisfaction scores during 90% of the year.

Employee Performance Expectation: Supervisors communicate with a minimum of one physician per month regarding our ability to improve medical imaging services and provide documentation of the meeting.

Source: Blake Medical Center, Bradenton, FL, March 2003. Reprinted with permission.

tives. During the action planning phase of strategic planning, the following kinds of questions are answered:

- What work needs to be completed?
- How will the work be completed?
- When will the work be completed?
- What resources will be needed?
- How will success be measured?

Answers to these questions influence the organization's recruitment strategies. A human resource professional should be part of the strategic planning team and have a good understanding of what is coming up for the organization in the next 12 to 24 months. This knowledge is important in planning for the hiring needs for the organization. High-performing organizations do not wait until they have openings to start recruitment planning.

Organizations also need to pay close attention to succession planning and retention. Is your organization putting people into a job and then training them to take over a position at the next level? When openings come up, do you have qualified people who are given an opportunity to move up? What succession planning does for recruitment is that it enables the organization to recruit at a less skilled level, making the position possibly easier to fill. To advance performance excellence, organizations need to pay close attention to keeping their best people and preparing them to assume additional responsibilities. More about the creation of a learning organization is covered later in this chapter.

WORK SYSTEM ENABLERS

☐ Structures and jobs avoid the creation of silos and draw on the strengths of the various organizational components.

☐ Workforce deployment is appropriate to support organizational goals and strategies.

☐ Use of the workforce is flexible, putting the right employees in the right roles, according to their skills.

☐ An explicit strategy is in place to build teamwork among people at all levels of the organization.

☐ A formal organizationwide communications strategy is in place and includes opportunities for feedback from new, existing, and exiting employees.

☐ The employee performance management system steers the workforce toward embodying and effectively pursuing the organization's strategic goals.

☐ Employees' performance expectations are aligned with the organization's mission, goals, and objectives.

☐ Employee compensation and benefits programs, workplace facilities, and work/family arrangements support hiring/retaining the best talent available and getting the best performance from that talent.

☐ Department heads, supervisors, and staff are kept informed about organizational decisions, and expectations are clearly communicated.

☐ Formal mechanisms are in place for celebrating successes and, when appropriate, providing rewards/bonuses.

EDUCATION, TRAINING, AND DEVELOPMENT

Investment in people is fundamental to performance excellence. This means actively facilitating the learning, growth, and development of individuals. An extensive capability for and commitment to training must be an integral part of the organization's business strategy. The following training policy components are essential:

- The view that continuous training is the norm
- The assumption that training will be a life-long process
- The recognition of the need to update existing skills, replace redundant skills, and train for new skills
- The need for multiskilled individuals to cope with change

A commitment to continuous learning and improvement can help an organization to not only respond to change but also to anticipate change, create new opportunities for itself, and pursue a shared vision that is ambitious and achievable.

The Learning Organization

The dynamics of the healthcare industry demand a multidimensional approach to organizational learning. Because the delivery of health services involves a close relationship between humans and technology, optimizing the human side of this relationship is a key aspect of performance excellence. Proactive workforce planning and organizational learning must be emphasized. One of the greatest challenges to the healthcare industry over the next ten years will be to transfer the knowledge of current employees to tomorrow's workforce. The organizational learning system must provide opportunities to pass on lessons learned and first-hand experience in a complete yet efficient manner.

Training and development—or competence development—is a crucial issue for every healthcare organization. The ascendancy of the concept of "learning organizations" is a strong indication of the growing recognition of this imperative. The learning organization characterizes a new way of thinking, including not only formal but also informal aspects of development. The most striking feature of the learning organization is the level of integration between strategy and training and between the needs of the organization and the individual. Staff training and development are present in every function of high-performing healthcare organizations. They are an integral part of the basic workload.

Use the self-assessment tool below to discover how far along your organization is in developing a learning environment. While responding to the statements in the self-assessment, you will also discover what characteristics are prevalent in high-performing learning organizations.

 SELF-ASSESSMENT

Do You Have a Learning Organization?

Instructions
Below is a list of statements. Read each one carefully, and then decide the extent to which it actually applies to your organization, using the scale below:
4 = Applies fully
3 = Applies to a great extent
2 = Applies to a moderate extent
1 = Applies to little or no extent

Learning Dynamics: Individual, Group or Team, and Organization
___ People are encouraged and expected to manage their own learning and development.
___ People use skills such as active listening and effective feedback.
___ Individuals are trained and coached in learning how to learn.
___ Teams and individuals learn from careful reflection on problem situations and then apply their new knowledge to future actions.
___ People use a comprehensive systems approach when thinking and acting.

Organization Transformation: Vision, Culture, Strategy, and Structure
___ The senior leadership team supports the vision of a learning organization.
___ The organizational climate supports and recognizes the importance of learning.
___ People learn from failures as well as successes.
___ Learning opportunities are incorporated into daily operations and programs.
___ The organization has few management levels in order to maximize communication and learning across all levels.

People Empowerment: Employee, Manager, Customer, and Community
___ We strive to develop an empowered workforce that is able to learn and perform.
___ Authority is decentralized and delegated.
___ Managers coach, mentor, and facilitate learning.
___ We actively share information with our patients/other customers to obtain their ideas so that we can learn and improve services.

___ We participate in joint learning opportunities with suppliers, community groups, professional associations, and academic institutions.

Knowledge Management: Acquisition, Creation, Storage and Retrieval, and Transfer and Use

___ People monitor performance trends outside of our organization by looking at what others do (e.g., by benchmarking best practices, attending conferences, examining published research).

___ People are trained in the skills of creative thinking and experimentation.

___ We often implement pilot projects to test new ways of delivering services.

___ Systems and structures exist to ensure that important knowledge is made available to those who need and can use it.

___ We continue to develop new strategies and mechanisms for sharing learning throughout the organization.

Technology Application: Information Systems and Technology-Based Learning

___ Computer-based information systems enhance our organizational learning.

___ People have ready access to the information superhighway (e.g., through local area networks, the Internet, electronic medical library searches).

___ Learning facilities such as training and conference rooms incorporate electronic multimedia support.

___ We support just-in-time learning with a system that integrates high technology learning systems, coaching, and actual work into a seamless process.

___ People have access to information when they need it (i.e., as the desired task is being performed).

___ Grand total for these five categories (maximum score = 100)

How to interpret your score:

81–100: Congratulations! You are well on your way to becoming a learning organization.

61–80: Keep on moving! Your organization has a solid learning foundation.

40–60: A good beginning. Your organization has some important building blocks for the journey toward becoming a learning organization.

Below 40: It is time to make some drastic changes if you want to become a learning organization.

It is not enough to tell managers and staff what competencies are necessary for their job. Learning organizations provide opportunities for existing staff to gain those competencies. For example, Central Du-Page Health provides managers with a host of ideas and strategies for strengthening important leadership skills and behaviors. Some of the suggestions involve formal training, but many are simply techniques that managers can employ to gain additional skills or change behaviors. Figure 7.6 provides the learning and development suggestions for one of the key leadership competencies: serving others.

Align Training with Strategy

In high-performing organizations, staff member training needs are identified in connection with the strategic planning process. This consists predominantly of an analysis of skills and competencies necessary for achieving strategic objectives and the development of a training plan. The training needs assessment may be simple and brief, or it may be very elaborate, as the situation requires depending on the difficulty of the job and the detailed breakdown of the envisaged training.

 SELF-ASSESSMENT

Is there sufficient linkage between your strategic goals and staff development and training activities? Test this relationship by responding to the statements below. The more statements you respond to in the affirmative, the more likely the linkage between strategy and training is weak or nonexistent.

	Yes	No
• We have a staff training and development function, but it has little to do with achieving the organization's strategic objectives.	—	—
• People in our organization do not have the skills necessary to achieve all of our strategic objectives.	—	—
• Nobody knows for sure if staff training and development does any good.	—	—
• Money for staff training flows like water, but people do not seem to get the skills that we really need to be a successful organization.	—	—
• Employees receive training, but managers do not participate in any leadership development training.	—	—
• People participate in training and development, but how much they apply what they have learned is unknown.	—	—
• Training here mainly means going into a classroom and having a break from work.	—	—

Staff training and development must be systematically undertaken, and identifying training needs is the key first step. To ensure that people in the organization are competent and able to respond quickly to

FIGURE 7.6 CENTRAL DUPAGE HEALTH SKILLS DEVELOPMENT
GUIDE FOR MANAGERS

Competency Category: Serving Others

Potential Development Activities:

- Address conflicts by communicating directly to the involved party. Keep the issue between you and that person(s), avoiding gossip. This will establish trust and honesty in the relationship.
- In staff meetings, encourage two-way communication, solicit agenda items from employees, and allow employees time to raise issues.
- Return phone calls promptly.
- Make a point of updating the appropriate people even when nothing new has developed.
- Be attuned to body language in listening to others, such as move from behind your desk, maintain eye contact, nod when in agreement or understanding.
- Establish communication guidelines for the team, which could include such things as:
  — There are no "dumb ideas."
  — Members are expected to listen to each other proactively and respectfully.
  — Open and honest opinions are welcome.
  — Rank does not have its privilege.
- Facilitate understanding of individual work and communication styles for each member and of the implications of the different styles on day-to-day work functions.

Source: Central DuPage Health, Winfield, IL, March 2003. Reprinted with permission.

new demands, workforce education must be linked to the organization's mission and strategic goals. Without such a linkage, there is no guarantee that resource-intensive employee training activities will actually help the organization reach its business objectives. Achieving strategic goals often requires new workforce competencies and/or reinforcement of existing skills. By planning for the training needs associated with each strategic goal, the organization can integrate learning opportunities into its training system. Thus senior leaders can ensure that the workforce is adequately prepared to keep up with the ever-changing tasks that need to be performed.

Creating this linkage is a six-step process, as follows:

1. Review the organization's strategic goals and objectives.
2. Identify relevant departmental objectives.
3. Identify staff competencies necessary to meet departmental objectives.
4. Identify knowledge/skill gaps.
5. Identify learning need priorities.
6. Plan and execute learning opportunities.

The experiences at Blake Medical Center serve as an example to describe these steps. Blake uses a systematic process that is tied to the strategic planning cycle to create an organizationwide training plan that is linked to strategic goals and objectives. The process starts in the fall of each year with the management team finalizing the organization's strategic plan for the upcoming year. The plan details strategies and measurable facility-based objectives. One facility-based objective in 2003 was to reduce the incidence of surgical infections. Once the organizationwide strategic plan is complete, the department directors define objectives for their area that are related to each relevant facility-based objective. Blake's 2003 strategic objectives for the 3-North patient care unit and the food and nutritional services department are shown in Figure 7.7. Department objectives are defined only for relevant facility-based objectives; hence, there is no objective set in food services for the facility-based objective related to the reduction of infections in patients with central lines.

In late December and early January the hospital's director of staff development meets with each department director to discuss the strengths and weaknesses of past educational activities, the content areas for department-specific education related to next year's strategic objectives, and any other issues that are affecting staff training needs. Department directors are asked to complete the competency survey form in Figure 7.8 prior to this meeting.

The department's strategic objectives are only one factor considered in the development of staff training plans. Other factors that influence the training plans include the following:

- Results of staff surveys regarding their training needs
- Addition of new products/equipment/procedures that require training
- Regulatory requirements and accreditation standards

FIGURE 7.7 FACILITY-BASED OBJECTIVES AND DEPARTMENT
OBJECTIVES

Facility-Based Objective	3-North Patient Care Unit Objective	Food and Nutrition Services Department Objective
Reduce incidence of skin breakdown.	Achieve 95% compliance with skin care initiatives as evidenced in 2003 audit reports.	Respond to skin breakdown consult within 24 hours and begin appropriate supplement per dietitian's recommendation.
Improve accuracy of patient identification.	Enforce medication administration safety policies and practices as evidenced through increased near miss reporting and reduction in medication errors.	Train within 3 days of hire each new employee and in-service all employees who pass trays at least 2 times per year. New employees will be monitored and signed off by supervisor before passing trays independently.
Maintain employee safety.	Employees with lost time due to physical injuries reduced to less than 2%.	Reduce employee accidents by 10 percent. Conduct a job hazard analysis for high risk, high volume activities.
Reduce infections in patients with central lines.	Meet organizational objective of <2% infection rate in patients with central lines.	
Meet or exceed overall patient satisfaction scores as established by Tampa Bay Division.	Achieve 3.56 score (very satisfied patient responses) or .20 mean score improvement to customer Gallup survey.	Department meets or exceeds food service scores for Division.
Continue to exceed company-wide physician satisfaction scores.	Achieve 3.20 or .20 mean score improvement on physician satisfaction.	Quality of food as evaluated by physicians through Gallup survey exceeds division mean.

FIGURE 7.7 *(continued)*

Facility-Based Objective	3-North Patient Care Unit Objective	Food and Nutrition Services Department Objective
Continue to exceed company-wide employee satisfaction scores.	Achieve overall grand mean score of 3.70 or improve mean score by .20 on employee satisfaction annual Gallup survey.	Department meets or exceeds division mean for employee satisfaction rated through annual Gallup survey
Continue to offer patient support groups for all main service lines and provide community education programs.	Participate annually in American Cancer Society Breast Cancer Awareness Project.	Offer monthly diabetes self-management classes. Registered dietitians to speak at community events as requested.
Participate in a minimum of two community health screening and health care patient education.	Participate annually in hospital sponsored health fairs or health screenings.	Offer weekly Trim Team classes.
Demonstrate community involvement at all levels of the organization.	Achieve 24 staff hours of community service annually.	Each manager, dietitian, and supervisor participates in one community activity per year as a representative of hospital.
Achieve 100% compliance with Code of Conduct.	Achieve 100% staff involvement in code of conduct education.	Achieve 100% staff involvement in code of conduct education.
Insure financial health by implementing strategies for cost reduction and revenue generation.	Achieve 97% compliance with "point of use" supply scanning. Achieve 95% or better on productivity measures.	Participate in 2 cost savings initiatives per year.

Source: Blake Medical Center, Bradenton, FL, March 2003. Reprinted with permission.

FIGURE 7.8 STAFF DEVELOPMENT DEPARTMENT COMPETENCY SURVEY

Department: _____ Director: _____

Please review the attached report of all recorded staff development activities for your departmental staff in 2002. Your evaluation of the effectiveness of last year's program and projection for future needs provide important data for staff development planning.

1. What were the major strengths of your staff development program in 2002? Any weaknesses?

2. To meet your department objectives in 2003, you have identified specific content areas for staff education. Please list below content areas that will require additional educational resources. Requests for additional resources might include up-to-date reference materials, audiovisual aids, teaching assistance or advice.

Content Area	Additional Resources Required	Date Needed
1.		
2.		
3.		
4.		

Please return the completed form to the Staff Development Department. Data is used to evaluate the staff development efforts of Blake Medical Center and to plan for future needs. Thanks for your help in meeting Blake Medical Center staff's development needs.

Date submitted: _____

Source: Blake Medical Center, Bradenton, FL, March 2003. Reprinted with permission.

- Results of ongoing monitoring activities (e.g., quality evaluations, infection control, safety, risk management)
- The patients served and the nature of the care provided by the department
- Information management issues
- Training needs generated by advances made in healthcare management, healthcare science, and technology
- Findings from department performance appraisals of individuals

The training director and manager jointly identify staff competencies necessary to meet department objectives or other priorities. They also jointly determine where there are staff knowledge/skill gaps. Through this discussion, the priority learning needs of the department are established, and these priorities are then incorporated into a staff education plan for the next 12 months. By the end of these meetings, all departments at Blake Medical Center have a staff education plan that is linked directly to the facility-based and department objectives for the upcoming year. Mandatory training—such as that required by the Joint Commission on Accreditation of Healthcare Organizations, the Occupational Safety and Health Administration, or other state or federal agencies—is also incorporated into the department education plans.

Linking learning to organizational priorities may require a change in the current role of staff educators from being reaction oriented to being proactive strategic partners with the organization. To support the mission and strategic goals, staff educators must become organizational development experts rather than just designers and deliverers of training (Spath 2002).

☑ **SELF-ASSESSMENT**

Do the staff training plans in your organization ensure that

❏ Competent staff are available to achieve strategic goals and objectives and to fulfill the day-to-day obligations of the organization?

❏ All employees have the necessary knowledge, skills, and attitudes to perform their jobs?

❏ The organization can respond to market, regulatory, organizational, technological, and other developments?

❏ The organization can make the best possible use of its human resources?

❏ There is a learning culture based on excellence and high performance?

❏ All services are of high quality and at a minimum correspond with performance expectations?

❏ Staff education and training support organizational strategic objectives; build employee knowledge, skills, and capabilities; and contribute to improved employee performance.

❏ Staff education and training balance short- and longer-term organizational and employee needs, including developing, learning, and career progression.

❏ Input is obtained from employees and their supervisors/managers on education and training needs, expectations, and training program design.

❏ The organization's workforce education plan includes key developmental and training needs, including diversity training, management, and leadership development.

❏ Employee knowledge and skills are reinforced through formal and on-the-job learning.

❏ Human resource/staff development professionals are actively involved in the organization's strategic planning process.

❏ The organization's operating budget spent on staff training and development is comparable with industry benchmarks.

STAFF WELL-BEING AND SATISFACTION

Senior leaders in high-performing organizations seek to maintain a work environment and staff support climate that contributes to the well-being, satisfaction, and motivation of all staff. Many factors affect these needs, including effective employee problem or grievance resolution; safety factors; employee views of management; employee training, development, and career opportunities; employee preparation for changes in technology or the work organization; work environment and other work conditions; workload; cooperation and teamwork; recognition; benefits; communications; job security; compensation; and equal opportunity. Many of these factors are addressed earlier in this chapter. This section focuses on what the organization does to assess and improve staff member well-being and satisfaction.

The Baldrige Criteria suggest that organizations have a systematic process for identifying key elements that affect staff satisfaction and techniques to measure the success of workplace improvements. Once leaders at Ellsworth County (Kansas) Medical Center recognized employees as vital customers of the organization, a process was put in place to identify key elements of employee satisfaction and measures of success. These initiatives are described by Roger Pearson in the case study below.

ECMC CASE STUDY

When ECMC started operations in 1993, it had approximately 55 employees. There had never been a human resources department, and creating a new department was not high on the priority list given that the organization had just emerged from bankruptcy. The office manager was responsible for payroll and maintenance of personnel files, and I handled any personnel policies or issues. To encourage increased participation in the review and revision of personnel policies, I formed a human resources committee made up of a group of managers. This committee functioned as a source of information and expertise to me, and membership was reserved for selected managers. By fall 2001, ECMC had grown to 137 employees. The old structures were no longer adequate to meet the human resource needs of our organization. With the advent of our new organizational recognition of employees as customers and with the creation of the Vision 20:20 model, the human resources committee had to become more instrumental in moving our organization forward.

The first order of business was to expand the committee to include all managers. The committe then created a mission statement: "Developing Employee Commitment to Excellence." An internal surveying process and national literature review identified key requirements that employees have concerning their work: it must be meaningful, there must be a supportive environment, that environment must be safe, and there must be opportunity for growth and development. To enable the organization to provide timely and rapid improvements (Baldrige core values) when addressing employee needs, the committee formed four subcommittees: compensation, recruitment, growth and development, and work/life balance. Each subcommittee is composed of a manager as chair and as many hourly employees as appropriate to accomplish committee programs and tasks. Each subcommittee developed a mission statement to guide its efforts and identified required elements and measurements of effectiveness for those efforts. (These are summarized in Figure 7.9.) Overall effectiveness of human resource activities is measured through employee satisfaction scores.

Subcommittee	Mission	Measures of Effectiveness
Compensation	Ensure accurate and equitable compensation to all ECMC employees.	• Benefits/salary ratio • Payroll accuracy
Recruitment	Enroll world-class individuals into our vision.	Position fill rate
Growth and Development	Enrich employee's lives by enhancing self worth.	Not defined as of February 2004
Work/Life Balance	Create an environment that allows employees to catch the energy and release their potential.	Work environment assessment score

Source: Ellsworth County Medical Center, Ellsworth, Kansas. Reprinted with permission.

The following is a partial list of projects and activities that the human resources committee and its subcommittees have thus far accomplished:

- Implement quarterly market adjustment to compensation.
- Standardize shift differential system for nights and weekends.
- Identify behavior standards aligned with the organization's mission, vision, and values.
- Develop standardized 360-degree evaluation system focusing on behavior standards.
- Develop standardized job description format to include behavior standards.
- Develop a standardized approach to employee application processing and interviewing.
- Develop standardized Internet training and competency testing.

- Develop scholarship program to support continued skill development.
- Implement employee communication and suggestion system.

Each subcommittee reports monthly to the human resources committee on the status of projects underway, seeks guidance and direction on possible future projects, and reports results on the metrics specified for that committee. Since ECMC is still in the beginning phase of subcommittee development, specific subcommittee trended results data are not available at the time this is written. However, overall employee satisfaction has been measured through two surveying cycles. Internally trended results show employee satisfaction has improved 7 percent from the prior year, with improvement in scores on 14 of 16 survey statements. And comparative results from a national database place ECMC employee satisfaction and morale at the 73rd and 78th percentile, respectively.

This is a work in progress as we learn about different measures and the effectiveness of each for reflecting ECMC's focus on employees as customers. Employees' involvement with these various activities has provided them with opportunities to become engaged, to assume personal accountability for outcomes and results, and to be part of the overall communication and learning process at ECMC. This in turn has facilitated everyone's involvement in patient service process improvement activities.

* * * * *

Measuring Work Environment

The first thing to recognize about the work environment is that much of it cannot be quantitatively measured. Yes, it is possible to count things like absenteeism, staff turnover, grievances or strikes, and other job-related actions. However, much of what makes up the work environment cannot be discretely counted, such as attitudes, behaviors, and the quality of work processes. To evaluate these aspects of the work environment, it is more appropriate to rely on qualitative surveys and observations.

An organization's work environment is the product of individual and group values, attitudes, competencies, and patterns of behavior. Organizations with a positive culture of excellence are characterized by communications founded on mutual trust, shared perceptions of the importance of quality, and confidence in the efficacy of performance improvement initiatives.

The absence of a positive work environment is often more visible. A variety of symptoms identify the absence or breakdown of the work climate. These symptoms, detailed in Figure 7.10, have been found to be precursors to declining performance in a healthcare organization and eventually may lead to serious quality or patient safety problems (Meyer and Natalie 1997; Baron and Kreps 2000).

Because of a staffing shortage in many healthcare organizations, an extensive amount of research has been done to identify factors that reduce staff turnover and improve recruitment of new hires. The reasons that staff members are satisfied with their work tend to vary and include flexible work hours, enjoyment of coworkers, congenial relations with medical staff and supervisors, individual learning and growth opportunities, peer support, participation in decision making, and being in a setting that provides outstanding patient care.

The "Strategies to Recruit and Retain Hospital Pharmacists" study conducted by the University HealthSystem Consortium, the Public Hospital Pharmacy Coalition, and the National Association of Public Hospitals and Health Systems (2000) found the most effective retention tactic to be the adoption of flexible scheduling. The availability of good retirement and benefits packages was also effective for enticing employees to stay. In addition, the offer of competitive salaries proved to be an attractive retention tool, with hospitals that increased salaries to levels competitive with those of retail pharmacies experiencing a reduction in vacancy rates. The opportunity for greater clinical involvement for pharmacists was also cited as an effective retention tactic. Some hospitals reported that providing employees with the opportunity to get a broader range of experience through new or challenging work assignments was effective as well.

This study provided specific examples of the methods adopted by several hospitals and institutions to effectively lower—and in some cases eliminate altogether—pharmacy vacancy rates. For example, Parkland Health and Hospital Systems in Dallas, Texas, achieved a vacancy rate of less than 1 percent by allowing its pharmacists to develop their clinical roles, instituting a tuition reimbursement program for employees seeking additional degrees, and paying higher wages for night and weekend shifts. Robert Wood Johnson Hospital in New Brunswick, New Jersey, reported zero pharmacist position vacancies following the initiation of a program that included flexible scheduling and job sharing (including retaining staff as per diem employees) and tuition reimbursement.

FIGURE 7.10 SYMPTOMS OF A PROBLEMATIC WORK
ENVIRONMENT

- Adversarial relationships laterally or horizontally within the organization
- Staff members blamed for problems
- Emergence of strong subcultures
- Physicians and/or staff members afraid to raise concerns for fear of retribution
- Staff afraid to report patient incidents or staff injuries
- Excessive forced overtime
- Excessive staff injuries
- Excessive sick time
- Excessive grievances
- Deviation from procedures or regulatory/accreditation requirements
- High staff turnover
- Lack of commitment to performance improvement
- Lack of consistency in manager or staff attitudes about what issues are important
- Lack of ownership of problems
- Lack of preventive maintenance
- Lack of teamwork
- Low buy-in to the organization's strategic goals and objectives
- Low staff morale
- Little or no communication between levels in the organization
- Little or no forward thinking in daily activities
- Management that "hides" behind the chain of command
- Overemphasis on people doing the right thing
- Procedures that do not work as written
- Reaching financial goals viewed as more important than managing quality and patient safety
- Evidence of recurring problems
- Top management unaware of the "real" work environment
- Unwillingness to face difficult problems or correct them
- Physicians and/or staff not reporting or discussing problems they are aware of

Note: Adapted from material in Meyer and Natalie (1997) and Baron and Kreps (2000).

Initial staff turnover leads to even more turnover, and quality re-placements are increasingly hard to find. The high costs associated with staff turnover are forcing many hospitals and other healthcare organizations to reevaluate their practices and to implement new hiring, training, and incentive initiatives to address this problem (ASHP 1994). However, many of these initiatives miss an important issue: the lack of a positive and supportive work culture (CMS 2002).

☑ SELF-ASSESSMENT

☐ Does your organization periodically analyze workplace conditions that affect staff commitment?

☐ Do you know what factors are critical to recruiting and retaining staff as well as supervisors and managers?

☐ Does your organization have a system for regularly assessing workplace climate and physician/staff satisfaction?

☐ Does your organization regularly review and identify trends and improvement opportunities in staff recruitment, retention, and satisfaction?

☐ Does your organization regularly examine the processes, systems, structures, and interactions among managers and staff in all departments that support or impede business objectives?

☐ Do you know what activities and behaviors are required to build long-term staff commitment and retention?

☐ Has your organization implemented staff retention and performance strategies that are aimed at enhancing recruitment, selection, training, and management activities?

Workplace Satisfaction Surveys

If your organization does not currently measure workplace satisfaction, now is the time to start. The organization's efficiency may be hampered by the attitudes of your staff members, and patient satisfaction can be adversely affected by staff dissatisfaction. Senior leaders need to understand the workplace issues that may be holding back the organization's performance excellence journey so that effective improvement strategies can be designed. There are a number of survey instruments that an organization can use to evaluate staff satisfaction. It is important to understand what you want to measure before choosing the right survey instrument.

Work attitude surveys are used to measure an employee's perception of various aspects of his or her work, such as job satisfaction, role clarity, role conflict, autonomy, participation in decision making, and overall involvement. Following are examples of statements that employees might be asked to rate on an attitude survey:

— I am able to act independently of my supervisor when performing my job function.
— I know what my job responsibilities are.

Organizational commitment surveys are used to assess staff issues such as job security, loyalty, trust in management, and level of employee alienation or helplessness. Examples of statements that employees might be asked to rate on an organizational commitment survey are as follows:

— I really feel as if this organization's problems are my problems.
— I feel a sense of pride or accomplishment as a result of the type of work that I do.

Organizational climate surveys measure staff perceptions about what it is like to work in the organization. Numerous facets of the organization's environment can be evaluated, such as fairness, safety, support, communication, flexibility, and continuous learning. Some examples of statements that employees might be asked to rate on an organizational climate survey follow:

— I am kept informed about changes that affect my work.
— There are adequate opportunities to pursue professional development activities.

Figure 7.11 is a short employee survey that incorporates questions addressing all three workplace dimensions. The survey is based on questions developed by the Gallup Organization, which has been conducting research on employee satisfaction for more than 30 years. Staff satisfaction surveys can measure any issue, from performance management to perceptions of patient safety, and they can be conducted organization-wide or in specific departments or functions.

Figure 7.11 Sample Staff Satisfaction Survey

Respond to the statements by circling the number that corresponds with the extent to which the statement is true for your organization.

Use a 5-point scale, ranging from 5 = strongly agree to 1 = strongly disagree.

Statement	*Score*				
1. I know what is expected of me at work.	5	4	3	2	1
2. I have the materials and equipment I need to do my work right.	5	4	3	2	1
3. At work, I have the opportunity to do what I do best every day.	5	4	3	2	1
4. In the last seven days, I have received recognition or praise for doing good work.	5	4	3	2	1
5. My supervisor seems to care about me as a person.	5	4	3	2	1
6. There is someone at work who encourages my development.	5	4	3	2	1
7. At work, my opinions seem to count.	5	4	3	2	1
8. The mission/purpose of this facility makes me feel that my job is important.	5	4	3	2	1
9. My fellow employees are committed to doing quality work.	5	4	3	2	1
10. In the last six months, someone at work has talked to me about my progress.	5	4	3	2	1
11. I would recommend this facility to a family member or friend looking for employment.	5	4	3	2	1
12. I am satisfied with my work experience at this facility.	5	4	3	2	1

If you want to know how employees feel, you need to ask them. Satisfaction surveys should be conducted on a regular basis in all healthcare organizations, large or small. Surveys should also be conducted after major projects are completed while the experience is still fresh in the employees' mind. In addition to surveys, conduct listening sessions with employees to address issues or concerns regarding the work environment. Hearing the words of staff members and observing how they talk about their work experiences can provide a very valuable perspective. Implement a suggestion system, and provide a means for employees to anonymously identify areas of conflict that may be affecting staff satisfaction with the workplace.

In addition to general workforce satisfaction surveys, additional measures should be used to track the success of actions intended to improve workplace satisfaction. These measures may include the following:

- Number of staff members who participate in meetings and employee forums
- Number of employee suggestions provided and percentage of suggestions implemented or referred up the chain of command
- Number of manager-staff or staff-staff conflicts that are addressed
- Level of workforce participation in the development of solutions to issues causing staff dissatisfaction

Share employee satisfaction information with managers and senior leaders at regular briefings. This helps the organization develop strategic plans to improve employee satisfaction as well as the day-to-day experience of staff members. Some senior leaders and managers operate behind the scenes and have little, if any, direct contact with staff. Why not invite some of these individuals to employee focus groups and staff meetings? The more they understand the needs of employees, the better they will be able to meet those needs or support others in the organization who can meet them.

A vital component of the organization's business intelligence is information about staff well-being and satisfaction. Maintain an employee satisfaction database so that managers and supervisors can be kept fully abreast of how staff members are feeling about their relationship with the organization.

Improving Staff Satisfaction

Examine the results of staff satisfaction surveys and focus groups to identify issues dealing with job satisfaction, quality of work life, and satisfaction with supervision. After identifying the concerns of the workforce, determine what actions can be taken to improve satisfaction. Use employee participation when determining these actions, and obtain the commitment of the workforce to attaining these goals.

❑ Organizational belief that satisfied employees create satisfied customers

❑ Organizational commitment to workforce excellence and recognition that people are the most important asset

❑ Systems for regularly measuring and assessing staff members' work attitudes, organizational commitment, and perception of the workplace climate

❑ Staff feedback used to improve the work climate via services, benefits, and policies

❑ Workplace improvements tailored to the needs of different categories and types of employees and to individuals, as appropriate

❑ Needs of the diverse workforce considered when improving staff satisfaction; improvements might include counseling, career development and employability services, recreational or cultural activities, non-work-related education, day care, job rotation and/or sharing, special leave for family responsibilities and/or for community service, flexible work hours, outplacement, and retiree benefits

NOTE

1. More information about Passport can be found on the SSM Health Care web site, www.ssmhc.com.

REFERENCES

Aiken, L. 2001. "Evidence-Based Management: Key to Hospital Workforce Stability." *Journal of Health Administration Education* (Special issue): 117–24.

American Society of Hospital Pharmacists (ASHP). 1994. "ASHP Technical Assistance Bulletin on the Recruitment, Selection, and Retention of Pharmacy Personnel." *American Journal of Hospital Pharmacy* 51: 1811–15.

Baron, J., and D. Kreps. 2000. *Strategic Human Resources: Frameworks for General Managers.* New York: John Wiley and Sons.

Bauman, A., L. O'Brien-Pallas, M. Armstrong-Stassen, J. Blythe, R. Bourbonnais, S. Cameron, D. Irvine Doran, M. Kerr, L. McGillis Hall, M. Vézina, M. Bud, and L. Ryan. 2001. *Commitment and Care: The Benefits of a Healthy Workplace for Nurses, Their Patients and the System.* Toronto: The Change Foundation and the Canadian Health Services Research Foundation.

Centers for Medicare & Medicaid Services (CMS). 2002. *Report to Congress: Appropriateness of Minimum Nurse Staffing Ratios in Nursing Homes.* [Online document; retrieved 1/04.] www.cms.gov/medicaid/reports/rp1201home.asp.

Cott, C. 1997. "We Decide, You Carry it Out: A Social Network Analysis of Multidisciplinary Long-Term Care Teams." *Social Science & Medicine* 45 (9): 1411–21.

Institute of Medicine (IOM). 2003. *Keeping Patients Safe: Transforming the Work Environment of Nurses.* Washington, DC: National Academies Press.

McConnell, E. 2000. "Reducing Turnover and Improving Health Care in Nursing Homes: The Potential Effects of Self-Managed Work Teams." *The Gerontologist* 40 (3): 358–63.

Meyer, J., and A. Natalie. 1997. *Commitment in the Workplace: Theory, Research, and Applications.* Thousand Oaks, CA: Sage.

Sibery, D., and D. Boynton. 2002. "The Learning Transformation Process in a Health Care System." In *Effective Staff Development in Health Care Organizations: A Systems Approach to Successful Training*, edited by P. Spath, ch. 3. San Francisco: Jossey-Bass Publishers/AHA Press.

Spath, P. 2002. *Effective Staff Development in Health Care Organizations: A Systems Approach to Successful Training.* San Francisco: Jossey-Bass Publishers/AHA Press.

University HealthSystem Consortium, Public Hospital Pharmacy Coalition, and National Association of Public Hospitals and Health Systems. 2000. "Strategies to Recruit and Retain Hospital Pharmacists." [Online article; retrieved 3/04.] www.phpcrx.org.

Veterans Health Administration High Performance Development Office. 2003. *Workforce Competencies at Veterans Health Administration Facilities.* Oklahoma City, OK: Veterans Health Administration.

CHAPTER EIGHT

Achieving Sustainable Gains: Process Management

FORWARD-THINKING HEALTHCARE organizations are preoccupied with process management. Why? Because process management is how you make your organization perform better. Getting a grip on your processes—understanding what they are, how they work, how to measure and compare them, and, most important, how to improve them—is the essence of the Baldrige program. Managing processes is at the core of any business or clinical improvement.

The Baldrige category of Process Management addresses how healthcare services are monitored, designed, implemented, and improved. In addition, it examines how key support and supplier/partnering processes are handled. Highlights of the Process Management category include the following:

- How the organization responds rapidly to changing customer requirements
- How the organization designs, implements, and manages healthcare services
- How decisions and changes are made to meet customer demands
- How key processes are designed and improved
- How support processes are managed
- Performance requirements of key customers
- The organization's actions/plans to improve the use of supplies and partners to achieve performance goals

Healthcare organizations tend to place short-term emphasis on process improvement actions and believe that they are managing processes. However, process management involves more than ad hoc improvement projects; rather, it has a broader context; it involves the activities of planning, monitoring, and improving processes as well as organizational learning. Process improvement—the activity of elevating the performance of a process—is only one component of process management. Rentzhog's (1998) description of processes and projects helps distinguish between process management and improvement actions:

> Processes can be seen as a canal that ships are sailing through. Ships in this context are projects, such as new product development projects, market research projects, et cetera. The aim of process management is to continuously work on gaining increased understanding for the canal and its curves and maelstroms in order to make it more streamlined. The crew on the ship ought to systematically capture information about the canal and report it to the canal team who will turn the information into improvement actions.

The Baldrige Criteria embrace the broad view of process management. The Process Management category poses questions about process design, operational performance, and evaluation and continuous improvement. In addition, the criteria encourage healthcare organizations to involve patients, other customers, and suppliers in the system to improve quality. Patients and other customers provide information that helps the organization to focus its improvement efforts on those performance characteristics that have the greatest impact on quality. Suppliers provide products or services that affect the organization's ability to achieve performance goals. By working with suppliers to clarify current needs or to share process improvements, the organization can reduce problems such as faulty equipment or inadequate service.

Process management has been rediscovered and reinvented many times over the years, yet three simple principles remain constant: leadership, direction, and method.

Leadership. If the organization is to get to where it wants to be, leadership is clearly called for. Although managing processes is important, leadership is needed to enable the individual steps toward better results. This involves getting people to challenge assumptions about how tasks get done and then optimizing the whole system, not just a department or a single process.

Direction. Someone needs to figure out where the organization should be. The organization's leaders must set targets that are based in part on patient/customer expectations and changing organizational needs and direction. The targets must be integrated with the actions and behaviors of people in the organization.

Method. Everyone—from staff to physicians to leadership—needs to understand key healthcare processes and be able to monitor and improve them. This requires using all of the learning at one's disposal to deploy resources in the right area. The various improvement methodologies—Kaizen, rapid cycle improvement, Six Sigma, lean thinking—all have a part to play in advancing healthcare excellence. There is a long list of process improvement methods, and people have to learn to use them in the right context.

Process management is a key element in an organization's performance excellence journey because it is how value is created and increased over time. If process management is not practiced or supported, then the basic mission of the organization is in question.

 REFLECTION

Is process management evident in your organization, or are people primarily focused on the activity of process improvement? What is lacking in the process management in your organization?

- Leadership?
- Direction?
- Method?

LEADERSHIP

Sustained process improvement can only take place in a healthcare organization that has adopted a process management philosophy. While many reasons can explain this, the primary reason is that process improvement is both enabled and constrained by existing processes and organizational structures. To fulfill its mission, the organization must ensure that processes and structures are purposefully designed around the mission.

Process management involves overseeing the way work activities, people, and the organization's structure combine to produce useful health services. The success of process management is based on performance standards that are derived from strategic goals and objectives. Goals and objectives in turn are based on the mission and enhanced by knowledge gained in part through customer research, benchmarking, and analysis.

Process management cannot simply be delegated to managers in the organization. To create and sustain an environment that promotes continual improvement, it is necessary for leaders to set the tenor, provide support, and clear away barriers. Leaders must ensure that the healthcare organization has a clear mission and strategic goals and objectives that are effectively communicated. Many of the general issues related to leadership support of performance excellence are covered in Chapter 3 and are not reiterated here. However, some specific leadership elements are crucial to the success of process management and bear reinforcing.

First, senior management must be committed to change. Genuine hands-on commitment must take the form of action, not rhetoric. Joel Barker's (1990) words shout loud and clear at all leaders: "Vision without action is merely a dream. Action without vision just passes the time. Vision with action can change the world." Leadership creates the structure that encourages or discourages performance excellence. When an organization finds itself going in the wrong direction or aiming at the wrong target, the best leaders can make things right again. Stephen Covey (1990) popularized a key tenet of performance excellence: Begin with the end in mind. To get to this end, an organization needs a path—a strategic plan. The plan not only establishes direction, priorities, and constraints but it also aligns the entire organization and incorporates accountability for the system.

Second, leaders must create a culture that promotes organizational learning. Think about what stops ideas from spreading in a healthcare organization:

- Fear of losing credit for a good idea
- Disregard for the leadership or goals of the organization
- Lack of knowledge about how to move ideas up the chain of command
- Belief that only a few people (in one's inner circle) have ideas worth pursuing

- Stove-piped organization that discourages knowledge of or contact with others outside of a specified area or professional discipline
- Difficulty when people want to communicate with one another
- The time it takes to share ideas, especially if there is no immediate need for them
- Fear of losing indispensability if unique skills are made available to others
- Inertia

Here is an example from my consulting work. During an engagement at a midsize hospital, I had the unpleasant opportunity to witness a senior vice president screaming at his management team, "Are you all brainless? Doesn't a single one of you understand anything about managing?" As might be predicted, this group of middle managers seldom moved positive ideas around, and they seldom volunteered anything that they thought could arouse his ire.

An example from another of my client hospitals illustrates just how difficult it is to create a culture that supports bringing ideas forward and overcoming the fear of making a mistake. A multidisciplinary group working on a process improvement project came up with some innovative ideas for reducing patient wait times in the emergency department. As the group was finalizing ideas to present to the chief operating officer (COO), one long-time employee suddenly exclaimed, "We can't present these ideas! The COO might not like them, and you know that at this hospital you have to be careful about what you say to management!" All of the group's previous enthusiasm for their recommendations quickly dissipated. I asked the employee why he believed that the COO would not listen to the group's ideas. He told the story of a former middle manager who had, many years before, stood up at a strategic planning meeting and tried to bring up a controversial topic. "By the next week, the middle manager was gone!" When I later inquired about this situation, it turned out that the outspoken middle manager had been in trouble for poor performance and was already on the way out. However, the belief that senior leaders did not want to hear new ideas or address sensitive subjects was still deeply embedded in the organization. This example illustrates how deeply instilled assumptions in an organization can disrupt or completely halt the free flow of ideas.

Are people willing to bring ideas forward in your organization? What stops ideas from spreading? How can senior leaders overcome barriers to organizational learning?

Third, process management requires some investments. People must receive training in problem solving, process improvement tools, and team building. While training can be a substantial expenditure in terms of financial and human resources, it is one of the better investments that can be made. Senior leaders in healthcare organizations should pay heed to the advice of President Lincoln: "If I had six days to chop down a tree, I would spend five days sharpening my axe." Improving processes with a "dull axe" makes the job more difficult, time consuming, and less effective than it needs to be. Staff training is covered in Chapter 7.

Fourth, process management requires patience and discipline. Experience demonstrates that process improvements do not come as quickly as one would like. There are some false starts. Some parts of the organization lag behind others. People may be threatened by process changes or increased employee involvement in decision making. A temptation arises to accept quick-fix process tweaks rather than commit resources to sustainable process redesign and system enhancements. It is no coincidence that Deming's (1986) first principle of total quality management is "practice constancy of purpose." Leaders should be willing to stick with it for years, as the journey toward performance excellence takes a long time. The challenges of immediate problem response must not derail the organization's long-term improvement goals.

 REFLECTION

Are employees adequately trained in process improvement and communication skills? Do senior leaders have the will and the energy to allow sufficient time for people to make genuine efforts toward changing things for the better?

DIRECTION

If the purpose of process improvement is unclear or if managers have very different thoughts about improvement goals, such confusion will have adverse operational effects. Eliminating confusion starts during the strategic planning process, when the organization develops goals and objectives that describe where it wants to be. The objectives statements should specifically quantify desired results and time frames for achieving these results. The strategic planning process, detailed in Chapter 4, provides a foundation for process improvement activities: the key processes selected for improvement and the purpose of improvements are derived from the organization's strategic goals and objectives.

Process improvement activities help to put the organization's strategies into action. However, the linkage between strategic objectives and specific improvement projects can become blurred. Consider the case study below. Although the organization had set an objective performance goal, the improvement project team headed in a much different direction than intended.

CASE STUDY

A strategic goal of the long-term rehabilitation hospital was to improve patient and family satisfaction. Overall satisfaction survey scores in 2002 ranged from 3.8 to 4.0 (on a scale of 1 to 5). The goal was to improve the average score to 4.5 by the end of 2003. An interdepartmental performance improvement team was formed to address this goal. The team started out by reviewing the complaints that had been received from patients and families in 2002. It appeared that many of these complaints would be prevented if caregivers developed closer, more consistent relationships with patients and their family members. For the past few years several members of the improvement team had been frustrated with the hospital's high rate of turnover among nurses and aides. These team members convinced everyone else that the turnover rate was the primary cause of patient and family complaints. Thus, the team decided to work on reducing employee turnover. As of January 2004 the turnover among nurses and aides had slightly decreased, but patient and family satisfaction scores still averaged right around 4.0.

* * * * *

After the organization sets strategic objectives, physicians, managers, and staff members are then asked to undertake activities intended to help the organization achieve these goals. Some objectives are a no-brainer; the people charged with achieving them need no further direction. However, strategic objectives may not be clearly communicated, or the objectives can morph into something else as the project progresses. In such situations, process improvement projects fall short of senior leaders' expectations. To keep this from happening, it is very important to provide process improvement teams with the "what" (objectives and targets) and the "why" (the strategic goal). The team's progress should be monitored to be sure it stays on track toward achieving the targets.

 SELF-ASSESSMENT

Are the people responsible for improving key processes in your organization provided with

❏ A clear mission/purpose?
❏ A vision and success criteria?
❏ An understanding of how the improvement activity fits into the larger picture?
❏ Ongoing feedback on the team's progress toward goal attainment?

Improvement Priorities

Another component of the direction principle is setting priorities for improvement. Although strategic imperatives should be used to set improvement priorities, leaders are frequently presented with suggestions outside of the strategic planning process. These recommendations may come from employees, patients and other customers, or external licensing or accreditation groups. The apparent urgency to fix these varied and random problems can quickly paralyze even the best organization.

One of the measures of a good leader is the ability to distinguish the important from the urgent to prevent the distortion of priorities. Otherwise, the organization will spend lots of financial and human resources on improvement projects that do not quite make it to completion before some urgent new problem comes along. The list of process improvement projects a healthcare organization could pursue is lengthy. The performance gaps are countless, and endless innovation possibilities can be uncovered, so the leaders have to choose. Selecting improvement projects has both a strategic and a tactical component. The strategic decisions are based on goals and priorities established during the planning process. The tactics are about leveraging the organization's financial and human resources for maximum performance gains.

Because process improvement projects are resource intensive, senior leaders must carefully evaluate many factors before initiating a project. Issues to be considered include—but are not limited to—the following:

- Does the issue represent a high priority for improvement for the organization?
- Does the issue represent a substantial risk to patient or staff safety?
- Will the organization receive substantial negative publicity or loss of license or accreditation if the concern is not addressed?
- Will failure to conduct the improvement project result in the deterioration of staff or physician morale and/or loss of trust in the leadership's commitment to quality patient care?

Some healthcare organizations use a scoring system to evaluate issues suggested as candidates for improvement actions. The quality council (or another leadership group) uses the scoring matrix to select improvement projects based on predefined criteria. Figure 8.1 illustrates the scoring system used by one organization. Issues requiring one-time improvement actions are not subjected to a formal assessment process. The scoring criteria are applied to issues that are likely to take longer than 30 days to resolve and/or will require the formation of a project team.

The Baldrige Criteria address priority setting in the Leadership category, which deals with how the senior leaders ensure that improvement activities are tied to the organization's key objectives and success factors. The goal of all improvement activities should be to move the organization toward the desired future state. Improvement actions must support rather than conflict with each other, and it is up to senior leaders to make this happen.

METHOD

The method for improving processes that is most familiar to people in healthcare organizations is Plan-Do-Check-Act (PDCA), which Shewhart and Deming developed when they adapted the scientific method

FIGURE 8.1 SCORING SYSTEM FOR SELECTING IMPROVEMENT PROJECTS

Issue: _____

Impact of this Issue on:	Score 0	Score 1	Score 2	Score 3	Rating
Health/safety of patients or staff	No injury or risk of injury	May cause minor injury	May cause serious or permanent injury	May cause death	
Quality of patient care	Low impact on patient care/ outcomes	Possible impact on patient care/ outcomes	Moderate impact on patient care/ outcomes	High impact on patient care/ outcomes	
Regulatory or accreditation compliance	Not currently a requirement	Will be required in two to three years	Will be required in one to two years	A current requirement	
Patient/other customer satisfaction	Minimal or no effect on satisfaction	Possible positive effect on satisfaction	Probable positive effect on satisfaction	Patients/other customers have voiced a need to resolve this issue	
Achievement of strategic goals	Affects 0–25% of strategic goals	Affects 25–50% of strategic goals	Affects 50–75% of strategic goals	Affects 75–100% of strategic goals	
Achievement of mission and vision	Minimal or no effect on mission and vision	Possible effect on mission and vision	Probable effect on mission and vision	Important to mission and vision	
Impact on physician/ staff satisfaction	Minimal or no effect on satisfaction	Possible positive effect on satisfaction	Probable positive effect on satisfaction	Physicians/ staff have voiced a need to resolve this issue	
				Total score for this issue:	

to organizational management. Process improvements occur by linking evidence from the work (Check) with decisions about what actions to take (Act). The evidence is used to propose hypotheses (Plan) and test them in trials or in real work (Do). The resulting data become more evidence to be used in another study. This cycle is illustrated in Figure 8.2.

The basic PDCA cycle can be an organization's primary model for all improvement projects. In 2002, when SSM Health Care in St. Louis became the first healthcare winner of the Baldrige award, all process improvement activities in the organization were guided by one continuous quality improvement model based on the PDCA cycle. The model is applied to business as well as clinical process improvement initiatives.

Often people confuse the process improvement model with the tools and techniques used during the application of the model. While an organization should have clearly defined steps for process improvement initiatives—the improvement model—during the life of an improvement project, many different tools may be used. These tools generally fall into five categories: basic quality tools, statistical tools, measurement tools, design tools, and management tools. Listed in Table 8.1 are examples of tools in each of these categories.

The PDCA improvement model is not written in a straight line for a reason: it is intended to be a model that is applied through recurring improvement cycles, as described below.

1. **Check** the evidence around you: How are your key processes performing? What are the needs and wants of patients and other customers? What are the organizational constraints? What are you trying to accomplish?
2. **Act** on the evidence to mitigate any adverse effects on your vision, strategic goals, or patient/customer satisfaction, but move swiftly to the next step.
3. **Plan** for improvements. Those involved in or affected by the process develop improvement actions based on the evidence. A question to be answered during the plan stage is, How will I know if a change is an improvement? Select process measures that correlate with expected results, and make predictions of how the changes will affect performance.
4. **Do** the trial or experiment. Collect data that can be used to accurately assess the effect of process changes.

FIGURE 8.2 PLAN-DO-CHECK-ACT CYCLE

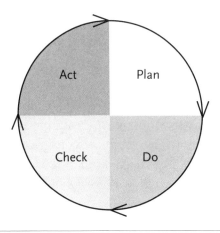

5. **Study** the results, comparing the effects of the process changes with the predicted outcomes. When expectations are realized, the theories about what will work (the plan) have been supported and the changes are implemented on a wider scale. When expected performance is not realized, the theories about what would work are wrong (not validated).

6. **Act** to make the changes, run new experiments, or do whatever is appropriate to the study findings. But before moving on, complete the next step.

7. **Plan** again to share the learning from the project—both the specifics of the process improvements and the general change principles—so that other people in the organization, even those in very different circumstances, may benefit from the lessons learned. This is key to knowledge management and organizational learning.

Familiar elements of the PDCA cycle can be found in any number of contemporary process improvement methodologies. For example, Six Sigma involves a highly structured improvement and design approach known as DMAIC (define-measure-analyze-improve-control). The tools and terminology may vary somewhat among the various improvement methods; however, the basic scientific approach still applies. Some of the currently popular process improvement methodologies are described later in this chapter.

TABLE 8.1 PROCESS MANAGEMENT TOOLS

Basic Quality Tools
- Flowchart
- Cause-and-effect diagram
- Pareto chart
- Check sheet
- Run/control chart
- Histogram
- Scatter diagram

Statistical Tools
- Statistical process control
- Design of experiments
- Gage repeatability and reproducibility study
- Multivariate analysis
- Regression analysis

Measurement Tools
- Cost of quality
- Benchmarking
- Audits
- Surveys

Design Tools
- Quality function deployment
- Failure mode and effect analysis
- Capability analysis
- Process maps/matrices

Management Tools
- Affinity diagram
- Interrelationship digraphs
- Matrix diagram
- Priorities matrix
- Activity network diagrams
- Tree diagrams
- Process decision program charts

Most process improvement models are patterned after the PDCA cycle. Figure 8.3 is a nonproprietary model showing the steps of process improvement. Often organizations develop a customized improvement model using terminology that is unique to their values and culture.

☑ **SELF-ASSESSMENT**

❑ What are the steps in your organization's process improvement model?
❑ Is the process improvement model described in written documentation such as your performance improvement plan?
❑ Can managers and staff members describe the steps in your process improvement model?
❑ Do people in your organization follow this model for every process improvement project, including the design of new services?

Achieving Sustainable Gains: Process Management   195

FIGURE 8.3 PROCESS IMPROVEMENT MODEL

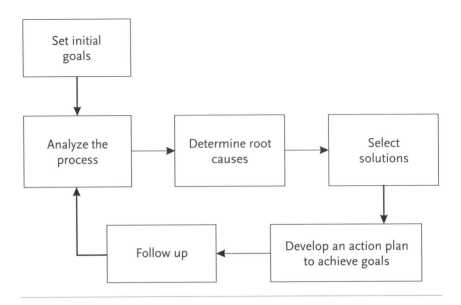

Which process improvement model will work best in your organization? Look for models that promote the following characteristics:

- *They make use of measurement and statistical analysis.* This is the scientific approach to process improvement and requires that process performance be assessed and understood prior to making changes. Measurement and statistical analysis are also used to evaluate the effects of changes to the system.
- *They rely on the knowledge of people.* Most process information does not reside in a database. Rather, information about processes is in the minds of the people who do the work: the process owners. It is not just individual knowledge that is important but also the collective knowledge of all of those who are involved with the process. The knowledge of patients, other customers, and suppliers is also valuable for understanding and improving processes.
- *They use quantitative methods.* The term *quantitative methods* refers to statistical and other graphical tools that summarize data in a structured way (Brassard and Ritter 1994). These methods help with the identification, understanding, and control of factors related to good or poor performance.

- *They encourage people to identify the common and special causes of performance problems.* Common causes are sources of variation due to either the system itself or the way the system is managed. Special causes are sources of variation due to isolated abnormalities or exceptional occurrences in the system. Actions taken on special causes can lead to immediate results, but actions taken on common causes can generate the greatest and most lasting benefits.
- *They help the organization to be proactive.* By anticipating and preventing poor performance, the organization's overall effectiveness is improved, and limited resources are used efficiently. The organization should also be able to use the improvement model in conjunction with strategic planning to identify and respond to new requirements.
- *They are cyclical.* Status quo is not good enough. Changes in strategic goals, resources, and operational constraints require healthcare organizations to continually seek out new and better ways to achieve their mission. The process improvement model should support the ongoing monitoring of performance and the use of new knowledge to address emerging needs.

ROLE OF SENIOR LEADERS

Do senior leaders need to understand the intricacies of each process improvement step and every tool? Probably not, which is why organizations employ quality managers and data analysts and provide training for project facilitators and team members. However, senior leaders do need to know enough to be able to distinguish between busywork and worthwhile process improvement activities. Plus, senior leaders should be actively encouraging the use of process improvement tools that have proven to work well in other industries. These tools include statistical process control, quality function deployment, benchmarking, failure modes and effects analysis, process mapping, and design of experiments. For those who wish to learn more about the various improvement models and tools, a list of additional resources is included in Figure 8.6 near the end of this chapter.

When it comes to process improvement, the most important objectives are that senior leaders create and support an environment in which people are constantly working on the system to continually improve it and that these improvements actually make a difference in terms of organizational performance. How can these objectives be achieved? By asking important questions about the process improvement activities in your organization.

Question: *Are we focused on improving our key processes?*

Performance excellence does not occur within the context of a single department or project. A department-by-department or project-by-project approach can yield short-term gains, but this approach is essentially self-limiting. Walled inside their functional silos, managers and their staff often focus on taking care of their own part of patient care or support processes. Yet, at their broadest, processes can span the entire organization and cut across all major functions or departments. The work activities of individuals or departments make up the myriad tasks within the broader process. Therefore, work activities and individual tasks at all levels must be effectively planned and organized as part of the larger, cross-functional picture. A process is defined as a series of work activities that produce output products and services. Activities take place through the interactions of people and things (e.g., technology, equipment). Process factors must be methodically analyzed and changed so that individuals and departments work together more efficiently and effectively. Processes are improved when they are more predictable, cost less, and contribute more to meeting strategic goals.

It is not possible to improve everything at all times. So the Baldrige Criteria suggest that organizations focus improvement activities on the key healthcare services and delivery processes that are most important to patients and other customers and to the organization's mission success. Key processes include activities or a group of tasks (e.g., physician ordering of a medication and pharmacist filling of the order are two tasks in the process of medication administration). An organizational focus on key processes provides a framework for prioritizing improvement opportunities and measuring performance. Most importantly, by identifying key processes, the organization can concentrate on using process improvement tools and techniques in areas that have the greatest impact on the organization's mission and strategic goals.

The selection of key processes starts with an understanding of the organization's core business. In other words, ask yourself, Why does the organization exist? To answer this question, one hospital identified the following four primary reasons for its existence:

1. Diagnosing patients
2. Treating and caring for patients
3. Planning and managing healthcare provision
4. Learning from patient treatment and care

These statements form a definition of the hospital's core business. Each component was examined to identify key processes. Questions such as those on the matrix in Figure 8.4 were used to select key processes for the core business. Ideally, definition of the organization's core business and selection of key processes is done during strategic planning sessions to ensure adequate input from senior leaders as well as managers and physicians.

To help identify your organization's key processes, the following are some examples that are common to many healthcare providers:

- Patient registration/admission
- Diagnostic exams, tests, and procedures
- Treatment planning and execution
- Nursing care
- Complimentary services (e.g. dietary, pharmacy, physical therapy)
- Purchasing
- Recruiting/hiring
- Staff development
- Billing
- Budgeting
- Information management

Question: *Are we measuring performance of key processes?*
Senior leaders need to understand how well key processes are performing and how well they are managed to meet the demands of patients and other customers. In addition, key processes must positively contribute to the achievement of strategic goals and objectives.

At a minimum, your organization should be measuring the performance of critical activities in key processes. Critical activities are those tasks that directly affect the achievement of strategic goals or those that are known to be problematic (e.g., not meeting the needs of managers, patients, or other customers). Look for red flags such as staff member

FIGURE 8.4 KEY PROCESS SELECTION MATRIX

Questions

Core Business	What do our patients and other customers value the most?	What processes are vital to our vision and mission?	What processes are critical to regulatory/accreditation compliance?
Diagnosing patients			
Treating and caring for patients			
Planning and managing healthcare provision			
Learning from patient treatment and care			

or patient complaints, long cycle times, and limited availability of improved technologies. When selecting critical activities for measurement and improvement, consider the following five questions:

1. How much do patients and other customers care about the activity?
2. Can the activity be improved/fixed?
3. Based on prior performance, how broken is the activity?
4. How important is the activity to the organization's mission and strategy?
5. What resources will be needed to improve the activity?

In a presentation at the American College of Healthcare Executives's 2004 Congress on Healthcare Management, Michael McEachern, FACHE, chief operating officer at Ascension Health Corporation's St. Vincent's Hospital in Birmingham, Alabama, described how his organization selected and deployed improvement strategies for key processes (McEachern 2004). During strategic planning, the organization identified 10 to 12 high-leverage processes—those with the greatest potential for cost and quality recovery if improvements were to be made. Each vice president was given the responsibility for improving one or more of these processes. A black belt–level Six Sigma specialist was assigned to the vice presidents to oversee and facilitate improvement projects in the critical activities of these key processes. At six-month increments, performance results and progress toward improvement are measured. The approach at St. Vincent's Hospital elevated process measurement and improvement to the strategic level, with a focus on critical activities in key processes that are important to the organization. Projects are staffed with adequate resources, and progress is regularly monitored.

Question: *Are we systematically improving processes?*

Once a process has been selected for improvement, the organization's model used for improving processes kicks in. Whether it is the PDCA model or some variant of it, the improvement project should follow the organization's prescribed steps. For simplicity's sake, the non-proprietary improvement model illustrated in Figure 8.3 is used here to describe the steps of a process improvement project.

Set Initial Goals

Process improvement starts with a clear definition of what you are trying to accomplish. The team of people involved in the process improvement initiative must understand the gap—or opportunity for improvement—in whatever it is assessing. Goal statements should be specific and based on facts. A good goal statement is

- specific,
- supported by evidence (quantified),
- clear in defining the problem—not the symptoms, and
- free of assumed causes and solutions.

Setting initial goals allows the organization to describe the ideal situation in the future state. The goals describe the outcome of fixing gaps between expected and actual performance. Senior leaders should establish goals for interdisciplinary or interdepartmental improvement projects. Generally, managers or division heads define the goals for projects confined to one department or unit.

 KEY POINT

Often the goals for process improvement initiatives are too general and do not clearly state the gap between actual and expected performance. Process improvement goals should be checked for clarity to ensure that they

- state the problem clearly and in specific terms,
- include data or evidences of the problem,
- describe the negative results or barriers that result from the problem, and
- avoid assuming solutions.

Analyze the Process

The main purposes of analyzing the process are to

- break the process down to its major steps,
- make sure information about the process is gathered and organized,
- expose tentative causes of process problems, and
- eliminate ambiguity about where improvements are needed.

Measurement and analysis tools are particularly important during this phase of the project. One of the characteristics of a Six Sigma project is the extensive use of process flowcharting, data collection, retrospective data mining using the design-of-experiments model, and statistical analysis of process performance. However, there are no specific tools that must be used for every process improvement activity. What is most important is that people gain a thorough understanding of the process as it now exists. At the end of analysis, the team should have a clear, specific understanding of the improvement opportunities within the process.

 KEY POINT

Process improvement project teams should rely on factual information to eliminate perceptions or hunches so that a well-framed description of process problems can be developed.

Determine Root Causes

It is now time to single out the cause of the problems that are affecting process performance—the root cause. A root cause is the most influential action, inaction, or condition that brings about an effect or a result. A root cause is one that prevents the process from achieving desired expectations. It is important to separate symptoms from what causes them.

To determine the root cause(s) of process problems identified in the previous step, the improvement team determines what could cause the effects or symptoms described in the problem that it has identified. All possible causes are brainstormed, and the primary or root causes are identified. Usually the root causes influence more than one of the problem areas identified in the situation analysis. Once the root causes are identified, the team is ready to develop process improvement solutions.

 KEY POINT

Improvement project facilitators must be properly trained to assist the people involved in the project to select and use the right improvement tools and techniques to identify root causes.

Select Solutions

When choosing solutions, the first thing to do is to brainstorm ideas. The intention is to capture as many possible solutions as the team can think of. Ideas for improvement may come from other departments or organizations that have tackled similar process problems. They may have procedures in place or experience and knowledge that would be useful. Often the project team has talked a lot about the process while analyzing the problems, and now is the time to consider improvement ideas that were discussed earlier in the project.

Once a list of possible solutions has been created, similar solutions are combined to condense the list. It can be helpful to develop a set of criteria or questions for evaluating alternative solutions. Examples include the following:

- If this course of action is implemented, is it plausible that the project goals will be reached?

- Will this course of action have a positive or negative impact on the goals of any other project? Is it dependent on the successful implementation of any other improvement actions?
- Is this a solution that will better satisfy the needs of our patients and other customers?
- Are we organized to implement this course of action? If not, what must be changed to accommodate implementation?
- How long will it take to implement this change? Will other constraints occur as a result?
- Will the improvement solution make the process more predictable? Less costly?
- How will the solution help the organization achieve its strategic goals and objectives?

Although some improvement actions may appear obvious, resist the temptation to implement the solution until all alternatives have been considered.

 KEY POINT

Improvement actions should not be formulated until the process has been thoroughly evaluated and alternative solutions have been analyzed.

Develop an Action Plan

Once "best guess" solutions are selected, a systematic plan for testing the solutions is devised. The improvement project is not complete until the actions have been validated as effective; in other words, the actions do indeed achieve the desired goals. Actions plans should contain the following specific elements:

- Time frame for completion
- Important steps that are necessary for achieving the goals
- People/departments responsible for the important steps
- Additional resources that may be needed to complete the action plan
- Milestones detailing when important steps are to be completed
- Measures of success

KEY POINT

Improvement plans should contain the specific accomplishments to be achieved and how progress toward completion of the improvement goal will be measured.

Follow Up

The purpose of the follow-up phase is to see how the redesigned process is actually working in the real world. After strategies are put into action they may have to change if improvement goals are not met. Management must be vigilant in monitoring the effects of process changes; otherwise, so-called temporary fixes remain in place for years without any understanding of how the actions are affecting performance. Follow-up is one of the commonly omitted steps of process improvement.

Ideally, to ensure that progress is being made, monitoring reports should be produced on a regular basis. Quarterly or monthly reports are preferable. Progress reports on improvement activities can be in the form of data tables or presented in charts or graphs. Whatever format is used, the report should be concise and the information boiled down to help participants make sense of the data.

 KEY POINT

The purpose of monitoring the results of improvement actions is not to punish but to ensure the best performance in meeting the needs of the organization and its customers.

Question: *Are we incorporating the needs of patients and other customers, suppliers, and partners into our process improvement activities?*

The work processes in a healthcare organization should be built around the delivery of services that are valued by patients and other stakeholders. To achieve this goal, organizations must have formal mechanisms to determine customer and other stakeholder requirements, expectations, and preferences. More about gathering this input is described in Chapter 5. To improve the performance of key processes, information about customer demands should be considered. Such information typically includes the following:

- Outcomes of collaborations with patients and other stakeholders to determine how well the process fulfills what matters to them
- Measures of current satisfaction
- Measures of current process capability to create value for patients and other stakeholders

Thomas Royer, M.D., president/CEO of CHRISTUS Health in Irving, Texas, encourages senior leadership teams to actively participate in candid conversations with patients and families. Royer suggests that interactions between senior leaders and patients take place during hospital rounds or with randomly chosen patient-family focus groups (Spath 2003a).

Patient satisfaction concepts have taken hold in most healthcare organizations; however, an often-overlooked element in improvement activities is the requirements of suppliers and partners (e.g., vendors, other healthcare institutions, community health services). Are relevant suppliers and partners involved in improvement projects? It is especially important to engage partners when the process spans the continuum of care. Recipients of healthcare services will be better served if all customers, suppliers, and partners are actively involved in process redesign activities.

Question: *Are we making good process measurement and improvement decisions?*

The concepts of quality control and continuous improvement have become commonplace in many healthcare organizations. Yet while staff members and physicians were learning to use basic quality tools such as Pareto analysis and flowcharting, the rigor of process improvement techniques in other industries was rapidly advancing. Today, world-class companies are using a wide range of comprehensive methods to make fact-based decisions about how to improve their products and services. Thus far, many healthcare organizations have lagged behind other industries in the use of graphical and statistical analysis tools in performance improvement efforts. There is still heavy reliance on limited or subjective data and individual judgment. Years of healthcare delivery characterized by inefficiencies, service delays, marginal customer satisfaction, adverse events, and burned-out employees make it imperative for healthcare organizations to find better ways to measure and improve processes. Many of the performance improvement techniques used in other industries can be applied to health service processes to make them better managed, more predictable, and better controlled. Through the acquisition of quantitative information and the use of graphical and statistical analysis tools, healthcare processes can be improved, and those improvements can be sustained.

Common process management tools were listed in Table 8.1 earlier in this chapter. People in many healthcare organizations are still using only the basic quality tools (e.g., flowchart, Pareto chart, histogram) to analyze and improve processes. This practice is holding back those organizations from achieving ever-greater process improvements as well as long-term quality gains. What tools should be used to improve healthcare processes? The answer is the topic of many journal articles and books and well beyond the space limitations of this chapter. It is enough to say here that other industries, including service industries, have many more tools in their process management toolbox than the average healthcare organization. Not until the late 1990s did healthcare organizations begin to apply statistical process control techniques, even though Shewhart introduced the concepts in the 1920s and Deming popularized them in the 1940s. Since the mid-1940s, human factors engineering has been used in various industries to reduce the risk of human errors, yet even today many healthcare organizations have not applied this learning to improve patient safety.

 KEY POINT

High-performing organizations use a large variety of process measurement and design techniques. Many of the basic quality tools are valuable and regularly used; however, these are not the only tools in the process management toolbox of high-performing organizations. The same should be true for healthcare organizations seeking to advance performance excellence.

Shown in Figure 8.5 are descriptions of process measurement and design tools that, when used in conjunction with basic QI tools, could greatly improve process management in healthcare organizations.

Question: *Are we able to sustain our gains?*

"I thought we fixed that two years ago" is an all-too-common statement in healthcare organizations. Financial and human resources are expended on improvement projects, and processes are undergoing

FIGURE 8.5 PROCESS MEASUREMENT AND DESIGN TOOLS

Analysis of variance (ANOVA): A basic statistical technique for analyzing experimental data. It subdivides the total variation of a data set into meaningful component parts associated with specific sources of variation to test a hypothesis on the parameters of the model or to estimate variance components.

Benchmarking: A systematic process for evaluating and improving the products, services, and work processes of an organization.

Control chart: A chart with upper and lower control limits on which values of some statistical measure for a series of samples or subgroups are plotted. The chart frequently shows a central line to help detect a trend of plotted values toward either control limit.

Correlation analysis: An evaluation of the relationship between two data sets of variables.

Design of experiments (DOE): A branch of applied statistics dealing with planning, conducting, analyzing, and interpreting controlled tests to evaluate the factors that control the value of a parameter or group of parameters.

Failure mode and effects analysis (FMEA): A procedure by which each potential failure mode in a system is analyzed to determine (1) the effects on the process, (2) the severity of each potential failure mode, (3) causes of the failure, and (4) the actions to be taken to repair the failure.

Fault tree analysis: A form of safety analysis that uses a fault tree to graphically display all possible faults leading up to a given event. This can also be used proactively to identify and correct potential faults that could lead to an adverse event.

Process capability: A statistical measure of the inherent process variability for a given characteristic. The most widely accepted formula for process capability is six sigma.

Process map: A type of flowchart depicting the steps in a process, with identification of responsibility for each step and for the key measures.

Quality function deployment (QFD): A structured method in which customer requirements are translated into appropriate technical requirements for each stage of product development and production. The QFD process is often referred to as "listening to the voice of the customer."

Regression analysis: A statistical technique for determining the best mathematical expression to describe the functional relationship between one response and one or more independent variables.

FIGURE 8.5 *(continued)*

Reliability modeling: A technique that is used to assess the probability that a process will perform consistently under specified conditions for a specified time period.

Simulation modeling: A technique that helps to visualize, analyze, and predict the performance of a system without the cost and risk of disrupting current work processes.

Statistical process control (SPC): The application of statistical techniques to control a process.

Sources: ASQ (2004); Spath (2000); Barry, Murcko, and Brubaker (2002); Brue (2002); Chaplin and Terninko (2000).

almost constant redesign. Yet familiar problems seem to creep back into the system to disrupt the performance of key processes. Backsliding is an age-old condition that often applies to many aspects of life. It would be presumptuous to offer a cure for one of humankind's oldest maladies in a paragraph or two. However, there are some red flags that senior leaders can watch for. Healthcare organizations trying to advance performance excellence sometimes make common mistakes that could be avoided with forethought and a little knowledge of the pitfalls of process improvement.

Change things rather than behaviors. Process improvements that come undone can often be traced back to a failure to change the attitudes or behaviors of people doing the work. Often process improvement efforts focus on standardizing or streamlining work steps, and, unfortunately, the human part of the process is overlooked. For instance, one hospital implemented a bar-coded patient identification system to reduce medication errors. However, the nurses found the process to be too cumbersome and began to develop short-cuts. Soon nurses were making duplicate copies of the patients' wristband so they could check the bar codes at the nursing station rather than in patient rooms (Spath 2003b). The potential for a medication administration error is obvious. Modifying attitudes and behaviors is important. Otherwise people will lapse into the old way of doing things without giving the new process a chance to become a habit.

Failure to train people. Giving people a clear vision of where the organization is going is all important. Of equal importance is the education of people in the use of the process improvement skills that they need to get the job done. Just as cheerleading alone will not improve a football team's chances of winning, neither will cheerleading alone ensure sustainable performance improvements. Everyone involved in process improvement should know how to apply the organization's fundamental improvement model and, at a minimum, know how to use basic QI tools.

Failure to test redesigned processes. Changes in the way people do their work are often implemented without a clear understanding of how the change affects other parts of the system: other people, processes, and services. One important way to ensure that improvements are sustainable is to test possible process changes with a small subset of patients or activities. If the changes appear to achieve the intended goals, then the process changes can be spread to all patients or activities. Learning can occur from as small a subset of patients or activities as five to ten. Quantitative and qualitative data should be collected during the pilot phase for the purpose of learning what effect specific changes in a process will have on related processes and systems.

Ordering change, ignoring support. For healthcare organizations to get better every day, it takes knowledge, diligence, effort, focus, and resources. Senior leaders cannot simply give people a book about process improvement, tell them which processes to improve, and then turn and walk away. Change will not happen. The result will be short-lived improvements. Leaders must take an active role in steering the improvement efforts of the organization. Otherwise, resources will not be optimized, and improvement projects will suffer a shotgun effect: scattered efforts, diluted objectives, and an obscured vision.

Question: *Is the organization getting optimal value from process improvement projects?*

To gain full value from process improvement initiatives, the lessons learned should be shared throughout the organization. Lessons learned are the knowledge or understanding gained by the improvement experience. The experience may be positive, such as better process performance, or negative, such as solutions that did not work as intended.

High-performance organizations recognize the importance of learning from the past to ensure future successes. These organizations commonly use several mechanisms to capture and disseminate lessons learned from performance improvement projects. For some organizations, the principal source for collection and sharing of lessons is a secure web-based communication system that managers are required to review on an ongoing basis. Many organizations use staff meetings, newsletters, training conferences, or program reviews to communicate lessons. Sioux Valley Hospitals and Health System, based in Sioux Falls, South Dakota, hosts an annual Quality Fair to share lessons learned and recognize successful improvement initiatives. This regional healthcare partnership includes more than 140 facilities in South Dakota, Minnesota, Iowa, and Nebraska. At the systemwide Quality Fair, which was first held in 1999, up to five teams from each facility share information about their improvement projects. Virginia Bynum, Ph.D., CHE, vice president at Sioux Valley, reports that participation in the fair has grown rapidly over the years, and it is now the biggest quality exhibition in the upper Midwest and quite possibly the nation. At the Quality Fair in May 2003, facilities across the system sent 123 teams, with more than 750 people participating. The project teams chosen to exhibit their initiatives are selected at the facility level. Several of the facilities have their own Quality Fair to choose who will go to the systemwide fair.

Improving the organization's lesson-learning systems can help ensure that knowledge gained from past experiences is applied to future improvement initiatives. Some examples of what can be done to improve knowledge sharing follow:

- Articulate the relationship between improvement projects and lesson learning in the organization's performance improvement plan.
- Designate an individual to serve as the lesson-learning coordinator to lead and manage efforts to share lessons learned in improvement projects.
- Develop ways to broaden and implement mentoring and storytelling as additional mechanisms for lesson sharing.
- Identify incentives to encourage more collection and sharing of lessons among employees and improvement project teams, such as links to performance evaluations and awards.
- Solicit user input on the value of the organization's current lesson-sharing efforts to determine how knowledge can be better disseminated.

- Initiate information technology pilot projects to evaluate the usefulness of electronic information sharing.
- Track and report on the effectiveness of the lesson-learning efforts using objective performance measures.

A common barrier to sharing lessons learned from improvement projects is the perception that people will be punished if an improvement action does not achieve its intended goal. Overcoming this barrier requires strong support from the organization's leaders. Intolerance of mistakes will cripple any knowledge-sharing efforts.

Sharing lessons learned during improvement projects should be part of the organization's larger knowledge management strategy. The elements of knowledge management are addressed in greater detail in Chapter 6.

CONTEMPORARY IMPROVEMENT MODELS

In the past few years, a number of hybrid process improvement methodologies have been introduced into the business world, and some are beginning to be applied in healthcare organizations. Whether these methodologies have staying power has yet to be determined. Following are four of the currently popular process improvement models:

1. Kaizen
2. Rapid cycle improvement
3. Six Sigma
4. Lean thinking

 KEY POINT

No process improvement model will solve all of your organization's problems. There are always new and better process improvement tools and techniques. The trick is to understand these new methods quickly and integrate them into your model of continuous improvement.

A brief description of the four improvement methodologies is provided below. For those who would like more comprehensive information, a list of additional resources is provided later in this section.

Kaizen

Kaizen means "continuous improvement." It comes from the Japanese words *kai*, meaning school, and *zen*, meaning wisdom. The Japanese way of process improvement encourages small improvements day after day, continuously and never ending. Like many process improvement models, Kaizen can be viewed as an organizational philosophy as much as a systematic improvement technique. Kaizen activities can be conducted in several ways. First and most common is to change processes to make the work more efficient or safer. Employers are encouraged to be actively involved in process improvements with the help of colleagues or a Kaizen support group. The second way is to improve the equipment used by employees, for example, by switching to intravenous pumps that do not have a free-flow setting to prevent medication administration errors. The third way is to improve the procedures that employees are expected to follow. All of these alternatives can be combined into one improvement initiative.

The application of Kaizen to a process improvement initiative follows a pattern very similar to that of the PDCA model. Depending on the objectives of the improvement project, there are many ways to implement the Kaizen procedure. Listed below are the common project steps.

1. *Form a Kaizen team and gather information.* In this step, the facts of the process are examined (e.g., start and end points, customer requirements).
2. *Describe the current process.* The team examines how the process works right now using flow charts or other process diagrams.
3. *Decide on the improvement goal.* After gathering detailed information about the current process, the team identifies the specific improvement goal.
4. *Develop alternative solutions.* The Kaizen methodology suggests that seven alternative solutions be developed.
5. *Evaluate and select the best solution.* This is a data-driven step in which the team considers the advantages and disadvantages of the alternative solutions developed in step four.
6. *Test the best solution.* To confirm the possibility of implementing the solution selected in step five, the change is pilot tested or simulated.

7. *Estimate benefits.* The potential benefits (e.g., cost savings, efficiency improvements, error reduction) of the solution are quantified.

8. *Gather results and analyze them.* Continue to monitor the process to confirm that the solution achieved the expected benefits.

In 1986, Masaaki Imai, with his book *Kaizen, the Key to Japan's Competitive Success*, was the first person to introduce the concept of Kaizen outside Japan. Since then, Kaizen has become a well-known and widely used philosophy in organizational improvement. Imai offers the following ten basic tips necessary to begin the journey of Kaizen implementation in an organization (Imai 1986):

1. Discard conventional fixed ideas.
2. Think of how to do it, not why it cannot be done.
3. Do not make excuses. Start by questioning current practices.
4. Do not seek perfection. Do it right away even if for only 50 percent of the target.
5. Correct it right away if you make a mistake.
6. Do not just spend money for Kaizen; use your wisdom.
7. Wisdom is brought out when you are faced with hardship.
8. Ask "Why?" five times, and seek root causes.
9. Seek the wisdom of ten people rather than the knowledge of one.
10. Kaizen ideas are infinite.

Rapid Cycle Improvement

Rapid cycle improvement (RCI) is an improvement process based on the PDCA model (Langley et al. 1996). Many of the Kaizen philosophies and improvement tools are incorporated into the RCI model. The model entails four steps: set the aim (the goal), define the measures (the expected improvements), make changes (the action plan), and test those changes (the solution).

Setting the aim involves taking a clear and deliberate look at what is to be accomplished. Questions that can help the project team establish aims are as follows:

• Is it measurable? (Will we know if it was achieved?)
• Is it a stretch goal?

- Is it right for the time frame?
- Is it consistent with the organizational mission?
- Does it matter to patients and families?
- Can we think of at least a few things to try that will help achieve the aim?
- Does the project team match the aim?
- Is it outcome oriented?

The aim or goal drives the next step: defining the measure. The measure describes what the process should be able to accomplish if a solution is successful. Key measures that operationalize the aim are chosen. For example, for the goal of improving patient satisfaction in a hospice unit, a measure might be the average time from pain assessment to administration of medication.

The third step is to select process changes that are expected to achieve the aim. Ideas for process changes can come from many sources: project team members, frontline staff, the literature, other organizations, professional colleagues, and so forth. The last RCI step is to test the changes using a rapid cycle PDCA process. The process is considered *rapid cycle* because the team focuses on small, concrete changes that can be quickly put into action in a pilot situation. Thus, the solution can be evaluated in a very short time. If the changes do not work, another PDCA cycle is initiated until a workable solution is found.

Rather than conduct a comprehensive (and often time intensive) analysis of a process, RCI relies on small process changes and careful measurement of the effect of these changes. This PDCA approach uses an accelerated method (usually less than four to six weeks per improvement cycle) to collect and analyze data and make informed changes based on that analysis. This is then followed by another improvement cycle to evaluate the success of the change. The ongoing repetition of these improvement cycles serves as the basis for continuous improvement and allows for the creation of internal performance benchmarks. Because RCI is based on the PDCA model, most people are familiar with the tools and techniques used for the improvement projects. An added benefit of using RCI is that only those people/departments that tend to be early adopters of innovation need to be involved in the pilot tests of process changes. If these pilot studies are widely visible and the data support the value of process changes, the late adopters are more willing to support the changes (Bergman 1999).

Many healthcare improvement initiatives are using the RCI model, including the breakthrough projects sponsored by the Institute for Healthcare Improvement and the Medicare quality improvement initiatives sponsored by the Centers for Medicare and Medicaid Services and overseen by state quality improvement organizations. Rapid cycle improvement has been successfully applied to both the operational aspects of healthcare delivery and clinical patient care processes.

Six Sigma

Six Sigma is a disciplined, data-driven approach aimed at the near elimination of defects from every product, process, and transaction. Six Sigma's goal is breakthrough knowledge leading to demonstrated process improvements. These improvements enable companies to do things better, faster, and at lower cost while offering superior consumer satisfaction.

Six Sigma has its foundation in total quality management philosophies and incorporates concepts from many other approaches, such as reengineering, balanced scorecards, voice of the customer, and design of experiments. One of the major contributions of Six Sigma is a reorientation to the definition of what constitutes acceptable quality.

Six Sigma is the term used in statistics to denote a 99.9997 percent defect-free yield for a process. Six Sigma as a process improvement methodology has long been applied to manufacturing processes. In recent years, healthcare organizations have also begun to use the tools and see results. Key characteristics of the Six Sigma improvement methodology are the following (Barry, Murcko, and Brubaker 2002; Brue 2002):

- *Process variation control.* To achieve an almost perfect level of quality, Six Sigma focuses on reducing the variations that can occur in a process. The gap between process capability and how the process currently performs is seen as an improvement opportunity.
- *Results oriented.* The potential impact on performance (financial, clinical, operational) is projected prior to the start of a Six Sigma project, and an evaluation is made at the end to determine if the goals have been met.
- *Data driven.* Detailed information about the process is gathered and analyzed to reveal defects in procedures that, once corrected, will

allow the process to operate within six standard deviations of average performance.

Initiation of a Six Sigma project is similar to any performance improvement activity. Leaders select projects based on the organization's strategic goals and likelihood that the project will lead to significant improvements. Six Sigma projects follow a highly structured and disciplined process, typically the DMAIC (pronounced *dee-MAY-ick*) methodology. This process improvement method involves the following five steps:

1. *Define* the problem.
2. *Measure* the problem.
3. *Analyze* the data.
4. *Improve* the system.
5. *Control* and sustain the improvement.

Each DMAIC step has defined goals, critical checkpoints, and relevant process improvement tools. Active leadership oversight is important to ensure that the project stays on track, adequate resources are allocated, and the steps are completed with sufficient rigor.

To be effective, Six Sigma projects must be overseen and led by people who have been adequately trained (Barry, Murcko, and Brubaker 2002; Brue 2002). Leading the initiatives are Six Sigma black belts and green belts, individuals who are intensively trained to evaluate and solve process problems using the DMAIC methodologies. A wide array of Six Sigma tools are used; some of them are highly scientific and statistical in nature, whereas others are common sense. Training in the Six Sigma methodology and tools is usually conducted at all levels of the organization. The champions, process owners, and project sponsors usually come from the leadership team. They identify the strategic direction and process focus areas and select and manage improvement projects. Project leaders (black belts) are trained in subjects such as the following (Barry, Murcko, and Brubaker 2002; Brue 2002):

- *Project guidelines and selection*: project selection, common problems, defining the scope of the project, team selection, teamwork leadership, communications, team members roles, and how productive teams work

- *Team behavior*: stages of individual and team growth as it applies to performance, how paradigms affect projects, gains in understanding self and others and in skills to reduce interpersonal relationship tensions to improve productivity
- *Data collection*: how to measure waste, cycle time, service processes, service strategies, service projects, management responsibilities, and performance measurements and understanding products versus services
- *How to use data*: data analysis tools and techniques such as using the normal distribution, dependent and independent variables, and probability distributions within which to analyze data
- *Project management*: critical path methodology for managing projects, executing and reporting on projects, and aspects of managing people; how to define, measure, analyze, and improve elements of the project
- *Control charts*: common-cause and special-cause variation, responsibility to investigate, different kinds of signals, how to construct and analyze X bar R charts, XmR charts, C charts and u charts, and p charts and np charts.
- *Statistical tests*: for example, correlation and regression analysis of variance
- *Process design*: design of experiments, failure mode and effect analysis, root cause analysis, modeling, and fault tree analysis
- *Problem solving*: concepts of the theory of inventive problem solving, reliability diagramming to assess how processes and systems handle failure

Typically a black belt will have undertaken a training program consisting of a minimum of 20 to 25 days of training and carried out one improvement project over his or her three- to six-month training period. Green belts—individuals who serve as project team members—receive much the same training as black belts; however, they lack the experience to facilitate an actual project. Organizations using Six Sigma often employ highly trained individuals, known as master black belts. These people are site experts and trainers of black and green belts. Six Sigma consultants suggest that an organization train and maintain ten black belts and one master black belt per 1,000 employees (Bendell 2000).

Six Sigma projects in healthcare organizations tend to focus on the operational aspects of service delivery rather than clinical decision-making activities. Examples of processes selected by hospitals for Six Sigma projects include the following:

- Patient registration/admission
- Patient flow/bed control
- Turnaround of diagnostic test results
- Timeliness of emergency room treatment
- Surgery scheduling
- Inventory control
- Supply chain management
- Billing accuracy
- Insurance denials
- Human resource management

Lean Thinking

The manufacturing industry has been using lean techniques for several years to improve productivity, eliminate waste, improve the quality of products, and lower costs. Now these techniques are being applied to processes in healthcare organizations. Some quality specialists view Kaizen and lean thinking as synonymous because the goals of the process improvement activities are similar: reduce costs, improve quality, and decrease cycle time. The basic principles of lean thinking are as follows:

- Eliminate waste (retain only value-added activities).
- Concentrate on improving value-added activities.
- Respond to the voice of the customer.
- Optimize processes across the organization.

The fundamental objective of lean thinking is to provide perfect value to the customer through a perfect value creation process that has zero waste. Another view is that everything done in a healthcare organization should add to the value of the services provided to patients, their families, and other customers. Some activities are of obvious value (e.g., diagnostic testing), while others seem far removed (e.g., clerical services). However, inefficiencies in clerical activities may detract from the organization's ability to provide excellent patient care. Lean thinking encourages viewing every activity to ensure that it is supporting a customer, regardless of whether the support is direct or indirect. To translate this concept to healthcare, management needs to shift its focus from optimizing separate tasks or activities to optimizing the flow of an entire process or group of linked processes. The goal is to eliminate waste along the entire value stream of a process instead of improving just the individual steps.

The simplest versions of lean thinking involve little more than a quick look at a process followed by some immediate changes based mainly on subjective decisions. Although this produces change very quickly, long-lasting performance improvement is unlikely. At the other extreme is a massive data collection effort that includes a comprehensive analysis of process flow. This can take several months or even years to complete before any actual changes are made. The ideal use of lean thinking is somewhere between these two extremes. It is critical to do enough data collection and process analysis to improve the process based on facts rather than opinions. The amount of data required will depend on the nature and condition of the processes. Optimizing the process flow comes from having the right data and knowing how to use it.

Value-added activities are those steps in a process that contribute to the organization's overall goals and business objectives. Fundamentally, *going lean* is a process improvement methodology that involves the following two primary steps:

1. Analyze the steps of the process to determine which steps add value and which do not. This involves asking questions such as those that follow:
   - Does this step create value for the customer?
   - Is it capable of producing a good result every time?
   - Is it able to produce the right result at the right time?
   - Is the capacity adequate so that wait time is not excessive, or is there too much capacity?
2. Link the value-added steps to optimize process flow and eliminate the unnecessary steps. This involves asking questions such as the following:
   - Do all the steps in the process occur in a tight sequence with little waiting? Does the information flow smoothly?
   - Does each step only occur at the command of the next downstream step and within the time available?

- Are demand signals filtered to remove unnecessary variation and levelled to smooth the workload?

While lean thinking may appear to be a process improvement model that is only applicable to manufacturing, it is being successfully applied in healthcare organizations. Often, lean thinking is a natural complement to Six Sigma. For example, the data gathered during the analysis of process flow can be used to identify high-priority/high-impact areas for Six Sigma projects.

For those who would like more in-depth descriptions of the four process improvement models described in this chapter, Figure 8.6 contains a list of additional resources.

Selecting the Right Method

The most important drivers of process management are leadership, creativity and innovation, and employee involvement. Probably only 20 percent of the gains made in a healthcare organization can be directly attributed to the tools and techniques. What is already known and proven about process management is voluminous and rigorous. This knowledge runs the risk of being lost and rediscovered in ever-more diluted forms as quality specialists reinvent it from their own perspective. Champions of each improvement method will tell you that implementation of their model will yield the best results. Yet it is hard to forget that the champions of yesterday's process improvement fads voiced the same enthusiasm. However, do not discount new process improvement methodologies as not being valuable.

The tools and techniques in these new improvement models can help healthcare organizations find better ways of solving problems, growing revenue, satisfying patients, and—best of all—innovating. These methodologies are really nothing more than names given to a collection of tools and scripted improvement techniques that can be integrated with the organization's existing process management activities. No methodology will solve all problems, which is why cross-training internal quality specialists in the multiple methodologies helps to ensure that the right tools are applied at the right time and place.

To select the best approach for a particular improvement project, it is helpful to understand the primary theory behind the model and the intended effect of the improvement efforts. Table 8.2 provides a comparison of the four improvement models presented in this chapter.

FIGURE 8.6 PROCESS IMPROVEMENT MODEL RESOURCES

Kaizen

Regan, M. D. 2000. *The Kaizen Revolution*. Chelan, WA: Holden Press.

Tozawa, B., and N. Bodek. 2002. *The Idea Generator: Quick and Easy Kaizen*. Vancouver, WA: PCS Press.

Lean Thinking

George, M. 2003. *Lean Six Sigma for Service: How to Use Lean Speed and Six Sigma Quality to Improve Services and Transactions*. New York: McGraw-Hill Trade.

Womack, J., and D. Jones. 1996. *Lean Thinking: Banish Waste and Create Wealth in Your Corporation*. New York: Simon & Schuster.

Rapid Cycle Improvement

Institute for Healthcare Improvement. *Breakthrough Series Guides* (several guides are available for various improvement topics). Boston: Institute for Healthcare Improvement.

Morath, J., and J. Turnbull. 1998. *The Quality Advantage: A Strategic Guide for Health Care Leaders*. San Francisco: Jossey-Bass.

Six Sigma

Barry, R., A. C. Murcko, and C. E. Brubaker. 2002. *The Six Sigma Book for Healthcare: Improving Outcomes by Reducing Errors*. Chicago: Health Administration Press.

Brue, G. *Six Sigma for Managers*. 2002. Milwaukee, WI: ASQ Quality Press.

Caldwell, C., and C. Denham. 2001. *Medication Safety and Cost Recovery: A Four-Step Executive Guide*. Chicago: Health Administration Press.

Rath & Strong Management Consultants. 2000. *Rath & Strong's Six Sigma Pocket Guide*. Lexington, MA: Rath & Strong.

General Reference

Revelle, J. 2004. *Quality Essentials: A Reference Guide from A to Z*. Milwaukee, WI: ASQ Quality Press.

 PROCESS MANAGEMENT ENABLERS

❑ Leadership-driven process management
❑ Process management activities focused on supporting and improving key processes
❑ Evaluation and improvement of processes based on strategic objectives and patient/other customer feedback

TABLE 8.2 COMPARISON OF IMPROVEMENT MODELS

Improvement Model	Primary Theory	Intended Effect
Kaizen	Improve performance through incremental process changes.	Simple, quick-strike tactics plug the holes in the process.
Rapid Cycle Improvement	Improve performance through incremental process changes.	Achieve predefined measures of success.
Six Sigma	Reduce process variation.	Reduce variation in complex processes.
Lean Thinking	Remove waste.	Create value-added processes.

- ❏ A consistently applied, rigorous model for process improvement
- ❏ Data-driven process improvement decisions using the basic quality tools as well as graphical and statistical analysis tools
- ❏ Adequately resourced improvement activities
- ❏ Employees trained in process improvement tools and techniques
- ❏ Regular monitoring of the progress of improvement activities
- ❏ Pilot testing of improvement actions prior to full implementation
- ❏ Ongoing measurement of key processes and critical activities to ensure that gains are sustainable
- ❏ Mechanisms for sharing improvements and applying best practices in all parts of the organization

REFERENCES

American Society for Quality (ASQ). 2004. "Online Quality Glossary." [Online information; retrieved 2/04.] www.asq.org/info/glossary/.

Barker, J. 1990. *Discovering the Future Series: The Power of Vision, the Business of Paradigms, and Paradigm Pioneers*. Video. Burnsville, MN: Charthouse Learning Corporation.

Barry R., A. Murcko, and C. Brubaker. 2002. *The Six Sigma Book for Healthcare: Improving Outcomes by Reducing Errors*. Chicago: Health Administration Press.

Bendell, T. 2000. "What is Six Sigma?" *Quality World* 26 (1): 14–17.

Bergman, D. 1999. "Evidence-Based Guidelines and Critical Pathways for Improvement." *Pediatrics* 103 (1, Suppl.): 225–32.

Brassard, M., and D. Ritter. 1994. *The Memory Jogger II: A Pocket Guide of Tools for Continuous Improvement and Effective Planning*. Methuen, MA: GOSL/QPC.

Brue, G. 2002. *Six Sigma for Managers*. Milwaukee, WI: ASQ Quality Press.

Chaplin, E., and J. Terninko. 2000. *Customer Driven Healthcare: QFD for Process Improvement and Cost Reduction*. Milwaukee, WI: ASQ Quality Press.

Covey, S. 1990. *The Seven Habits of Highly Effective People*. New York: The Free Press.

Deming, W. 1986. *Out of the Crisis*. Cambridge, MA: Massachusetts Institute of Technology, Center for Advanced Engineering Study.

Imai, M. 1986. *Kaizen, the Key to Japan's Competitive Success*. New York: McGraw-Hill/Irwin.

Langley G., K. Nolan, T. Nolan, C. Norman, and L. Provost. 1996. *The Improvement Guide: A Practical Approach to Improving Organizational Performance*. San Francisco: Jossey-Bass.

McEachern, M. 2004. " 'Good to Great' in Healthcare: Financial Turnaround Lessons from 2002 and 2003." Presentation with C. A. Caldwell, Jr., A. D. Jimenez, and T. R. Day at the 2004 Congress on Healthcare Management sponsored by the American College of Healthcare Executive, Chicago, March 2.

Rentzhog. O. 1998. *Process orientation: A basis for organisation of tomorrow* (in Swedish), p. 30. Lund, Sweden: Studentlitteratur.

Spath, P. 2003a. "Do You Hear Me Now?" *Hospital and Health Networks* 77 (12): 36–40, 49.

———. 2003b. "Automation: Friend or Foe?" *For the Record* 15 (13): 34–37.

———. 2000. *Patient Safety Improvement Guidebook*. Forest Grove, OR: Brown-Spath & Associates.

CHAPTER NINE

Measuring Your Progress

THE FINAL SECTION in the Baldrige Criteria is Organizational Performance Results. If an organization applies for the Baldrige National Quality Award, documenting results is an important factor in award scoring. The organization's internal performance trends—as well as comparisons with competitors or industry standards—are taken into consideration by the examiners. The Results section defines criteria for measurement in the following six areas:

1. Healthcare results
2. Patient-focused and other customer–focused results
3. Financial and market results
4. Staff and work system results
5. Organizational effectiveness results
6. Governance and social responsibility results

Organizational results have the greatest weight in the Baldrige award scoring system. In the 2004 criteria, 450 of the 1,000 possible total points were assigned to the results category. To receive the maximum number of points, healthcare organizations must exhibit the following characteristics (Baldrige National Quality Program 2004):

• Current performance is excellent in most areas of importance to the key organizational requirements.

- Excellent improvement trends and/or sustained excellent performance levels are reported in most areas.
- Evidence of healthcare sector and benchmark leadership is demonstrated in many areas.
- Organizational performance results fully address key customer, market, process, and action plan requirements.

Even organizations that choose not to apply for the Baldrige award will find the scoring assignment process useful for evaluating their progress toward performance excellence. The current edition of the Baldrige Health Care Criteria should be consulted to determine how the results are scored.

MEASURING PROGRESS IN THE EXCELLENCE JOURNEY

A healthcare organization seeking performance excellence does not necessarily have the greatest abilities or best outcomes. Senior leaders in those organizations are just committed to seeing what works and what does not. The performance excellence journey is very much like the Plan-Do-Check-Act process improvement model. Improvements in performance occur by comparing the organization's systems and processes with the Baldrige Criteria (Check). Where gaps exist, decisions are made as to what actions to take (Act). Changes intended to advance excellence are proposed (Plan) and tested in the real world of the organization (Do). Each Baldrige-based self-assessment becomes evidence to be used in the next improvement cycle.

Often organizational results—those high-level measures of performance on the organization's scorecard—are slow to substantiate significant improvements. Unfortunately, this can dampen people's enthusiasm for continuing the journey. It will be up to senior leaders to keep the passion for excellence alive. How can this be done? By focusing on the value of the journey, not just an elusive end point.

A comment that addresses this matter appeared recently in the "Quotable Quotes" section of the *Reader's Digest*. "Quotable Quotes" is a one-page section in each issue that lists a dozen or so remarks by different people—both living and dead—that succinctly make a point worth remembering. The quote, attributed to author Louis L'Amour, reads, "The trail is the thing, not the end of the trail. Travel too fast and you miss all you are traveling for." Performance excellence is a journey, and the journey itself can be measured and celebrated. There is certainly nothing wrong with an organization having strategic goals and being goal driven, but successes should not be judged merely by goal attainment. Along the performance excellence trail, a lot of positive changes should be happening, and these changes can be measured and celebrated just as much as performance results. The boxer Muhammad Ali was also quoted on that same page of "Quotable Quotes" as saying, "The man who views the world at 50 the same as he did at 20 has wasted 30 years of his life." The trail is the thing. Organizational learning will occur as people travel the performance excellence journey, and the application of this learning can be measured.

The CEO and governing board at Ellsworth County (Kansas) Medical Center (ECMC) decided to apply for the Kansas Excellence Award not to gain another plaque for the hospital's lobby but to measure the organizational learning and resultant changes that were occurring along the trail to excellence. The Kansas award levels, like many state quality awards, serve as excellence journey mileposts for the applicant. A panel of examiners reviews the award application and writes a feedback report identifying the applicant's strengths and opportunities for improvements. In 2001, ECMC applied for and was awarded the Level I, or introductory level, Kansas Excellence Award. This award recognized the hospital's commitment to performance excellence; however, the journey was just getting underway, and much change was still needed. ECMC used the feedback from the application process to begin to refine the structures and systems that support performance improvement. The next milepost for ECMC was the submission of an application for the Level II award in 2002. Feedback from the application process provided ECMC with a deeper understanding of how to deploy the Baldrige concepts in the organization.

When ECMC reapplied for the Level II award in 2003, the organization was much further along in its performance excellence journey and was able to show considerable advancement. ECMC received the Level II award (a Certificate of Progress), along with feedback on additional opportunities for advancing the Baldrige approach and deployment strategies throughout the organization. For ECMC, the intent of the state award application process has been to gain new learning and measure the organization's progress along the excellence journey; the award itself is a secondary consideration. Roger Pearson, CEO of ECMC, sums up the hospital's experiences to date in the case study below.

ECMC is benefiting from its continued participation in the Kansas Excellence Award program. The consensus feedback reports we receive provide valuable suggestions and recommendations on how to even more effectively apply Baldrige Criteria to our own organizational efforts. The award scoring process, which is conducted by unbiased examiners, helps us evaluate our progress at applying the criteria.

We have also seen improvements in organizational results since we started learning and using Baldrige principles. Patient and employee satisfaction scores have improved. Financial performance, as measured by net margin, has improved 14 percent; market share, as measured by patient origin studies, shows a 29.4 percent improvement; and business operations, as measured by days of revenue in accounts receivable, has improved 13.7 percent. These positive results are reported throughout the organization and to the governing board and the community. In addition, my observation is that there is increased frequency of consensus among managers and staff as to what is important to our customers and where to target improvement efforts. Staff members are monitoring and measuring results on a more consistent basis, and it appears that those managers who have been trained as examiners for the Kansas Excellence Award program have better problem-solving skills.

As I review the various stages of our journey in performance excellence, I am struck by the reality that the biggest change is not something our organization actually did. It is about what our organization is becoming. When ECMC initially started on this journey, I knew that QI [quality improvement] needed to be fixed—after all, it was broken, and we needed to do something. But as ECMC proceeded down the trail, I began to realize that organizational excellence is not a destination that you suddenly arrive at. Rather, it is a journey during which the CEO and the organization become something different than before. It is a culture change that allows employees to recognize and appreciate the opportunity to provide value and service to customers and to continually improve in that service. Traveling this journey takes faith, belief, and commitment to purpose.

Performance excellence is more like a marathon than a sprint. To sustain long-term, continual improvement, organizational systems must be in place and functioning in a coordinated, consistent manner. Now that

ECMC has had four years of learning, experience, and changes for the better, improving medical and clinical care systems and meeting the needs of the community are the next priorities. We have built an organizational foundation and a tradition of successes on which further improvements can more effectively be incorporated into our overall performance excellence journey. And when someone asks me, "How is ECMC doing?" I can reply, "Better than yesterday and not as good as tomorrow"—that is what a journey is all about.

*   *   *   *   *

The Baldrige Criteria are an excellent barometer for measuring an organization's progress along the performance excellence journey. First and foremost, senior leaders and managers learn a great deal about the organization just by completing an internal self-assessment using the full set of Baldrige Criteria. The self-assessment process can be repeated periodically (ideally annually) to determine how far the organization has progressed in institutionalizing the Baldrige concepts. The criteria provide a reliable, dependable, and repeatable method of measuring milestones in the organization's excellence journey. In addition, the self-assessment helps leaders to identify activities that can have the most leverage for improving performance. Self-assessment tools are available free of charge on the Baldrige National Quality Program web site (www.quality.nist.org), and state quality award programs offer complimentary assessment instruments. A list of these state programs is found in the appendix at the end of this book.

By applying for a quality award at the state or national level or by engaging an outside consultant familiar with the Baldrige Criteria, organizations can gain advice on how to further excellence through various strategies and initiatives. In addition, by applying for a quality award or by engaging a consultant for a facilitated self-assessment, organizations can better understand how to assess progress using the Baldrige Criteria scoring system. The scores, which serve as organizational mileposts along the excellence journey, can be somewhat confusing for the uninformed evaluator. In the case of ECMC, the CEO and several managers learned how to apply the scoring system as part of their training as examiners for the Kansas Excellence Award Program. However, feedback from the award examiners also proved very valuable to ECMC. If an

SSM *Health Care, St. Louis, MO*
2002 Award Winner
- Improved turnover rate for all employees from 21% in 1999 to 13% as of
  August 2002
- Attained national benchmark levels of patients receiving lipid-lowering
  agents to decrease morbidity and mortality in patients who have suffered a
  heart attack
- For four consecutive years, maintained an investment grade rating in the AA
  credit rating category (published by the two national rating agencies:
  Standard & Poor's and Fitch). This rating is attained by fewer than 1 percent
  of U.S. hospitals.

Baptist Hospital, Inc., Pensacola, FL
2003 Baldrige Award Winner
- Inpatient overall satisfaction for Baptist Hospital of Pensacola (BH) and Gulf
  Breeze Hospital (GBH) have been near the 99th percentile of the Press
  Ganey survey each quarter since 1998.
- Overall outpatient satisfaction for BH has been near the 99th percentile each
  quarter since 1999; for Baptist Medical Park, it has been near the 99th
  percentile since the third quarter of 2001.
- The employee turnover rate at BH declined from 27% in 1997 to 13.9% in
  2003, and the GBH turnover rate declined from 31% in 1997 to 14% percent
  in 2003. These levels for both hospitals are more favorable than the
  northwest Florida average and the national average and are at the
  best-in-class level.

Saint Luke's Hospital of Kansas City (SLH), Kansas City, MO
2003 Baldrige Award Winner
- Percentage rate of returns following ambulatory procedures is significantly
  lower for SLH at 14.2% compared with 39.18 % for similar size national
  teaching hospitals.
- SLH leads the nation in the percentage of diagnosed stroke patients receiving
  tissue plasminogen activator (tPA) to help restore circulation and reduce
  permanent brain injury. Twenty-seven percent of SLH patients received tPA in
  the second quarter of 2003 versus a national average of 3 percent.
- Percentage of minority managers at SLH has shown a positive trend since
  1998, increasing by 3 percent to 9.4 percent in 2003.

Sources: SSM Health Care, www.ssmhc.com; Baptist Hospital, Inc., www.bhcpns.org;
Saint Luke's Hospital of Kansas City, www.saint-lukes.org.

organization has its sights set on winning the National Baldrige Quality Award, the services of a knowledgeable consultant will most likely be necessary.

MEASURING RESULTS

There is nothing typical about the outcomes that organizations use to measure business results. While the Baldrige award application process requires that organizational results be reported for six different dimensions, what measurements are reported in those dimensions varies by organization. Some of the performance results reported by past winners of the Baldrige award in the healthcare category are listed in Figure 9.1.[1]

Consistent with the nonprescriptive philosophy of the Baldrige Criteria, the definition of what results are important is left to the organization. This decision is based on the areas of strategic significance defined by senior leaders. A description of the linkage between strategic planning and high-level measures of success, as well as examples of key results that healthcare organizations are measuring, are found in Chapters 4 and 6.

Organizations that use the Baldrige Criteria solely for internal self-assessment purposes can evaluate progress toward achieving key results by applying the Baldrige award scoring system found in the most current edition of the criteria. The results evaluation tools developed and distributed by state quality award programs can also be useful.

Use the self-assessment below to evaluate your organization's performance results. The questions are based on the Baldrige Health Care Criteria and the award scoring system.

☑ **SELF-ASSESSMENT**

Healthcare Results

☐ Current levels and trends for key measures of healthcare outcomes show sustained improvement.
☐ Current levels and trends for key measures of health service delivery show sustained improvement.
☐ Current levels and trends for key measures of patient safety show sustained improvement.

❏ Current levels and trends for key measures of patients' functional status show sustained improvement.

❏ Key measures of healthcare results consistently compare favorably with competitors and other organizations providing similar healthcare services.

Patient-Focused and Other Customer–Focused Results

❏ Current levels and trends for key measures of patient satisfaction show sustained improvement.

❏ Current levels and trends for key measures of other customer satisfaction show sustained improvement.

❏ Current levels and trends for key measures of patient/other customer loyalty and retention show sustained improvement.

❏ Current levels and trends for product and service attributes important to your patients and other customers show sustained improvement.

❏ Key measures show that patients/other customers consistently evaluate your performance as being better than that of competitors or alternative providers.

Financial and Market Results

❏ Key financial metrics demonstrate good to excellent levels with favorable trends that are sustained over several measurement periods for indicators such as revenue, profitability by market segment, operating margins, cost reduction, and asset utilization.

❏ Financial results demonstrate leading performance as compared with your best competitor, the industry average, and appropriate benchmarks from outside your industry.

❏ Current levels and trends of marketplace performance over several periods show increased market share, sustained business growth, and penetration of new markets.

❏ Key measures of financial and market results consistently compare favorably with competitors and other organizations providing similar healthcare services.

Staff and Work System Results

❏ Current levels and trends for key measures of staff well-being and satisfaction show sustained improvement.

❏ Current levels and trends for key measures of staff learning and development show sustained improvement.

❏ Current levels and trends for key measures of work system performance and effectiveness show sustained improvement.

❏ Key measures of staff and work system results consistently compare favorably with competitors and other organizations providing similar healthcare services.

Organizational Effectiveness Results

❏ Current levels and trends for key measures of key healthcare process productivity show sustained improvement.

❏ Current levels and trends for key measures of key healthcare process cycle time show sustained improvement.

❏ Current levels and trends for key measures of key healthcare process supplier and partner performance show sustained improvement.

❏ Current levels and trends for key measures of key support and business process productivity show sustained improvement.

❏ Current levels and trends for key measures of key support and business process cycle time show sustained improvement.

❏ Current levels and trends for key measures of key support and business process supplier and partner performance show sustained improvement.

❏ Current levels and trends for key measures of strategy effectiveness show sustained improvement.

❏ Key measures of organizational effectiveness results consistently compare favorably with competitors and other organizations providing similar healthcare services.

Governance and Social Responsibility Results

❏ Current levels and trends for key measures of fiscal responsibility show sustained improvement.

❏ Current levels and trends for key measures of organizational citizenship—such as being sensitive to issues of public concern, ensuring ethical behavior, contributions to community health, and similar measures—show sustained improvement.

❏ Current levels and trends for key measures of regulatory/legal compliance—such as audits, regulatory findings, environmental findings, warnings, and similar measures—show sustained improvement.

❏ Key measures of governance and social responsibility results consistently compare favorably with competitors and other organizations providing similar healthcare services.

From a performance standpoint, how high is up? To make it to the top and stay there, a healthcare organization not only has to be "good" but it also has to be seen as good by its leaders, managers, staff members, and customers. To determine whether or not your organization is good, consider the following question:

Where would you want your loved ones to receive healthcare services?

❏ At a facility that holds a current state license
❏ At a facility that holds a current state license and one or more accreditations from national accrediting groups
❏ At a facility that holds a current state license and one or more accreditations from national accrediting groups and where the senior leaders are actively using the Baldrige Criteria to advance performance excellence.

The importance of the performance excellence journey cannot be overstated. It must not be seen as being a "program of the month." It is a change in organizational focus—the way of doing things. It is a leadership-driven effort to continuously improve healthcare processes with the goal of forever-higher levels of performance. Organizational efforts are directed toward constantly seeking opportunities for improvement.

NOTE

1. If you would like to learn more about the Baldrige award experience and performance results for these three healthcare organizations, visit their web sites:
   - SSM Health Care: www.ssmhc.com
   - Baptist Hospital, Inc.: www.bhcpns.org
   - Saint Luke's Hospital of Kansas City: www.saint-lukes.org

REFERENCE

Baldrige National Quality Program. 2004. *Baldrige Health Care Criteria for Performance Excellence*, 61. Gaithersburg, MD: NIST.

Appendix: State Quality Award Programs*

*Current as of January 2004.

Alabama Quality Award
Phone: 205/348-8994
www.alabamaproductitycenter.com

Arizona State Quality Award
Phone: 602/636-1383
www.arizona-excellence.com

Arkansas Performance Excellence Awards
Phone: 501/373-1300
www.arkansas-quality.org

California Awards for Performance
   Excellence
Phone: 619/237-5100
www.calexcellence.org

Colorado Performance Excellence Award
Phone: 303/893-2739
www.coloradoexcellence.org

Connecticut Quality Leadership Award
Phone: 203/322-9534
www.ctqualityaward.org

Delaware Quality Award
Phone: 302/739-4271
http://www.accoladealliance.org/
DQA02.htm

Florida Governor's Sterling Award
Phone: 850/922-5316
www.floridasterling.com

Georgia Oglethorpe Award
Phone: 404/651-8405
www.georgiaoglethorpe.org

Hawaii State Award of Excellence
Phone: 808/545-4300, ext. 394

Illinois—The Lincoln Awards for
   Excellence
Phone: 630/637-1595
www.lincolnaward.org

Indiana Quality Improvement Award
Phone: 317/635-3058
www.bmtadvantage.org

Iowa Recognition for Performance
   Excellence
Phone: 319/398-7101
www.iowaqc.org

Kansas Excellence Award
Phone: 800/743-6767
www.kae.bluestep.net

Commonwealth of Kentucky Quality
   Award
Phone: 606/695-0066
www.kqc.org

Louisiana Performance Excellence Award
Phone: 337/482-6767
www.laqualityaward.com

Maryland Quality Awards
Phone: 301/403-4101
www.umcqp.umd.edu

Massachusetts Performance Excellence
   Award
Phone: 978/934-2403
www.massexcellence.com

Michigan Quality Leadership Award
Phone: 248/370-4552
www.michiganquality.org

Minnesota Quality Award
Phone: 612/462-3577
www.councilforquality.org

Mississippi Quality Award
Phone: 601/432-6349
www.sbcjc.cc.ms.us/acct/

Missouri Quality Award
Phone: 573/526-1727
www.mqa.org

Nebraska—The Edgerton Quality Awards
Phone: 402/471-3745
http://assist.neded.org/edgerton/

Nevada State Quality Award
Phone: 702/286-1876
www.nvqa.org

New Hampshire—Granite State Quality
    Award
Phone: 603/223-1312
www.gsqc.com

New Jersey—Governor's Award for
    Performance Excellence
Phone: 609/777-0940
www.qnj.org

New Mexico Quality Awards
Phone: 505/944-2001
www.qualitynewmexico.org

New York—The Empire State Advantage
Phone: 518/482-1747
www.empirestateadvantage.org

Ohio Award for Excellence—Best
    Practices in Quality Improvement
Phone: 330/672-2102
www.oae.org

Oklahoma Quality Award
Phone: 405/815-5295
www.oklahomaquality.com

Pennsylvania—Greater Pittsburgh Total
    Quality Award
Phone: 412/392-4500

Pennsylvania—Keystone Performance
    Excellence Award
Phone: 717/560-2910

Pennsylvania—Lancaster Chamber
    Performance Excellence Award
Phone: 717/397-3531
www.lcci.com

Rhode Island—Governor's Award for
    Competitiveness and Performance
    Excellence
Phone: 401/598-1398
www.ricpe.org

South Carolina Governor's Quality Award
Phone: 888/231-0578
www.scquality.com

Tennessee—Greater Memphis Pyramid
    of Excellence Award
Phone: 901/678-4268
www.gmaq.org

Tennessee Center for Performance
    Excellence
Phone: 615/214-3106
www.tncpe.org

Texas Award for Performance Excellence
Phone: 512/868-3456
www.texas-quality.org

University of Texas at Austin Center for
    Performance Award
Phone: 512/931-2332
www.utexas.edu/utcpe

Vermont Program for Performance
    Excellence
Phone: 802/655-1910
www.vermontquality.org

Wisconsin Forward Award
Phone: 608/663-5300
www.forwardaward.org

Index

About the Author

Patrice L. Spath is a health information management professional with extensive experience in performance improvement. She is president of Brown-Spath & Associates (www.brownspath.com), a healthcare publishing and training company based in Forest Grove, Oregon. Patrice has presented more than 350 educational programs on healthcare quality topics, including the workshop "Driving Performance Excellence," sponsored by the American College of Healthcare Executives. For the past 20 years she has consulted with healthcare organizations throughout the United States on methods for assessing and improving business and clinical performance.

Patrice has authored and edited numerous books and journal articles for Health Administration Press, AHA Press, Jossey-Bass Publishers, Aspen Publications, OR Manager, Inc., Brown-Spath & Associates, and other groups. Her most recent book, *Partnering with Patients to Reduce Medical Errors* (AHA Press, 2004) addressed groundbreaking patient safety improvement concepts. She writes the monthly "Quality-Cost Connection" column for *Hospital Peer Review* and serves as a quarterly guest columnist for *Hospital Case Management*.

In 1998, Patrice received the Legacy Award from the American Health Information Management Association in recognition of her significant contributions to the knowledge base of the profession. In 2001, the National Association for Healthcare Quality honored her with its Award for Excellence in Publication. Patrice has served on several national task groups, including the clinical practice guidelines panel of the Veterans Health Administration and the quality management practice standards task group of the Association for Perioperative Registered Nurses. She currently serves on the advisory board for WebM&M (http://webmm.ahrq.gov), an online case-based journal and forum on patient safety and healthcare quality that is supported by a contract from the Agency for Healthcare Research and Quality. Patrice can be contacted at patrice@brownspath.com.